# Principles of Organizational Management

# Principles of Organizational Management

James Carter

Willford Press
www.willfordpress.com

Published by Willford Press,
118-35 Queens Blvd., Suite 400,
Forest Hills, NY 11375, USA





ISBN: 978-1-68285-985-8

**Cataloging-in-Publication Data**

Principles of organizational management / James Carter.
p. cm.
Includes bibliographical references and index.
ISBN 978-1-68285-985-8
1. Management. 2. Organizational behavior. 3. Corporate culture.
4. Organizational effectiveness. 5. Personnel management. I. Carter, James.
HD31.2 .P75 2021
658--dc23

For information on all Willford Press publications
visit our website at www.willfordpress.com

WILLFORD PRESS

# Table of Contents

# Preface

The purpose of this book is to help students understand the fundamental concepts of this discipline. It is designed to motivate students to learn and prosper. I am grateful for the support of my colleagues. I would also like to acknowledge the encouragement of my family.

An organization comprises of multiple people which has a particular purpose. It is made up of a group of different people who aim to achieve the targeted goal. The management that focuses on adequate handling of all the processes and resources of the company is known as organizational management. Its main objective is planning, organizing, executing and controlling activities for the achievement of company's pre-established goals. The resources which are managed includes financial and human resources, facilities, knowledge, business relationships, etc. There is a growing need for organizational management. It helps in creating a clearer picture of goals of departments. It also assists in effective implementation of business plans. This book elucidates the concepts and innovative models around prospective developments with respect to organizational management. Most of the topics introduced herein cover new techniques and the applications of this field. This book, with its detailed analyses and data, will prove immensely beneficial to professionals and students involved in this area at various levels.

A foreword for all the chapters is provided below:

Chapter - What is Organizational Management?

Management of an organization by planning, structuring and directing its resources to achieve targeted goals is referred to as organizational management. It determines lines of authority, communication, duties and responsibility between each unit of the organization and its members. The topics elaborated in this chapter will help in gaining a better perspective about organizational management.

Chapter - Diverse Aspects of Organizational Management

Some of the aspects that fall under the domain of organizational management are organizational communication, organizational development, organizational culture, organizational architecture, organizational diagnostics, etc. This chapter discusses about these aspects of organizational management in detail.

Chapter - Organizational Behavior and Ethics

Organizational behavior studies human behavior in a work environment including job structure, performance, communication, leadership, etc. Organizational ethics refers to the principles, values and rules by which businesses operate. This chapter has been carefully written to provide an easy understanding of organizational behavior and ethics.

Chapter - Human Resource Management

Human resource management includes recruitment and selection of employees, providing training, improving the performance of employees and maintaining relations with them. This chapter closely examines these aspects associated with human resource management to provide an extensive understanding of the subject.

Chapter - Performance Management

Performance management focuses on the performance of an organization to meet their goals effectively and efficiently. Business performance management, enterprise performance management, behavior systems analysis, etc. comes within it. This chapter delves into the concepts related to performance management.

**James Carter**

# 1

# What is Organizational Management?

Management of an organization by planning, structuring and directing its resources to achieve targeted goals is referred to as organizational management. It determines lines of authority, communication, duties and responsibility between each unit of the organization and its members. The topics elaborated in this chapter will help in gaining a better perspective about organizational management.

Since all companies have operations, i.e. certain ways to create an optimal output from various input sources, whether it be manufacturing physical products or offering services, it is good to be familiar with the basics of managing these operations.

Operations management involves planning, organizing, and supervising processes, and make necessary improvements for higher profitability. The adjustments in the everyday operations have to support the company's strategic goals, so they are preceded by deep analysis and measurement of the current processes.

Operations management was previously called production management, clearly showing its origins in manufacturing. Historically, it all began with the division of production, starting as early as the times of ancient craftsmen, but spreading more widely only by adding the concept of interchangeability of parts in the eighteenth century, ultimately sparking the industrial revolution.

Still, it was not until Henry Ford took a twist on manufacturing with his famous assembly line concept, otherwise known as "bring work to men," that the management of production for improving productivity became a hot topic. From the 1950's and 1960's, it formed a separate discipline, besides bringing other concepts, such as Taylorism, production planning, or inventory control, to life.

As the economies in the developed world were gradually shifting to be service-based, all the corporate functions, including product management, started to integrate them. The service side also began its approach by applying product management principles to the planning and organizing of processes, to the point where it made more sense to call it operations management.

## Multidisciplinary Nature

Operations management is now a multidisciplinary functional area in a company, along with finance and marketing. It makes sure the materials and labor, or any other input, is used in the most effective and efficient way possible within an organization – thus maximizing the output.

Operations management requires being familiar with a wide range of disciplines. It incorporates general management, factory- and equipment maintenance management by tradition. The operations manager has to know about the common strategic policies, basic material planning, manufacturing and production systems, and their analysis. Production and cost control principles are also of importance. And last, but not least, it has to be someone's who is able to navigate industrial labor relations.

## Required Skills

The skills required to perform such work are as diverse as the function itself. The most important skills are:

- Organizational abilities: Organizing processes in an organization requires a set of skills from planning and prioritizing through execution to monitoring. These abilities together help the manager achieve productivity and efficiency.
- Analytic capabilities/understanding of process: The capability to understand processes in your area often includes a broad understanding of other functions, too. An attention to detail is often helpful to go deeper in the analysis.
- Coordination of processes:. Once processes are analyzed and understood, they can be optimized for maximum efficiency. Quick decision-making is a real advantage here, as well as a clear focus problem-solving.
- People skills: Flaws in the interactions with employees or member of senior management can seriously harm productivity, so an operation manager has to have people skills to properly navigate the fine lines with their colleagues. Furthermore, clear communication of the tasks and goals serves as great motivation and to give a purpose for everyone.
- Creativity:. Again, problem-solving skills are essential for a creative approach if things don't go in the right direction. When they do, creativity helps find new ways to improve corporate performance.
- Tech-savviness: In order to understand and design processes in a time when operations are getting increasingly technology-dependent, affinity for technology is a skill that can't be underestimated. Operations managers have to be familiar with the most common technologies used in their industries, and have an even deeper understanding of the specific operation technology at their organizations.

## The Major Principles of Operations Management

Some of the fundamentals of the everyday work in operations management worth expanding a little more. Below you will find two major approaches that are important to understand the driving forces behind the decisions about planning, designing and organizing processes.

They are both embracing the idea of focusing on the delivery: supporting the organization to deliver better results, by an optimized input of materials, equipment, technology, and human resources.

## The Ten Principles of OM by Randall Schaeffer

Randall Schaeffer is an experienced manufacturing and operations management professional, an industrial philosopher, and regular speaker at conferences organized by APICS, the leading US association of supply chain and operations management. He presented his list of 10 principles of operations management at an APICS conference in 2007, saying the violation of these principles had caused the struggle US manufacturing companies were experiencing.

- Reality: Operations management should focus on the problem, instead of the techniques, because no tool in itself would present a universal solution.
- Organization: Processes in manufacturing are interconnected. All elements have to be predictable and consistent, in order to achieve a similar outcome in profits.
- Fundamentals: The Pareto rule is also applicable to operations: 80% of success comes from a strict adherence to precisely maintaining records and disciplines, and only 20% comes from applying new techniques to the processes.
- Accountability: Managers are expected to set the rules and the metrics, and define responsibilities of their subordinates, as well as regularly check if the goals are met. Only this way would the workers put in the necessary efforts.
- Variance: Variance of processes has to be encouraged, because if managed well, they can be sources of creativity.
- Causality: Problems are symptoms: effects of underlying causes. Unless the causes are attacked, the same problems will appear again.
- Managed passion: The passion of employees can be a major driver of company growth, and it can be instilled by the managers if not coming naturally.
- Humility: Instead of a costly trial and error process, managers should acknowledge their limitations, "get help, and move on".
- Success: What is considered success will change over time, but always consider the interest of the customer. In order to keep them, all the other principles have to be revised occasionally.
- Change: There will always be new theories and solutions, so you should not stick to one or the other, but embrace the change, and manage for stability in the long term.

## The 16 Principles of Operations Management by Dr. Richard Schonberger

- Team up with customers: Know what they buy and use, and organize product families accordingly.
- Continual, rapid improvement: Aim for non-stop improvement to always deliver the best quality, aim for a quicker response to customer demand, and always offer maximum flexibility. Thus, it gives more value, in a more flexible way.
- Unified purpose: Involve frontline employees in strategic discussions to make sure they understand the purpose of their work and have their say in what to change.
- Know the competition: Know their customers, their best practices, and their competitive edges.

- Focus: Allow no variations that the customers don't buy or demand.
- Organize resources: Set priorities in organizing resources in a way the operations are close to the customer rate of use or demand.
- Invest in HR: Offer cross-training options, job rotation, and improvements in work safety and health. Also offer more rewards and recognitions.
- Maintain equipment: Always think of improvement of current assets first, instead of a new purchase.
- Simple "best" equipment: Keep the equipment as simple and flexible as possible, at a reasonable cost.
- Minimize human error: Improve the equipment and keep frontline workers accountable.
- Cut times: Shorten product path to customer by making processes and delivery faster.
- Cut setup: Be prepared to support different processes and get all information and tools ready for on-demand production.
- Pull system: Improve the workflow and cut the waste by producing on demand.
- Total quality control: Use only the best materials, processes, and partners.
- Fix causes: Focus on controlling the root causes that really affect cost and performance.
- Visibility management: Promote corporate achievements; let the market know about your improvements in competence or productivity.

## The Activities of Operations Management

There are three major groups of activities performed by operations management, deriving from its planning or designing, organizing, and supervising functions. All activities involve considering assets, costs, and human resources, and are preceded by a thorough analysis of processes.

## Design

Before planning processes or designing products, operations management should be busy analyzing the market to test the demands. If it delivers promising results, e.g. a niche to target or a new product or service to develop, you can start planning.

In most cases, planning involves designing a new product, from the initial concept to the actual launch, with several testing phases involved. During planning, you will have to consider both technical and business requirements.

Sometimes the processes need to be updated: designing a new supply chain or other logistics processes. If your product is a service, process design aims for a variety of requirements and customer contact levels.

Again in other cases, it's about a new facility: your company decides to expand its operations, and you will have to decide on the location of the facility, its capacity, and its layout.

Plans should always support the business objectives: they are in focus when considering the costs and finding the best matching quality and capacity, or calculating inventory and human labor needs.

Therefore, it is important to set proper measures in the planning phase, to know if the actual performance meets them, or there is need for adjustments. Capacity is one of these measures, as is product quality, or delivery times. The initial figures are usually estimates based on the market analysis conducted beforehand.

## Management/Organization

So you have a facility for production, your product design is ready, and so is the way it will be produced: with what material and human resources, at what costs, with what workflow.

This is a solid starting base for maximizing the efficiency of your operations. Still, you will need constant and competent management to correct the accidental mistakes in planning, to adjust production to changing costs or regulations, and keep them efficient on many levels.

The operations manager selects and schedules the processes for an optimal result and does the same with materials for an ideal quality and capacity. Organizing the maintenance of the equipment is also part of the quality management activities. Furthermore, the inventory and the whole supply chain has to be managed in order to produce more efficiently.

As in all management functions, the management of human resources is an essential activity. In operations management, the planning of actual employment levels can have a great impact on whether an organization can operate effectively.

## Improve

There is always room to improve when it comes to the processes used, the quality and capacity achieved, or as far as the level of inventory and human resources are concerned.

A great deal of operations management's tasks, therefore, comes from these needs, and this is where long-term planning steps in. But remember, changes made according to these plans are only as good as the improvement they bring in business terms.

# 2

# Diverse Aspects of Organizational Management

Some of the aspects that fall under the domain of organizational management are organizational communication, organizational development, organizational culture, organizational architecture, organizational diagnostics, etc. This chapter discusses about these aspects of organizational management in detail.

## Organizational Communication

We define organizational communication' as the sending and receiving of messages among interrelated individuals within a particular environment or setting to achieve individual and common goals. Organizational communication is highly contextual and culturally dependent. Individuals in organizations transmit messages through face-to face, written, and mediated channels.

Organizational communication helps us to: 1) accomplish tasks relating to specific roles and responsibilities of sales, services, and production; 2) acclimate to changes through individual and organizational creativity and adaptation; 3) complete tasks through the maintenance of policy, procedures, or regulations that support daily and continuous operations; 4) develop relationships where "human messages are directed at people within the organization-their attitudes, morale, satisfaction, and fulfillment"; and 5) coordinate, plan, and control the operations of the organization through management. Organizational communication is how organizations represent, present, and constitute their organizational climate and culture—the attitudes, values and goals that characterize the organization and its members.

Organizational communication largely focuses on building relationships and interacting with with internal organizational members and interested external publics. As Mark Koschmann explains, we have two ways of looking at organizational communication. The conventional approach focuses on communication within organizations. The second approach is communication as organization – meaning organizations are a result of the communication of those within them. Communication is not just about transmitting messages between senders and receivers. Communication literally constitutes, or makes up, our social world. Much of our communication involves sending and receiving relatively unproblematic messages and acting on that information. Other times things are a bit more complex, such as when you need to resolve conflict with a close friend or family member.

There is much more going on in these situations then merely exchanging information. You are actually engaging in a complex process of meaning and negotiating rules created by the people involved.

For organizations to be successful, they must have competent communicators. Organizational communication study shows that organizations rely on effective communication and efficient communication skills from their members. A number of surveys identify effective oral and written communication as the most sought after skills by those who run organizations. The U.S. Department of Labor reported communication competency as the most vital skill necessary for the 21st century workforce to achieve organizational success. The Public Forum Institute maintained that employees need to be skilled in public presentation, listening, and interpersonal communication to flourish in an organization.

Organizations seek people who can follow and give instructions, accurately listen, provide useful feedback, get along with coworkers and customers, network, provide serviceable information, work well in teams, and creatively and critically solve problems and present ideas in an understandable manner. Developing organizational communication awareness and effectiveness is more than just having know-how or knowledge. Efficient organizational communication involves knowing how to create and exchange information, work with diverse groups or individuals, communicate in complicated and changing circumstances, as well as having the aptitude or motivation to communicate in appropriate manners.

## Classical Management Perspective

The original perspective for understanding organizational communication can be described using a machine metaphor. At the beginning of the industrial age, when people thought science could solve almost every problem, American Frederick Taylor, Frenchman Henri Fayol, and German Max Weber tried to apply scientific solutions to organizations. They wanted to determine how organizations and workers could function in an ideal way. Organizations during the industrial revolution wanted to know how they could maximize their profits so the classical management perspective focused on worker productivity.

The machine metaphor of classical management suggests that three basic aspects should exist in organizations: Specialization, Standardization, and Predictability. Those who advocated this perspective argued that every employee should have a specialized function, thus, essentially any individual could perform a job if they are properly trained. If one individual fails to do the job, they are easily replaceable with another person since people are seen as simply parts of a machine.

Taylor developed his Theory of Scientific Management from his early days as a foreman in a machine shop. Little did he know how drastically he was going to influence organizations and our notions of working life. Taylor could not understand why organizations and individuals would not want to maximize efficiency. In Copley's biography about Taylor he reveals a man who was driven by perfection: "The spectacle of a [man] doing less than [his] best was to him morally shocking. He enthusiastically believed that to do anything less than your best is to add to the sum of the world's unrighteousness". However, workers were not always as enthusiastic about efficiency and quality as Taylor, especially given the significant difference in status and pay between management and labor. For the common laborer during the industrial revolution, this new approach to employment meant possibly losing your job if a "scientific" formula showed that fewer workers could do the same job.

During this time, Weber was also developing his ideas about bureaucracy. He was fascinated with what the ideal organization should look like, and believed that effective hierarchies helped organizations operate effectively. Precise rules, a division of labor, centralized authority, and a distinctly defined hierarchy should be driven by rational thought void of emotion and outside influence. These qualities would allow organizations to operate in a somewhat predictable manner — employees knew what to expect and who was in charge, and management could make decisions based on familiar, relevant information rather than irrational feelings.

Fayol's theory of classical management focused on how management worked, specifically looking at what managers should do to be most effective. For Fayol, organizational members should be clear who is in charge, and everyone should know their role in an organization. He argued that organizations should be grouped in a precise hierarchy that limits the flow of communication to top-down communication.

Theory X is an example of a classical management theory where managers micro-manage employees by using reward-punishment tactics, and limiting employee participation in decision-making. This theory sees employees as basically lazy or unmotivated. Because of this, managers must closely supervise their workers. Those that do not do their work are disposable parts of the machine. This allows for management to mistreat and abuse their employees, ultimately lowering the very thing they were after, greater productivity.

Organizations using this approach can still be found today. Have you ever had a boss or manager who treated you like an interchangeable part of a machine who had little value? If so, you've experienced aspects of the classical management perspective at work. While scientific approaches to organizations were an interesting starting point for determining how to communicate, the classical management approach fell short in many ways. Thus, development and refinement continued to occur regarding ways to understand organizational communication.

## Human Relations Perspective

Because classical management was so mechanical and did not treat people as humans, organizational scholars wanted to focus on the human elements of organizations. The human relations approach focuses on how organizational members relate to one another, and how individuals' needs influence their performance in organizations. In 1924 Elton Mayo and his team of Harvard scientists began a series of studies that were initially interested in how to modify working conditions to increase worker productivity, decrease employee turnover, and change the overall poor organizational effectiveness at the Hawthorne Electric Plant near Chicago.

Mayo's team discovered that, no matter what changes they made to the work environment (such as adjusting lighting and temperature levels, work schedules, and worker isolation), worker productivity increased simply due to the fact that researchers were paying attention to them. Simply paying attention to workers and addressing their social needs yielded significant changes in their productivity. This is where the term "The Hawthorne Effect" developed. Mayo's work provided an impetus for a new way of looking at workers in organizations.

Maslow's hierarchy suggests that human beings are actually motivated to satisfy their personal needs. His theory is still of interest to us today as we try to comprehend the relevance of human relations in the workplace. Papa, Daniels and Spiker s describe McGregor's contributions: "As management theorists became familiar with Maslow's work, they soon realized the possibility of connecting higher-level needs to worker motivation. If organizational goals and individual needs could be integrated so that people would acquire self-esteem and, ultimately, self-actualization through work, then motivation would be self-sustaining". Remember that Theory X managers do not trust their employees because they think workers are inherently unmotivated and lazy. At the other end of the managerial spectrum, Theory Y managers (those that take a human relations perspective to employees) assume that workers are self motivated, seek responsibility, and want to achieve success. As a result of this changing perspective, managers began to invite feedback and encourage a degree of participation in organizational decision making, thus focusing on human relationships as a way to motivate employee productivity. Today many companies make employees happy by keeping them well rested and supplying them with ways to catch up on sleep even at work.

## Human Resources Perspective

The Human Resources perspective picks up where human relations left off. The primary criticism of human relations was that it still focused on productivity, trying to achieve worker productivity simply by making workers happy. The idea that a happy employee would be a productive employee makes initial sense. However, happiness does not mean that we will be productive workers. As a matter of fact, an individual can be happy with a job and not work very hard. Another reason scholars tried to improve the human relations perspective was because manipulative managers misused it by inviting participation from employees on the surface, but not really doing anything with the employees' contributions. Imagine your boss encouraging everyone to put their ideas into a suggestion box but never looking them.

Human Resources attempts to truly embrace participation by all organizational members, viewing each person as a valuable human resource. Employees are valuable resources that should be fully involved to manifest their abilities and productivity. Using this approach, organizations began to encourage employee participation in decision making.

An example of the human resources perspective is William Ouchi's Theory Z. Ouchi believed that traditional American organizations should be more like Japanese organizations. Japanese culture values lifetime employment, teamwork, collective responsibility, and a sound mind and body. This contrasts with many American work values such as short-term employment, individualism, and non-participation. Many U.S. companies implemented Japanese organizational concepts such as quality circles (QC), quality of work life (QWL) programs, management by objectives (MBO), and W. E. Deming's notion of total quality management (TQM). Each of these approaches was designed to flatten hierarchies, increase participation, implement quality control, and utilize teamwork. Human Resources works "by getting organizational participants meaningfully involved in the important decisions that regulate the enterprise".

## Systems Perspective

Collectively, individuals in organizations achieve more than they can independently. The systems perspective for understanding organizations is "concerned with problems of relationships, of structure, and of interdependence rather than with the constant attributes of objects". An organization is like a living organism and must exist in its external environment in order to survive. Without this interaction an organization remains what we call closed, and withers away.

All organizations have basic properties. Equifinality means that a system (organization) can reach its goals from different paths. Each professor that teaches public speaking, for example, does so in a different way but, the end result is that the students in each of the classes as completed a course in public speaking. Negative entropy is the ability of an organization to overcome the possibility of becoming run down. Companies like Apple do everything they can to stay ahead of their competition and keep their products ahead of the curve. Requisite variety means that organizations must be responsive to their external environment and adjust when needed. Apple is always under pressure to come up with the newest and best technology. When Apple goes a long time without doing so, the public begins to be critical. Homeostasis points to an organization's need for stability in a turbulent environment. When gas prices go up, for example, organizations impacted by these rising costs take steps to ensure their survival and profitability. Complexity states that the more an organization grows and interacts, the more elaborate it becomes. Think about how huge companies such as Verizon must have elaborate organizational systems in place to deal with all of its employees and customers in a competitive market place.

If an organization is a system, how do we use the role of communication to analyze interactions among organizational members? Karl Weick's Theory of Organizing suggests that participants organize through their communication and make sense of unpredictable environments through interactions. Simply put, organizations exist as a result of the interactions of people in those organizations. An organization is more than just a physical building with people inside. Communication is the "process of organizing" implying that communication actually is the organization. Regardless of whether the focus is on the message or the meaning, systems theory stresses the interdependence of integrated people in organizations and the outcomes they produce as a result of their interactions.

## Cultural Perspective

Each organization has unique characteristics and cultural differences such as language, traditions, symbols, practices, past-times, and social conveniences that distinguish it from other organizations. Likewise, they are rich with their own histories, stories, customs, and social norms.

Fast food restaurants such as In-and-Out and Chipotle have a culture of serving high quality food at a fast rate, yet they are very different organizations. Chipotle's company motto is "good food is good buisness" (Chipotle.com). We can understand organizations by seeing them as unique cultures.

Simply put, the cultural perspective states that organizations maintain: 1) Shared values and beliefs, 2) Common practices, skills, and actions, 3) Customarily observed rules, 4) Objects and artifacts, and 5) Mutually understood meanings. Shockley-Zalabak contends, "Organizational culture reflects the shared realities and shared practices in the organization and how these realities create and shape organizational events". Not every individual in an organization shares, supports, or engages in organizational values, beliefs, or rules in a similar manner. Instead, organizational culture includes various perspectives in a continually changing, emerging, and complex environment.

Some people try to treat culture as a "thing." However, organizational cultures emerge through interaction. Members share meaning, construct reality, and make sense of their environment on an ongoing basis. As Morgan states, "There is often more to culture than meets the eye and our understandings are usually much more fragmented and superficial than the reality itself".

When we become involved with organizations, we learn from other people in the organization "the correct way to perceive, think, and feel". There are three interdependent levels that provide insight into how culture works in organizations:

- Artifacts are the first type of communicative behavior we encounter in organizations. Artifacts aresymbols used by an organization to represent the organization's culture. You might observe artifacts such as office technology, office architecture and arrangement, lighting, artwork, written documents, personal items on desks, clothing preferences, personal appearance, name tags, security badges, policy handbook, or web sites. You might observe routine behavior such as work processes, patterned communication (greetings), non-verbal characteristics (eye contact and handshakes) rituals, ceremonies, stories, or informal/formal interactions between supervisor and subordinate. All of these are artifacts that tell us something about an organization's cultural values and practices. What artifacts represent the college or university you are attending right now?
- Values are an organization's preference for how things should happen, or strategies for determining how things should be accomplished correctly. Hackman and Johnson believe that values "serve as the yardstick for judging behavior". Many times there is a disconnect between what an organization says it values, and their actual behavior. Disney espouses family values, for example, yet many of their subsidiary companies produce media that do not hold up these values. A way around this for Disney is to make sure to use other names, such as Touchstone Pictures, so that the Disney name is not attached to anything antithetical to "family values".
- Basic assumptions are the core of what individuals believe in organizations. These "unconscious, taken-for-granted beliefs, perceptions, thoughts, and feelings" ultimately influence how you experience the world as an organizational member. Unspoken beliefs reveal how we treat other individuals, what we see as good and bad in human nature, how we discover

truth, and our place in the environment. Basic assumptions guide how organizations treat employees and provide services to customers. Imagine that you work overtime almost everyday without pay. Why would you do this? Maybe you hold the basic assumption that people who work hard ultimately get ahead by being given promotions and pay raises. Imagine if you did this for years with no recognition or acknowledgement.

## Challenges in Organizational Communication

Ineffective communication can cause many problems that can impact relationships, productivity, job satisfaction, and morale as we interact in organizations. Gerald Goldhaber summarizes Osmo Wiio's "laws" of communication that are good to remember as you interact in increasingly complex organizations. Wiio pessimistically warns that: 1) If communication can fail, it will fail, 2) If a message can be understood in different ways, it will be misunderstood in the manner that does the most damage, 3) The more communication there is, the more tricky it is for the communication to be successful, and 4) There is always someone who thinks they know better what you said than you do.

One of the greatest challenges facing organizations is the practice of ethics. Ethics are a basic code of conduct (morals) that individuals and groups use to assess whether something is right or wrong.

Many organizations practice a climate of "survival of the fittest" as individuals scramble their way up the ladder of success at any cost. Comedian Jimmy Durante posited this advice: "Be nice to people on your way up because you might meet 'em on your way down." Obviously, not every organization has this type of cutthroat culture, but with an inherent hierarchy and imbalance of power, organizations are ripe for unethical behaviors. Because of the competitive nature of many business climates, and the push for profits, organizational and individual ethics are often tested.

Do organizations have a moral responsibility to act ethically outside of their capitalistic and legal obligations? "Since 1985, more than two-thirds of Fortune 500 firms have been convicted of serious crimes, ranging from fraud to the illegal dumping of hazardous waste". The Chevron Corporation, the second largest oil company in the U.S., is just one example of an unethical organization. Tax evasion and several environmental infractions, including dumping over 18 billion gallons of toxic waste into the Amazon rainforest, are examples of their ethical behavior. Other unethical practices common in organizations include exploiting workers, tax loopholes, overbilling, and dumping toxins. Despite these unfortunate, immoral practices, all of us have an obligation to communicate ethically in all aspects of our lives, including organizations.

Differences in perception and the failure to clarify communication can lead to miscommunication at interpersonal as well as organizational levels. Organizationally, communication failure occurs due to information overload, communication anxiety, unethical communication, bad timing, too little information, message distortion, lack of respect, insufficient information, minimal feedback, ineffective communication, and even disinterest or apathy. To be successful in our organizational environments, we need to be earnest participants, as well as active listeners, to ensure effective communication and mutual satisfaction. Organizations cannot successfully operate without effective communication at every level.

## Early Underlying Assumptions

Some of the main assumptions underlying much of the early organizational communication research were:

- Humans act rationally. Some people do not behave in rational ways, they generally have no access to all of the information needed to make rational decisions they could articulate, and therefore will make unrational decisions, unless there is some breakdown in the communication process—which is common. Irrational people rationalize how they will rationalize their communication measures whether or not it is rational.
- Formal logic and empirically verifiable data ought to be the foundation upon which any theory should rest. All we really need to understand communication in organizations is (a) observable and replicable behaviors that can be transformed into variables by some form of measurement, and (b) formally replicable syllogisms that can extend theory from observed data to other groups and settings.
- Communication is primarily a mechanical process, in which a message is constructed and encoded by a sender, transmitted through some channel, then received and decoded by a receiver. Distortion, represented as any differences between the original and the received messages, can and ought to be identified and reduced or eliminated.
- Organizations are mechanical things, in which the parts (including employees functioning in defined roles) are interchangeable. What works in one organization will work in another similar organization. Individual differences can be minimized or even eliminated with careful management techniques.
- Organizations function as a container within which communication takes place. Any differences in form or function of communication between that occurring in an organization and in another setting can be identified and studied as factors affecting the communicative activity.

Herbert A. Simon introduced the concept of bounded rationality which challenged assumptions about the perfect rationality of communication participants. He maintained that people making decisions in organizations seldom had complete information, and that even if more information was available, they tended to pick the first acceptable option, rather than exploring further to pick the optimal solution.

In the early 1990s Peter Senge developed new theories on organizational communication. These theories were learning organization and systems thinking. These have been well received and are now a mainstay in current beliefs toward organizational communications.

## Communication Networks

Networks are another aspect of direction and flow of communication. Bavelas has shown that communication patterns, or networks, influence groups in several important ways. Communication networks may affect the group's completion of the assigned task on time, the position of the de facto leader in the group, or they may affect the group members' satisfaction from occupying certain positions in the network. Although these findings are based on laboratory experiments, they have important implications for the dynamics of communication in formal organizations.

There are several patterns of communication, such as "chain", "wheel", "star", "all-channel" network, and "circle".

## Interorganization Communication

## Flow Nomenclature

Abbreviations are used to indicate the two-way flow of information or other transactions, e.g. B2B is "business to business". Duplex point-to-point communication systems, computer networks, non-electronic telecommunications, and meetings in person are all possible with the use of these terms. Examples:

| In Business | In Governance | In Society |
|---|---|---|
| • B2B (business-to-business)<br>• B2C (business-to-consumers)<br>• B2E (business-to-employees)<br>• B2G (business-to-government) | • G2G (government-to-government)<br>• G2C (government-to-citizens)<br>• G2E (government-to-employees)<br>• G2B (government-to-business) | • C2B (consumer-to-business)<br>• C2C (consumer-to-consumer)<br>• or (customer-to-customer) or (citizen-to-citizen) |

## Interpersonal Communication

One-to-one or interpersonal communication between individuals may take several forms- messages may be verbal (that is, expressed in words), or non-verbal such as gestures, facial expressions, and postures ("body language"). Nonverbal messages may even stem from silence.

Managers do not need answers to operate a successful business; they need questions. Answers can come from anyone, anytime, anywhere in the world thanks to the benefits of all the electronic communication tools at our disposal. This has turned the real job of management into determining what it is the business needs to know, along with the who/what/where/when and how of learning it. To effectively solve problems, seize opportunities, and achieve objectives, questions need to be asked by managers—these are the people responsible for the operation of the enterprise as a whole.

Ideally, the meanings sent are the meanings received. This is most often the case when the messages concern something that can be verified objectively. For example, "This piece of pipe fits the threads on the coupling." In this case, the receiver of the message can check the sender's words by actual trial, if necessary. However, when the sender's words describe a feeling or an opinion about something that cannot be checked objectively, meanings can be very unclear. "This work is too hard" or "Watergate was politically justified" are examples of opinions or feelings that cannot be verified. Thus they are subject to interpretation and hence to distorted meanings. The receiver's background of experience and learning may differ enough from that of the sender to cause significantly different perceptions and evaluations of the topic under discussion. As we shall see later, such differences form a basic barrier to communication.

Nonverbal content always accompanies the verbal content of messages. When speaking about nonverbal communication, Birdwhistell says "it is complementary to (meaning "adds to") rather than redundant with (or repeating of) the verbal behavior". For example, if someone is talking about the length of an object, they may hold out their hands to give a visual estimate of it. This is reasonably clear in the case of face-to-face communication. As Virginia Satir has pointed out, people cannot help but communicate symbolically (for example, through their clothing or possessions) or through some form of body language. In messages that are conveyed by the telephone, a messenger, or a letter, the situation or context in which the message is sent becomes part of its non-verbal content. For example, if the company has been losing money, and in a letter to the production division, the front office orders a reorganization of the shipping and receiving departments, this could be construed to mean that some people were going to lose their jobs — unless it were made explicitly clear that this would not occur.

A number of variables influence the effectiveness of communication. Some are found in the environment in which communication takes place, some in the personalities of the sender and the receiver, and some in the relationship that exists between sender and receiver. These different variables suggest some of the difficulties of communicating with understanding between two people. The sender wants to formulate an idea and communicate it to the receiver. This desire to communicate may arise from his thoughts or feelings or it may have been triggered by something in the environment. The communication may also be influenced by the relationship between the sender and the receiver, such as status differences, a staff-line relationship, or a learner-teacher relationship.

Whatever its origin, information travels through a series of filters, both in the sender and in the receiver, and is affected by different channels, before the idea can be transmitted and re-created in the receiver's mind. Physical capacities to see, hear, smell, taste, and touch vary between people, so that the image of reality may be distorted even before the mind goes to work. In addition to physical or sense filters, cognitive filters, or the way in which an individual's mind interprets the world around him, will influence his assumptions and feelings. These filters will determine what the sender of a message says, how he says it, and with what purpose. Filters are present also in the receiver, creating a double complexity that once led Robert Louis Stevenson to say that human communication is "doubly relative". It takes one person to say something and another to decide what he said.

Physical and cognitive, including semantic filters (which decide the meaning of words) combine to form a part of our memory system that helps us respond to reality. In this sense, March and Simon compare a person to a data processing system. Behavior results from an interaction between a person's internal state and environmental stimuli. What we have learned through past experience becomes an inventory, or data bank, consisting of values or goals, sets of expectations and preconceptions about the consequences of acting one way or another, and a variety of possible ways of responding to the situation. This memory system determines what things we will notice and respond to in the environment. At the same time, stimuli in the environment help to determine what parts of the memory system will be activated. Hence, the memory and the environment form an interactive system that causes our behavior. As this interactive system responds to new experiences, new learnings occur which feed back into memory and gradually change its content. This process is how people adapt to a changing world.

## Formal and Informal

Informal and formal communication are used in an organization. Communication flowing through formal channels are downward, horizontal and upward whereas communication through informal channels are generally termed as grapevine.

Informal communication, generally associated with interpersonal, horizontal communication, was primarily seen as a potential hindrance to effective organizational performance. This is no longer the case. Informal communication has become more important to ensuring the effective conduct of work in modern organizations.

Grapevine is a random, unofficial means of informal communication. It spreads through an organization with access to individual interpretation as gossip, rumors, and single-strand messages. Grapevine communication is quick and usually more direct than formal communication. An employee who receives most of the grapevine information but does not pass it onto others is known as a dead-ender. An employee that receives less than half of the grapevine information is an isolate. Grapevine can include destructive miscommunication, but it can also be beneficial from allowing feelings to be expressed, and increased productivity of employees.

Top-down approach: This is also known as downward communication. This approach is used by the top level management to communicate to the lower levels. This is used to implement policies, guidelines, etc. In this type of organizational communication, distortion of the actual information occurs. This could be made effective by feedbacks.

Additionally, McPhee and Zaug (1995) take a more nuanced view of communication as constitutive of organizations (also referred to as CCO). They identify four constitutive flows of communication, formal and informal, which become interrelated in order to constitute organizing and an organization:

- Organizational self-structuring.
- Membership negotiation.
- Activity coordination.
- Institutional positioning.

## Perspectives

Shockley-Zalabak identified the following two perspectives, essentially as ways of understanding the organizational communication process as a whole.

## The Functional Tradition

According to Shockley-Zalabak, the functional tradition is "a way of understanding organizational communication by describing what messages do and how they move through organizations." There are different functions within this process that all work together to contribute to the overall success of the organization, and these functions occur during the repetition of communication patterns in which the members of the organization engage in. The first types of functions are message functions which are "What communication does or how it contributes to the overall functioning of the organization", and we describe message functions in three different categories which are organizational functions, relationship functions, and change functions. Organizing functions as Shockley-Zalabak states, are "Messages that establish the rules and regulations of a particular environment". These messages can include items such as newsletters or handbooks for a specific organization, that individuals can read to learn the policies and expectations for a certain company. Relationship functions are "Communication that helps individuals define their roles and assess the compatibility of individual and organizational goals". These relationship functions are a key aspect to how individuals identify with a company and it helps them develop their sense of belonging which can greatly influence their quality of work. The third and final subcategory within message functions are change functions, which are defined as "messages that help organizations adapt what they do and how they do it". Change messages occur in various choice making decisions, and they are essential to meet the employee's needs as well as have success with continual adaptations within the organization.

## The Meaning Centered Approach

According to Shockley-Zalabak, the meaning centered approach is "a way of understanding organizational communication by discovering how organizational reality is generated through human interaction". This approach is more concerned with what communication is instead of why and how it works, and message functions as well as message movement are not focused on as thoroughly in this perspective.

## Research

## Research Methodologies

Historically, organizational communication was driven primarily by quantitative research methodologies. Included in functional organizational communication research are statistical analyses (such as surveys, text indexing, network mapping and behavior modeling). In the early 1980s, the interpretive revolution took place in organizational communication. In Putnam and Pacanowsky's 1983 text Communication and Organizations: An Interpretive Approach. they argued for opening up methodological space for qualitative approaches such as narrative analyses, participant-observation, interviewing, rhetoric and textual approaches readings) and philosophic inquiries.

In addition to qualitative and quantitative research methodologies, there is also a third research approach called mixed methods. "Mixed methods is a type of procedural approach for conducting research that involves collecting, analyzing, and mixing quantitative and qualitative data within a single program of study. Its rationale postulates that the use of both qualitative and quantitative research provides a better and richer understanding of a research problem than either traditional research approach alone provides." Complex contextual situations are easier to understand when using a mixed methods research approach, compared to using a qualitative or quantitative research approach. There are more than fifteen mixed method design typologies that have been identified. Because these typologies share many characteristics and criteria, they have been classified into six different types. Three of these types are sequential, meaning that one type of data collection and analysis happens before the other. The other three designs are concurrent, meaning both qualitative and quantitative data are collected at the same time.

## Sequential Explanatory Design

To achieve results from a sequential explanatory design, researchers would take the results from analyzing quantitative data and get a better explanation through a qualitative follow up. They then interpret how the qualitative data explains the quantitative data.

## Sequential Exploratory Design

Although sequential exploratory design may resemble sequential explanatory design, the order in which data is collect is revered. Researchers begin with collecting qualitative data and analyzing it, then follow up by building on it through a quantitative research method. They use the results from qualitative data to form variables, instruments and interventions for quantitative surveys and questionnaires.

## Sequential Transformative Design

Researchers in line with sequential transformative design are led by a "theoretical perspective such as a conceptual framework, a specific ideology, or an advocacy position and employs what will best serve the researcher's theoretical or ideological perspective". Therefore, with this research design, it could be either the qualitative or quantitative method that is used first and priority depends on circumstance and resource availability, but can be given to either.

## Concurrent Triangulation Design

With a concurrent triangulation design, although data is collected through both quantitative and qualitative methods at the same time, they are collected separately with equal priority during one phase. Later, during the analysis phase, the mixing of the two methods takes place.

## Concurrent Embedded Design

In a concurrent embedded design, again, both qualitative and quantitative data is collected, although here one method supports the other. Then, one of the two methods (either qualitative or quantitative) transforms into a support for the dominant method.

## Concurrent Transformative Design

The concurrent transformative design allows the researcher to be guided by their theoretical perspective, so their qualitative and quantitative data may have equal or unequal priority. Again, they are both collected during one phase.

Mixed methods capitalizes on maximizing the strengths of qualitative and quantitative research and minimizing their individual weaknesses by combining both data. Quantitative research is criticized for not considering contexts, having a lack of depth and not giving participants a voice. On the other hand, qualitative research is criticized for smaller sample sizes, possible researcher bias and a lack of generalizability.

During the 1980s and 1990s critical organizational scholarship began to gain prominence with a focus on issues of gender, race, class, and power/knowledge. In its current state, the study of organizational communication is open methodologically, with research from post-positive, interpretive, critical, postmodern, and discursive paradigms being published regularly.

Organizational communication scholarship appears in a number of communication journals including but not limited to Management Communication Quarterly, Journal of Applied Communication Research, Communication Monographs, Academy of Management Journal, Communication Studies, and Southern Communication Journal.

## Current Research Topics

In some circles, the field of organizational communication has moved from acceptance of mechanistic models (e.g., information moving from a sender to a receiver) to a study of the persistent, hegemonic and taken-for-granted ways in which we not only use communication to accomplish certain tasks within organizational settings (e.g., public speaking) but also how the organizations in which we participate affect us.

These approaches include “postmodern”, “critical”, “participatory”, “feminist”, “power/political”, “organic”, etc. and adds to disciplines as wide-ranging as sociology, philosophy, theology, psychology, business, business administration, institutional management, medicine (health communication), neurology (neural nets), semiotics, anthropology, international relations, and music.

Currently, some topics of research and theory in the field are:

## Constitution

Example:

- How communicative behaviors construct or modify organizing processes or products?
- How communication itself plays a constitutive role in organizations?
- How the organizations within which we interact affect our communicative behaviors, and through these, our own identities?
- Structures other than organizations which might be constituted through our communicative activity (e.g., markets, cooperatives, tribes, political parties, social movements)?
- When does something “become” an organization? When does an organization become (an) other thing(s)? Can one organization “house” another? Is the organization still a useful entity/thing/concept, or has the social/political environment changed so much that what we now call “organization” is so different from the organization of even a few decades ago that it cannot be usefully tagged with the same word – “organization”?

## Narrative

Example:

- How do group members employ narrative to acculturate/initiate/indoctrinate new members?

- Do organizational stories act on different levels? Are different narratives purposively invoked to achieve specific outcomes, or are there specific roles of "organizational storyteller"? If so, are stories told by the storyteller received differently from those told by others in the organization?
- In what ways does the organization attempt to influence storytelling about the organization? Under what conditions does the organization appear to be more or less effective in obtaining a desired outcome?
- When these stories conflict with one another or with official rules/policies, how are the conflicts worked out? in situations in which alternative accounts are available, who or how or why are some accepted and others rejected?

## Identity

Example:

- Who do we see ourselves to be, in terms of our organizational affiliations?
- Do communicative behaviors or occurrences in one or more of the organizations in which we participate effect changes in us? To what extent do we consist of the organizations to which we belong?
- Is it possible for individuals to successfully resist organizational identity? what would that look like?
- Do people who define themselves by their work-organizational membership communicate differently within the organizational setting than people who define themselves more by an avocational (non-vocational) set of relationships?
- For example, researchers have studied how human service workers and firefighters use humor at their jobs as a way to affirm their identity in the face of various challenges. Others have examined the identities of police organizations, prison guards, and professional women workers.

## Interrelatedness of Organizational Experiences

Example:

- How do our communicative interactions in one organizational setting affect our communicative actions in other organizational settings?
- How do the phenomenological experiences of participants in a particular organizational setting effect changes in other areas of their lives?
- When the organizational status of a member is significantly changed (e.g., by promotion or expulsion) how are their other organizational memberships affected?
- What kind of future relationship between business and society does organizational communication seem to predict?

### Power

Example:

- How does the use of particular communicative practices within an organizational setting reinforce or alter the various interrelated power relationships within the setting? Are the potential responses of those within or around these organizational settings constrained by factors or processes either within or outside of the organization – (assuming there is an "outside")?
- Do taken-for-granted organizational practices work to fortify the dominant hegemonic narrative? Do individuals resist/confront these practices, through what actions/agencies, and to what effects?
- Do status changes in an organization (e.g., promotions, demotions, restructuring, financial/social strata changes) change communicative behavior? Are there criteria employed by organizational members to differentiate between "legitimate" (i.e., endorsed by the formal organizational structure) and "illegitimate" (i.e., opposed by or unknown to the formal power structure) behaviors? When are they successful, and what do we mean by "successful" when there are "pretenders" or "usurpers" who employ these communicative means?

## Organization Development

Organization development (OD) is the study of successful organizational change and performance. OD emerged from human relations studies in the 1930s, during which psychologists realized that organizational structures and processes influence worker behavior and motivation. More recently, work on OD has expanded to focus on aligning organizations with their rapidly changing and complex environments through organizational learning, knowledge management and transformation of organizational norms and values. Key concepts of OD theory include: organizational climate (the mood or unique "personality" of an organization, which includes attitudes and beliefs that influence members' collective behavior), organizational culture (the deeply-seated norms, values and behaviors that members share) and organizational strategies (how an organization identifies problems, plans action, negotiates change and evaluates progress).

Organization development as a practice involves an ongoing, systematic process of implementing effective organizational change. OD is both a field of applied science focused on understanding and managing organizational change and a field of scientific study and inquiry. It is interdisciplinary in nature and draws on sociology, psychology, particularly industrial and organizational psychology, and theories of motivation, learning, and personality. Although behavioral science has provided the basic foundation for the study and practice of OD, new and emerging fields of study have made their presence felt. Experts in systems thinking, in organizational learning, in the structure of intuition in decision-making, and in coaching (to name a few) whose perspective is not steeped in just the behavioral sciences, but in a much more multi-disciplinary and inter-disciplinary approach, have emerged as OD catalysts or tools.

Kurt Lewin is the founding father of OD, although he died before the concept became mainstream in the mid-1950s. From Lewin came the ideas of group dynamics and action research which underpin the basic OD process as well as providing its collaborative consultant/client ethos. Institutionally, Lewin founded the "Research Center for Group Dynamics" (RCGD) at MIT, which moved to Michigan after his death. RCGD colleagues were among those who founded the National Training Laboratories (NTL), from which the T-groups and group-based OD emerged.

Kurt Lewin played a key role in the evolution of organization development as it is known today. As early as World War II, Lewin experimented with a collaborative change-process (involving himself as consultant and a client group) based on a three-step process of planning, taking action, and measuring results. This was the forerunner of action research, an important element of OD, Lewin also initiated a learning method known as laboratory training, or T-groups. After Lewin's death in 1947, his close associates helped to develop survey-research methods at the University of Michigan. These procedures became important parts of OD as developments in this field continued at the National Training Laboratories and in growing numbers of universities and private consulting-firms across the country. Leading universities offering doctoral-level degrees in OD include Benedictine University and the Fielding Graduate University.

Douglas and Richard Beckhard, while "consulting together at General Mills in the 1950s coined the term organization development (OD) to describe an innovative bottom-up change effort that fit no traditional consulting categories".

The failure of off-site laboratory training to live up to its early promise was one of the important forces stimulating the development of OD. Laboratory training is learning from a person's "here and now" experience as a member of an ongoing training group. Such groups usually meet without a specific agenda. Their purpose is for the members to learn about themselves from their spontaneous "here and now" responses to an ambiguous situation. Problems of leadership, structure, status, communication, and self-serving behavior typically arise in such a group. The members have an opportunity to learn something about themselves and to practice such skills as listening, observing others, and functioning as effective group members. Herbert A. Shepard conducted the first large-scale experiments in Organization Development in the late fifties. He also founded the first doctoral program in organizational behavior at Case Western State University, and his colleague, Robert Blake, was also influential in making the term "organizational development" a more widely recognized field of psychological research.

As formerly practiced (and occasionally still practiced for special purposes), laboratory training was conducted in "stranger groups" - groups composed of individuals from different organizations, situations, and backgrounds. A major difficulty developed, however, in transferring knowledge gained from these "stranger labs" to the actual situation "back home". This required a transfer between two different cultures, the relatively safe and protected environment of the T-group (or training group) and the give-and-take of the organizational environment with its traditional values. This led the early pioneers in this type of learning to begin to apply it to "family groups" — that is, groups located within an organization. From this shift in the locale of the training site and the realization that culture was an important factor in influencing group members (along with some other developments in the behavioral sciences) emerged the concept of organization development.

## Core Values

Underlying Organization Development are humanistic values. Margulies and Raia articulated the humanistic values of OD as follows:

- Providing opportunities for people to function as human beings rather than as resources in the productive process.
- Providing opportunities for each organization member, as well as for the organization itself, to develop to their full potential.
- Seeking to increase the effectiveness of the organization in terms of all of its goals.
- Attempting to create an environment in which it is possible to find exciting and challenging work.
- Providing opportunities for people in organizations to influence the way in which they relate to work, the organization, and the environment.
- Treating each human being as a person with a complex set of needs, all of which are important to their work and their life.

This is a separate concept from change efforts known as:

- Operation management.
- Training and Development.
- Technological innovations, etc.

## Objectives

The objectives of OD are:

- To increase the level of inter-personal trust among employees.
- To increase employees' level of satisfaction and commitment.
- To confront problems instead of neglecting them.
- To effectively manage conflict.
- To increase cooperation and collaboration among employees.
- To increase organizational problem-solving.
- To put in place processes that will help improve the ongoing operation of an organization on a continuous basis.

As objectives of organizational development are framed keeping in view specific situations, they vary from one situation to another. In other words, these programs are tailored to meet the requirements of a particular situation. But broadly speaking, all organizational development programs try to achieve the following objectives:

- Making individuals in the organization aware of the vision of the organization.

Organizational development helps in making employees align with the vision of the organization.

- Encouraging employees to solve problems instead of avoiding them.
- Strengthening inter-personal trust, cooperation, and communication for the successful achievement of organizational goals.
- Encouraging every individual to participate in the process of planning, thus making them feel responsible for the implementation of the plan.
- Creating a work atmosphere in which employees are encouraged to work and participate enthusiastically.
- Replacing formal lines of authority with personal knowledge and skill.
- Preparing members to align with changes and to break stereotypes.
- Creating an environment of trust so that employees willingly accept change.

According to organizational-development thinking, organization development provides managers with a vehicle for introducing change systematically by applying a broad selection of management techniques. This, in turn, leads to greater personal, group, and organizational effectiveness.

## Change Agent

A change agent in the sense used here is not a technical expert skilled in such functional areas as accounting, production, or finance. The change agent is a behavioral scientist who knows how to get people in an organization involved in solving their own problems. A change agent's main strength is a comprehensive knowledge of human behavior, supported by a number of intervention techniques. The change agent can be either external or internal to the organization. An internal change agent is usually a staff person who has expertise in the behavioral sciences and in the intervention technology of OD. Beckhard reports several cases in which line people have been trained in OD and have returned to their organizations to engage in successful change-assignments. In the natural evolution of change mechanisms in organizations, this would seem to approach the ideal arrangement.

Researchers at the University of Oxford found that leaders can be effective change-agents within their own organizations if they are strongly committed to "knowledge leadership" targeted towards organizational development. In their three-year study of UK healthcare organizations, the researchers identified three different mechanisms through which knowledge leaders actively "transposed", "appropriated" or "contended" change concepts, effectively translating and embedding these in organizational practice.

The change agent may be a staff or line member of the organization who is schooled in OD theory and technique. In such a case, the "contractual relationship" is an in-house agreement that should probably be explicit with respect to all of the conditions involved except the fee.

## Sponsoring Organization

The initiative for OD programs often comes from an organization that has a problem or anticipates facing a problem. This means that top management or someone authorized by top management is aware that a problem exists and has decided to seek help in solving it. There is a direct analogy here to the practice of psychotherapy: The client or patient must actively seek help in finding a solution to his problems. This indicates a willingness on the part of the client organization to accept help and assures the organization that management is actively concerned.

## Applied Behavioral Science

One of the outstanding characteristics of OD that distinguishes it from most other improvement programs is that it is based on a "helping relationship". Some believe that the change agent is a physician to the organization's ills; that s/he does not examine the "patient", make a diagnosis, and write a prescription. Nor does s/he try to teach organizational members a new inventory of knowledge which they then transfer to the job situation. Using theory and methods drawn from such behavioral sciences as industrial/organizational psychology, industrial sociology, communication, cultural anthropology, administrative theory, organizational behavior, economics, and political science, the change agent's main function is to help the organization define and solve its own problems. The basic method used is known as action research. This approach, consists of a preliminary diagnosis, collecting data, feedback of the data to the client, data exploration by the client group, action planning based on the data, and taking action.

### Systems Context

## The Holistic and Futuristic view of Organization

OD deals with a total system — the organization as a whole, including its relevant environment — or with a subsystem or systems — departments or work groups — in the context of the total system. Parts of systems — for example, individuals, cliques, structures, norms, values, and products — are not considered in isolation; the principle of interdependency — that change in one part of a system affects the other parts — is fully recognized. Thus OD interventions focus on the total cultures and cultural processes of organizations. The focus is also on groups, since the relevant behavior of individuals in organizations and groups is generally a product of the influences of groups rather than of personalities.

## Improved Organizational Performance

The objective of OD is to improve the organization's capacity to handle its internal and external functioning and relationships. This includes improved interpersonal and group processes, more effective communication, and enhanced ability to cope with organizational problems of all kinds. It also involves more effective decision processes, more appropriate leadership styles, improved skill in dealing with destructive conflict, as well as developing improved levels of trust and cooperation among organizational members. These objectives stem from a value system based on an optimistic view of the nature of man — that man in a supportive environment is capable of achieving higher levels of development and accomplishment. Essential to organization development and effectiveness is the scientific method — inquiry, a rigorous search for causes, experimental testing of hypotheses, and review of results.

Self-managing work groups allows the members of a work team to manage, control, and monitor all facets of their work, from recruiting, hiring, and new employees to deciding when to take rest breaks. An early analysis of the first-self-managing work groups yielded the following behavioral characteristics:

- Employees assume personal responsibility and accountability for outcomes of their work.
- Employees monitor their own performance and seek feedback on how well they are accomplishing their goals.
- Employees manage their performance and take corrective action when necessary to improve their and the performance of other group members.
- Employees seek guidance, assistance, and resources from the organization when they do not have what they need to do the job.
- Employees help members of their work group and employees in other groups to improve job performance and raise productivity for the organization as a whole.

## Organizational Self-renewal

The ultimate aim of OD practitioners is to "work themselves out of a job" by leaving the client organization with a set of tools, behaviors, attitudes, and an action plan with which to monitor its own state of health and to take corrective steps toward its own renewal and development. This is consistent with the systems concept of feedback as a regulatory and corrective mechanism. To this end, OD scholars and practitioners use tools such as simulations with their clients, to be used in workshops and classroom settings.

The study of organizational effectiveness and improving organizational performance has developed alongside the study of leadership development with a greater focus on leadership development programs which focus on development of the individual.

## Understanding Organizations

Weisbord presents a six-box model for understanding organizations:

- Purposes: The organization members are clear about the organization's mission and purpose and goal agreements, whether people support the organization's purpose.
- Structure: How is the organization's work divided up? The question is whether there is an adequate fit between the purpose and the internal structure.
- Relationship: Between individuals, between units or departments that perform different tasks, and between the people and requirements of their jobs.
- Rewards: The consultant should diagnose the similarities between what the organization formally rewarded or punished members for.

- Leadership: Is to watch for blips among the other boxes and maintain balance among them.
- Helpful mechanism: What must the organization attend to in order to survive and thrive – procedures such as planning, control, budgeting, and other information systems.

## Modern Development

In recent years, serious questioning has emerged about the relevance of OD to managing change in modern organizations. The need for "reinventing" the field has become a topic that even some of its "founding fathers" are discussing critically.

With this call for reinvention and change, scholars have begun to examine organization development from an emotion-based standpoint. For example, deKlerk writes about how emotional trauma can negatively affect performance. Due to downsizing, outsourcing, mergers, restructuring, continual changes, invasions of privacy, harassment, and abuses of power, many employees experience the emotions of aggression, anxiety, apprehension, cynicism, and fear, which can lead to performance decreases. deKlerk suggests that in order to heal the trauma and increase performance, O.D. practitioners must acknowledge the existence of the trauma, provide a safe place for employees to discuss their feelings, symbolize the trauma and put it into perspective, and then allow for and deal with the emotional responses. One method of achieving this is by having employees draw pictures of what they feel about the situation, and then having them explain their drawings with each other. Drawing pictures is beneficial because it allows employees to express emotions they normally would not be able to put into words. Also, drawings often prompt active participation in the activity, as everyone is required to draw a picture and then discuss its meaning.

The use of new technologies combined with globalization has also shifted the field of organization development. Roland Sullivan defined Organization Development with participants at the 1st Organization Development Conference for Asia in Dubai-2005 as Organization Development is a transformative leap to a desired vision where strategies and systems align, in the light of local culture with an innovative and authentic leadership style using the support of high tech tools. Bob Aubrey introduced KDIs (Key Development Indicators) to help organisations go beyond performance and align strategy, organisations and individuals and argued that fundamental challenges such as robotics, artificial intelligence and genetics prefigure a regeneration of the field.

## Action Research

Wendell L French and Cecil Bell defined organization development (OD) at one point as "organization improvement through action research". If one idea can be said to summarize OD's underlying philosophy, it would be action research as it was conceptualized by Kurt Lewin and later elaborated and expanded on by other behavioral scientists. Concerned with social change and, more particularly, with effective, permanent social change, Lewin believed that the motivation to change was strongly related to action: If people are active in decisions affecting them, they are more likely to adopt new ways. "Rational social management", he said, "proceeds in a spiral of steps, each of which is composed of a circle of planning, action, and fact-finding about the result of action".

Lewin's description of the process of change involves three steps:

- "Unfreezing": Faced with a dilemma or disconfirmation, the individual or group becomes aware of a need to change.
- "Changing": The situation is diagnosed and new models of behavior are explored and tested.
- "Refreezing": Application of new behavior is evaluated, and if reinforced, adopted.

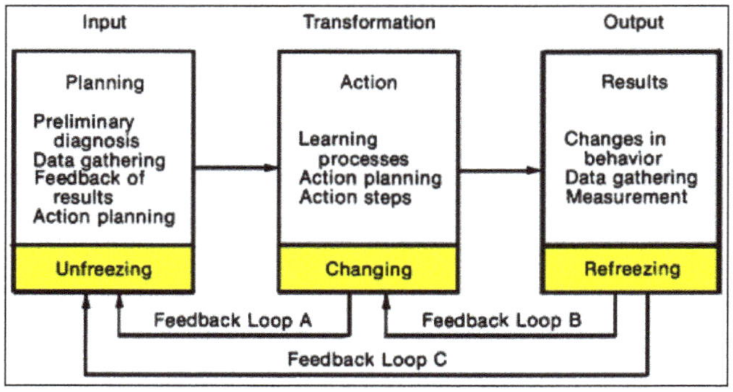


Systems Model of Action-Research Process.

Above figure summarizes the steps and processes involved in planned change through action research. Action research is depicted as a cyclical process of change. The cycle begins with a series of planning actions initiated by the client and the change agent working together. The principal elements of this stage include a preliminary diagnosis, data gathering, feedback of results, and joint action planning. In the language of systems theory, this is the input phase, in which the client system becomes aware of problems as yet unidentified, realizes it may need outside help to effect changes, and shares with the consultant the process of problem diagnosis.

The second stage of action research is the action, or transformation, phase. This stage includes actions relating to learning processes (perhaps in the form of role analysis) and to planning and executing behavioral changes in the client organization. feedback at this stage would move via Feedback Loop A and would have the effect of altering previous planning to bring the learning activities of the client system into better alignment with change objectives. Included in this stage is action-planning activity carried out jointly by the consultant and members of the client system. Following the workshop or learning sessions, these action steps are carried out on the job as part of the transformation stage.

The third stage of action research is the output, or results, phase. This stage includes actual changes in behavior (if any) resulting from corrective action steps taken following the second stage. Data are again gathered from the client system so that progress can be determined and necessary adjustments in learning activities can be made. Minor adjustments of this nature can be made in learning activities via Feedback Loop B. Major adjustments and reevaluations would return the OD project to the first, or planning, stage for basic changes in the program. The action-research model closely follows Lewin's repetitive cycle of planning, action, and measuring results. It also illustrates other aspects of Lewin's general model of change. As indicated in the diagram, the planning stage is a period of unfreezing, or problem awareness. The action stage is a period of changing, that is, trying out new forms of behavior in an effort to understand and cope with the system's problems. (There is inevitable overlap between the stages, since the boundaries are not clear-cut and cannot be in a continuous process). The results stage is a period of refreezing, in which new behaviors are tried out on the job and, if successful and reinforcing, become a part of the system's repertoire of problem-solving behavior.

Action research is problem centered, client centered, and action oriented. It involves the client system in a diagnostic, active-learning, problem-finding, and problem-solving process. Data are not simply returned in the form of a written report but instead are fed back in open joint sessions, and the client and the change agent collaborate in identifying and ranking specific problems, in devising methods for finding their real causes, and in developing plans for coping with them realistically and practically. Scientific method in the form of data gathering, forming hypotheses, testing hypotheses, and measuring results, although not pursued as rigorously as in the laboratory, is nevertheless an integral part of the process. Action research also sets in motion a long-range, cyclical, self-correcting mechanism for maintaining and enhancing the effectiveness of the client's system by leaving the system with practical and useful tools for self-analysis and self-renewal.

## OD Interventions

"Interventions" are principal learning processes in the "action" stage of organization development. Interventions are structured activities used individually or in combination by the members of a client system to improve their social or task performance. They may be introduced by a change agent as part of an improvement program, or they may be used by the client following a program to check on the state of the organization's health, or to effect necessary changes in its own behavior. "Structured activities" mean such diverse procedures as experiential exercises, questionnaires, attitude surveys, interviews, relevant group discussions, and even lunchtime meetings between the change agent and a member of the client organization. Every action that influences an organization's improvement program in a change agent-client system relationship can be said to be an intervention.

There are many possible intervention strategies from which to choose. Several assumptions about the nature and functioning of organizations are made in the choice of a particular strategy. Beckhard lists six such assumptions:

- The basic building blocks of an organization are groups (teams). Therefore, the basic units of change are groups, not individuals.
- An always relevant change goal is the reduction of inappropriate competition between parts of the organization and the development of a more collaborative condition.
- Decision making in a healthy organization is located where the information sources are, rather than in a particular role or level of hierarchy.
- Organizations, subunits of organizations, and individuals continuously manage their affairs against goals. Controls are interim measurements, not the basis of managerial strategy.
- One goal of a healthy organization is to develop generally open communication, mutual trust, and confidence between and across levels.
- People support what they help create. People affected by a change must be allowed active participation and a sense of ownership in the planning and conduct of the change.

Interventions range from those designed to improve the effectiveness of individuals through those designed to deal with teams and groups, intergroup relations, and the total organization. There are interventions that focus on task issues (what people do), and those that focus on process issues (how people go about doing it). Finally, interventions may be roughly classified according to which change mechanism they tend to emphasize: for example, feedback, awareness of changing cultural norms, interaction and communication, conflict, and education through either new knowledge or skill practice.

One of the most difficult tasks confronting the change agent is to help create in the client system a safe climate for learning and change. In a favorable climate, human learning builds on itself and continues indefinitely during man's lifetime. Out of new behavior, new dilemmas and problems emerge as the spiral continues upward to new levels. In an unfavorable climate, in contrast, learning is far less certain, and in an atmosphere of psychological threat, it often stops altogether. Unfreezing old ways can be inhibited in organizations because the climate makes employees feel that it is inappropriate to reveal true feelings, even though such revelations could be constructive. In an inhibited atmosphere, therefore, necessary feedback is not available. Also, trying out new ways may be viewed as risky because it violates established norms. Such an organization may also be constrained because of the law of systems: If one part changes, other parts will become involved. Hence, it is easier to maintain the status quo. Hierarchical authority, specialization, span of control, and other characteristics of formal systems also discourage experimentation.

The change agent must address himself to all of these hazards and obstacles. Some of the things which will help him are:

- A real need in the client system to change.
- Genuine support from management.
- Setting a personal example: listening, supporting behavior.
- A sound background in the behavioral sciences.
- A working knowledge of systems theory.
- A belief in man as a rational, self-educating being fully capable of learning better ways to do things.

A few examples of interventions include team building, coaching, Large Group Interventions, mentoring, performance appraisal, downsizing, TQM, and leadership development.

## Organizational Engineering

Organizational Engineering (OE) is a form of organizational development. It was created by Gary Salton of Professional Communications, Inc. It has been developing continuously since 1994 on both theoretical and applied levels.

The core premise of OE is that humans are information-processing organisms. It posits that individual behavior can be understood and predicted using engineering's basic model of:

```
INPUT > PROCESS > OUTPUT
```

This offers advantages over the more typical psychological approaches. Primary among these is that it requires only simple logic. There is no need to rely on unseen forces or "inherent" mental characteristics.

For example, life requires a person to navigate a host of relationships with people and things. People's lives tend to be relatively stable. They live in the same house, drive the same car, put the same children to bed in the evening and go to work to the same place each morning. This stability allows people to perfect a strategy that works in their typical situations. Since people tend to reuse things that work, this strategy becomes their general approach. They will try to use it even in unfamiliar situations. It becomes a characteristic approach.

OE calls the strategies people regularly use strategic styles. Styles are different combinations of the Input>Process>Output. Each mix produces a different but predictable pattern of behavior. For example, a person may elect to pay attention to detail (input). It is virtually certain that this will slow response. The more detail they require, the slower they will be. Others will probably infer that they are cautious or deliberate. This result is a certainty. It takes time to process information. Unless a way can be found to speed the chemical reactions between the neurons in the brain the result will always be the same.

OE applies the same kind of logic to define the range of possible behaviors. These relationships have been codified under the name of "I Opt." This is an acronym for "Input Output Processing Template". It is the basic measuring tool of Organizational Engineering.

## Tools for Individuals

The "I Opt" model uses a 24-statement survey to assess preferences. The survey is designed in a way that creates ratio measurement (exact, like a ruler). This contrasts more typical ordinal measurement (e.g., rank ordered – big-bigger-biggest or none-some-lots) used by most other tools. Exact measurement allows "I Opt" to derive formulas that can be used by a computer. Interpretation is unnecessary. The computer can provide a definitive answer.

Information processing is involved in almost every part of a person's life. This means that individual reports can be generated on a variety of interest areas. Standard computer programs in areas like learning, sales, leadership, change management and career direction are available. Additional reports can be programmed as the need for them becomes visible.

## Tools for Groups

Exact measurement allows "I Opt" infer probable outcomes embedded in a relationship of groups of people. For example, a person might prefer to rely on analysis to make decisions. Another might prefer spontaneous action. Both of these postures use different Input>Process>Output combinations. Both strategies will work to resolve issues. But the strategy of one forecloses the strategy of the other. It is predictable that there will be tension in the relationship. This requires no "interpretation." The direction and degree of tension can be calculated from the strength of the "I Opt" scores of each person.

Organizational Engineering uses Sociology—the science of groups—as its scaffold. The principles of sociology allow OE to extend its reach. Computer programs can analyze groups of 20 or more people all interacting simultaneously. There is no need to interview group participants. Everything is embedded in the numbers.

Sociology guides interpretation. Computer programs have been created to apply its principles to common situations. For example, TeamAnalysis analyzes groups assuming that everyone has equal power. It reveals the macro-dynamics that underlie group behavior. These become the basis of the advice the computer offers. The LeaderAnalysis takes the next step. It looks at a group and each person in the group from the viewpoint of the leader. It analyzes the leader-group match and produces specific counsel for the leader to consider in guiding the group.

"I Opt" models view groups as a system of relationships. In a system if you change a relationship you change system performance. No individual in the group has to change. Just their relationship to others in the group. It is hard to change people. It is relatively easy to change relationships. This means that the benefits can accrue quickly and will typically increase over time as the interaction patterns are refined.

## Tools for Firms

Firms are systems of groups. The output of the "I Opt" can be used to assess entire firms. This level of analysis uses the "I Opt" individual and group analytical components as investigatory tools.

The influence of groups upon groups is measured using the tools of practical geometry. The composite profiles of groups are overlaid. The magnitude and direction of overlaps are calculated. Likely outcomes of interactions are inferred. These are the macro-behavioral tendencies of the system of groups. It describes what will happen if the groups are allowed to interact without consistent guidance.

OE sees individual leaders as lynch pins between groups. This follows the Rensis Likert's concept of the linking pin model. The leader represents the group that he/she leads when that leader is participating in larger groups. Leaders also act as a corridor carrying information from the larger group back to their local one. The leader's "I Opt" profile will determine their understanding of the issues. It will also determine the likely actions that they will take.

The predictable behaviors of groups and leaders allow OE to plot likely outcomes. The same principles that apply to teams apply to firms. Change the relationships and you will change the outcomes. "I Opt" can define "what is causing what" in the system of groups and leaders. This allows it to pinpoint critical areas. This ability to focus on points of maximum effect reduces the cost and improves the timeliness of change.

The durable interaction of leaders and groups evolve into a corporate culture. The overlap of the composite profiles defines common perspectives. This is a basis of the "shared" values, beliefs and behaviors that define a culture. Alter the relationships of the groups and/or leaders and corporate culture can be changed in any direction desired.

## Applications

Consultants and internal groups within firms use OE and "I Opt" in a variety of ways. Improving team performance is a common use. The reports are easy to read, respectful in tone and mature in content. The non-judgmental nature of the reports means they can be and are used from the Board of Directors to factory floor work groups with equal positive effect.

The various "I Opt" individual analyzes are used as a component of educational programs in areas like leadership development, learning and career guidance. They are also used to facilitate education itself. For example, the TwoPerson Analysis is used as a tool to quickly launch mentoring relationships. Participants know each other's bias form the onset. They can compensate immediately rather than spending time "discovering" these in each other.

Another area of application is in the selection of people to fill specific roles. "I Opt" analysis can predict the relationship of an individual to both the leader and other group members. Taken in conjunction with other measures (e.g., competencies, experience, education, etc.) it can reduce the probability of inappropriate placements.

Overall, organizational engineering gives a way to understand, measure, predict and guide human behavior for both individuals and groups. Its objective is to produce visible, positive results of significant consequence and magnitude. It is able to consistently accomplish this objective in any situation that meets the mutual dependency criteria characteristic of goal directed organizations. This has been demonstrated in domestic and international contexts.

"I Opt" can be used with confidence. The measurement component of "I Opt" has been fully validated. It requires only a 6th-grade reading level to complete the required survey. The individual reports are written at an 8th-grade level. Group reports vary by the complexity of the group being assessed but typically require less than a 12th-grade level reading level.

## Organizational Culture

Organizational culture encompasses values and behaviors that contribute to the unique social and psychological environment of a business. The organizational culture influences the way people interact, the context within which knowledge is created, the resistance they will have towards certain changes, and ultimately the way they share (or the way they do not share) knowledge. Organizational culture represents the collective values, beliefs and principles of organizational members. It may also be influenced by factors such as history, product, market, technology, strategy, type of employees, management style, and national culture. Culture includes the organization's vision, values, norms, systems, symbols, language, assumptions, environment, location, beliefs and habits.

Ravasi and Schultz characterise organizational culture as a set of shared assumptions that guide behaviors. It is also the pattern of such collective behaviors and assumptions that are taught to new organizational members as a way of perceiving and, even thinking and feeling. Thus organizational culture affects the way people and groups interact with each other, with clients, and with stakeholders. In addition, organizational culture may affect how much employees identify with an organization.

Schein, Deal and Kennedy, and Kotter advanced the idea that organizations often have very differing cultures as well as subcultures. Although a company may have its "own unique culture," in larger organizations there are sometimes co-existing or conflicting subcultures because each subculture is linked to a different management team. Flamholtz and Randle suggest that one can view organizational culture as "corporate personality." They define it as it consisting of the values, beliefs, and norms which influence the behavior of people as members of an organization.

The term of culture in the organizational context was first introduced by Dr. Elliott Jaques in his book The Changing Culture of a Factory, in 1951. This is the published report of "a case study of developments in the social life of one industrial community between April, 1948 and November 1950". The "case" is a publicly held British company engaged principally in the manufacture, sale, and servicing of metal bearings. The study is concerned with the description, analysis, and development of the corporate group behaviours.

According to Dr. Elliott Jaques "the culture of the factory is its customary and traditional way of thinking and doing of things, which is shared to a greater or lesser degree by all its members, and which new members must learn, and at least partially accept, in order to be accepted into service in the firm" In simple terms, to the extent that people can share common wishes, desires and aspirations, they can commit themselves to work together. It is a matter of being able to care about the same things, and it applies to nations as well as to associations and organizations within nations.

Elaborating on the work in The Changing Culture of a Factory Dr. Elliott Jaques in his concept of requisite organization established the list of valued entitlements or organizational values that can gain from people their full commitment. Together they make an organizational culture or credo:

- Fair and just treatment for everyone, including fair pay based upon equitable pay differentials for level of work and merit recognition related to personal effectiveness appraisal.
- Leadership interaction between managers and subordinates, including shared context, personal effectiveness appraisal, feedback and recognition, and coaching.
- Clear articulation of accountability and authority to engender trust and confidence in all working relationships.
- Articulation of long-term organizational vision through direct communication from the top.
- Opportunity for everyone individually or through representatives to participate in policy development.
- Work for everyone at a level consistent with their level of potential capability, values and interests.
- Opportunity for everyone to progress as his or her potential capability matures, within the opportunities available.

The role of managerial leadership at every organizational level is to make these organizational values operationally real.

## Usage

Organizational culture refers to culture in any type of organization including that of schools, universities, not-for-profit groups, government agencies, or business entities. In business, terms such as corporate culture and company culture are often used to refer to a similar concept. The term corporate culture became widely known in the business world in the late 1980s and early 1990s. Corporate culture was already used by managers, sociologists, and organizational theorists by the beginning of the 80s. The related idea of organizational climate emerged in the 1960s and 70s, and the terms are now somewhat overlapping.

If organizational culture is seen as something that characterizes an organization, it can be manipulated and altered depending on leadership and members. Culture as root metaphor sees the organization as its culture, created through communication and symbols, or competing metaphors. Culture is basic, with personal experience producing a variety of perspectives.

The organizational communication perspective on culture views culture in three different ways:

- Traditionalism: views culture through objective things such as stories, rituals, and symbols.
- Interpretivism: views culture through a network of shared meanings (organization members sharing subjective meanings).
- Critical-interpretivism: views culture through a network of shared meanings as well as the power struggles created by a similar network of competing meanings.

Business executive Bernard L. Rosauer defines organizational culture as an emergence – an extremely complex incalculable state that results from the combination of a few ingredients. In "Three Bell Curves: Business Culture Decoded" Rosauer outlines the three manageable ingredients which (he claims) guide business culture:

- Employee (focus on engagement).
- The work (focus on eliminating waste increasing value) waste.
- The customer (focus on likelihood of referral).

Rosauer writes that the Three Bell Curves methodology aims to bring leadership, their employees, the work and the customer together for focus without distraction, leading to an improvement in culture and brand. He states: "If a methodology isn't memorable, it won't get used. The Three Bell Curves Methodology is simple (to remember) but execution requires strong leadership and diligence. Culture can be guided by managing the ingredients." Reliance of the research and findings of Sirota Survey Intelligence, which has been gathering employee data worldwide since 1972, the Lean Enterprise Institute, Cambridge, MA, and Fred Reichheld/Bain/Satmetrix research relating to NetPromoterScore.

## Classification of Cultural Types

Typology refers to the "study of or analysis or classification based on types or categories." Organizational culture and climate may be erroneously used interchangeably. Organizational culture has been described as an organization's ideals, vision, and mission, whereas climate is better defined as employees' shared meaning related to the company's policies and procedures and reward/consequence systems. Many factors, ranging from depictions of relative strength to political and national issues, can contribute to the type or types of culture that can be observed in organizations and institutions of all sizes. Below are examples of organizational culture types.

## Strong and Weak Typology of Organizational Culture

Flamholtz and Randle state that: "A strong culture is one that people clearly understand and can articulate. A weak culture is one that employees have difficulty defining, understanding, or explaining." Strong culture is said to exist where staff respond to stimulus because of their alignment to organizational values. In such environments, strong cultures help firms operate like well-oiled machines, engaging in outstanding execution with only minor adjustments to existing procedures as needed.

Conversely, there is weak culture where there is little alignment with organizational values, and control must be exercised through extensive procedures and bureaucracy.

Research shows that organizations that foster strong cultures have clear values that give employees a reason to embrace the culture. A "strong" culture may be especially beneficial to firms operating in the service sector since members of these organizations are responsible for delivering the service and for evaluations important constituents make about firms. Organizations may derive the following benefits from developing strong and productive cultures:

- Better aligning the company towards achieving its vision, mission, and goals.
- High employee motivation and loyalty.
- Increased team cohesiveness among the company's various departments and divisions.
- Promoting consistency and encouraging coordination and control within the company.
- Shaping employee behavior at work, enabling the organization to be more efficient.

Irving Janis defined groupthink as "a mode of thinking that people engage in when they are deeply involved in a cohesive in-group, when the members' strivings for unanimity override their motivation to realistically appraise alternative courses of action." This is a state in which even if group members have different ideas, they do not challenge organizational thinking. As a result, innovative thinking is stifled. Groupthink can lead to lack of creativity and decisions made without critical evaluation. Groupthink can occur, for example, when group members rely heavily on a central charismatic figure in the organization or where there is an "evangelical" belief in the organization's values. Groupthink can also occur in groups characterized by a friendly climate conducive to conflict avoidance.

## Healthy

Organizations should strive for what is considered a "healthy" organizational culture in order to increase productivity, growth, efficiency and reduce counterproductive behavior and turnover of employees. A variety of characteristics describe a healthy culture, including:

- Acceptance and appreciation for diversity.
- Regard for fair treatment of each employee as well as respect for each employee's contribution to the company.
- Employee pride and enthusiasm for the organization and the work performed.

- Equal opportunity for each employee to realize their full potential within the company.
- Strong communication with all employees regarding policies and company issues.
- Strong company leaders with a strong sense of direction and purpose.
- Ability to compete in industry innovation and customer service, as well as price.
- Lower than average turnover rates (perpetuated by a healthy culture).
- Investment in learning, training, and employee knowledge.

Additionally, performance oriented cultures have been shown to possess statistically better financial growth. Such cultures possess high employee involvement, strong internal communications and an acceptance and encouragement of a healthy level of risk-taking in order to achieve innovation. Additionally, organizational cultures that explicitly emphasize factors related to the demands placed on them by industry technology and growth will be better performers in their industries.

According to Kotter and Heskett, organizations with adaptive cultures perform much better than organizations with unadaptive cultures. An adaptive culture translates into organizational success; it is characterized by managers paying close attention to all of their constituencies, especially customers, initiating change when needed, and taking risks. An unadaptive culture can significantly reduce a firm's effectiveness, disabling the firm from pursuing all its competitive/operational options.

Healthy companies are able to deal with employees' concerns about the well-being of the organization internally, before the employees would even feel they needed to raise the issues externally. It is for this reason that whistleblowing, particularly when it results in serious damage to a company's reputation, is considered to be often a sign of a chronically dysfunctional corporate culture. Another relevant concept is the notion of "cultural functionality". Specifically, some organizations have "functional" cultures while others have "dysfunctional" cultures. A "functional" culture is a positive culture that contributes to an organization's performance and success. A "dysfunctional" culture is one that hampers or negatively affects an organization's performance and success.

## Management Types of Communication

There are many different types of communication that contribute in creating an organizational culture:

- Metaphors such as comparing an organization to a machine or a family reveal employees' shared meanings of experiences at the organization.
- Stories can provide examples for employees of how to or not to act in certain situations.
- Rites and ceremonies combine stories, metaphors, and symbols into one. Several different kinds of rites affect organizational culture:
    - Rites of passage: employees move into new roles.
    - Rites of degradation: employees have power taken away from them.

    - Rites of enhancement: public recognition for an employee's accomplishments.
    - Rites of renewal: improve existing social structures.
    - Rites of conflict reduction: resolve arguments between certain members or groups.
    - Rites of integration: reawaken feelings of membership in the organization.
- Reflexive comments are explanations, justifications, and criticisms of our own actions. This includes:
    - Plans: comments about anticipated actions.
    - Commentaries: comments about action in the present.
    - Accounts: comments about an action or event that has already occurred.
- Such comments reveal interpretive meanings held by the speaker as well as the social rules they follow.
- Fantasy Themes are common creative interpretations of events that reflect beliefs, values, and goals of the organization. They lead to rhetorical visions, or views of the organization and its environment held by organization members.

## Bullying Culture Type

Bullying is seen to be prevalent in organizations where employees and managers feel that they have the support, or at least implicitly the blessing, of senior managers to carry on their abusive and bullying behaviour. Furthermore, new managers will quickly come to view this form of behaviour as acceptable and normal if they see others get away with it and are even rewarded for it.

When bullying happens at the highest levels, the effects may be far reaching. That people may be bullied irrespective of their organisational status or rank, including senior managers, indicates the possibility of a negative ripple effect, where bullying may be cascaded downwards as the targeted supervisors might offload their own aggression on their subordinates. In such situations, a bullying scenario in the boardroom may actually threaten the productivity of the entire organisation.

## Personal Culture Type

Organizational culture is taught to the person as culture is taught by his/her parents thus changing and modeling his/her personal culture. Indeed, employees and people applying for a job are advised to match their "personality to a company's culture" and fit to it. Some researchers even suggested and have made case studies research on personality changing.

## National Culture Type

Corporate culture is used to control, coordinate, and integrate company subsidiaries. However differences in national cultures exist contributing to differences in the views on management. Differences between national cultures are deep rooted values of the respective cultures, and these cultural values can shape how people expect companies to be run, and how relationships between leaders and followers should be, resulting in differences between the employer and the employee regarding expectations. Perhaps equally foundational; observing the vast differences in national copyright (and taxation, etc.) laws suggests deep rooted differences in cultural attitudes and assumptions about property rights and sometimes about the desired root function, place, or purpose of corporations relative to the population.

## Multiplicity

Xibao Zhang carried out an empirical study of culture emergence in the Sino-Western international cross-cultural management (SW-ICCM) context in China. Field data were collected by interviewing Western expatriates and Chinese professionals working in this context, supplemented by non-participant observation and documentary data. The data were then analyzed objectively to formulate theme-based substantive theories and a formal theory.

The major finding of this study is that the human cognition contains three components, or three broad types of "cultural rules of behavior", namely, Values, Expectations, and Ad Hoc Rules, each of which has a mutually conditioning relationship with behavior. The three cognitive components are different in terms of the scope and duration of their mutual shaping of behavior. Values are universal and enduring rules of behavior; Expectations, on the other hand, are context-specific behavioral rules; while Ad Hoc Rules are improvised rules of behavior that the human mind devises contingent upon a particular occasion. Furthermore, they need not be consistent, and frequently are not, among themselves. Metaphorically, they can be compared to a multi-carriage train, which allows for the relative lateral movements by individual carriages so as to accommodate bumps and turns in the tracks. In fact, they provide a "shock-absorber mechanism", so to speak, which enables individuals in SW-ICCM contexts to cope with conflicts in cultural practices and values, and to accommodate and adapt themselves to cultural contexts where people from different national cultural backgrounds work together over extended time. It also provides a powerful framework which explains how interactions by individuals in SW-ICCM contexts give rise to emerging hybrid cultural practices characterized by both stability and change.

One major theoretical contribution of this "multi-carriage train" perspective is its allowance for the existence of inconsistencies among the three cognitive components in their mutual conditioning of behavior. This internal inconsistency view is in stark contrast to the traditional internal consistency assumption explicitly or tacitly held by many culture scholars. The other major theoretical contribution, which follows logically from the first one, is to view culture as an overarching entity which is made of a multiplicity of Values, Expectations, and Ad Hoc Rules. This notion of one (multiplicity) culture to an organization leads to the classification of culture along its path of emergence into nascent, adolescent, and mature types, each of which is distinct in terms of the pattern of the three cognitive components and behavior.

## Effects

Research suggests that numerous outcomes have been associated either directly or indirectly with organizational culture. A healthy and robust organizational culture may provide various benefits, including the following:

- Competitive edge derived from innovation and customer service.

- Consistent, efficient employee performance.
- Team cohesiveness.
- High employee morale.
- Strong company alignment towards goal achievement.

Although little empirical research exists to support the link between organizational culture and organizational performance, there is little doubt among experts that this relationship exists. Organizational culture can be a factor in the survival or failure of an organization – although this is difficult to prove given that the necessary longitudinal analyses are hardly feasible. The sustained superior performance of firms like IBM, Hewlett-Packard, Procter & Gamble, and McDonald's may be, at least partly, a reflection of their organizational cultures.

A 2003 Harvard Business School study reported that culture has a significant effect on an organization's long-term economic performance. The study examined the management practices at 160 organizations over ten years and found that culture can enhance performance or prove detrimental to performance. Organizations with strong performance-oriented cultures witnessed far better financial growth. Additionally, a 2002 Corporate Leadership Council study found that cultural traits such as risk taking, internal communications, and flexibility are some of the most important drivers of performance, and may affect individual performance. Furthermore, innovativeness, productivity through people, and the other cultural factors cited by Peters and Waterman also have positive economic consequences.

Denison, Haaland, and Goelzer found that culture contributes to the success of the organization, but not all dimensions contribute the same. It was found that the effects of these dimensions differ by global regions, which suggests that organizational culture is affected by national culture. Additionally, Clarke found that a safety climate is related to an organization's safety record.

Organizational culture is reflected in the way people perform tasks, set objectives, and administer the necessary resources to achieve objectives. Culture affects the way individuals make decisions, feel, and act in response to the opportunities and threats affecting the organization.

Adkins and Caldwell found that job satisfaction was positively associated with the degree to which employees fit into both the overall culture and subculture in which they worked. A perceived mismatch of the organization's culture and what employees felt the culture should be is related to a number of negative consequences including lower job satisfaction, higher job strain, general stress, and turnover intent.

It has been proposed that organizational culture may affect the level of employee creativity, the strength of employee motivation, and the reporting of unethical behavior, but more research is needed to support these conclusions.

Organizational culture also affects recruitment and retention. Individuals tend to be attracted to and remain engaged in organizations that they perceive to be compatible. Additionally, high turnover may be a mediating factor in the relationship between culture and organizational performance. Deteriorating company performance and an unhealthy work environment are signs of an overdue cultural assessment.

## Change

When an organization does not possess a healthy culture or requires some kind of organizational culture change, the change process can be daunting. Organizational culture can hinder new change efforts, especially where employees know their expectations and the roles that they are supposed to play in the organization. This is corroborated by Mar (2016:1) who argues that 70% of all change efforts fail because of the culture of an organization's employees. One major reason why such change is difficult is that organizational cultures, and the organizational structures in which they are embedded, often reflect the "imprint" of earlier periods in a persistent way and exhibit remarkable levels of inertia. Culture change may be necessary to reduce employee turnover, influence employee behavior, make improvements to the company, refocus the company objectives and/or rescale the organization, provide better customer service, and/or achieve specific company goals and results. Culture change is affected by a number of elements, including the external environment and industry competitors, change in industry standards, technology changes, the size and nature of the workforce, and the organization's history and management.

There are a number of methodologies specifically dedicated to organizational culture change such as Peter Senge's Fifth Discipline. There are also a variety of psychological approaches that have been developed into a system for specific outcomes such as the Fifth Discipline's "learning organization" or Directive Communication's "corporate culture evolution." Ideas and strategies, on the other hand, seem to vary according to particular influences that affect culture.

Burman and Evans argue that it is 'leadership' that affects culture rather than 'management', and describe the difference. When one wants to change an aspect of the culture of an organization one has to keep in consideration that this is a long term project. Corporate culture is something that is very hard to change and employees need time to get used to the new way of organizing. For companies with a very strong and specific culture it will be even harder to change.

Prior to a cultural change initiative, a needs assessment is needed to identify and understand the current organizational culture. This can be done through employee surveys, interviews, focus groups, observation, customer surveys where appropriate, and other internal research, to further identify areas that require change. The company must then assess and clearly identify the new, desired culture, and then design a change process.

Cummings & Worley give the following six guidelines for cultural change, these changes are in line with the eight distinct stages mentioned by Kotter:

- Formulate a clear strategic vision (stage 1, 2, and 3). In order to make a cultural change effective a clear vision of the firm's new strategy, shared values and behaviors is needed. This vision provides the intention and direction for the culture change.
- Display top-management commitment (stage 4). It is very important to keep in mind that culture change must be managed from the top of the organization, as willingness to change of the senior management is an important indicator. The top of the organization should be very much in favor of the change in order to actually implement the change in the rest of the organization. De Caluwé & Vermaak provide a framework with five different ways of thinking about change.

- Model culture change at the highest level (stage 5). In order to show that the management team is in favor of the change, the change has to be notable at first at this level. The behavior of the management needs to symbolize the kinds of values and behaviors that should be realized in the rest of the company. It is important that the management shows the strengths of the current culture as well; it must be made clear that the current organizational culture does not need radical changes, but just a few adjustments. This process may also include creating committees, employee task forces, value managers, or similar. Change agents are key in the process and key communicators of the new values. They should possess courage, flexibility, excellent interpersonal skills, knowledge of the company, and patience. As McCune puts it, these individuals should be catalysts, not dictators.
- The fourth step is to modify the organization to support organizational change. This includes identifying what current systems, policies, procedures and rules need to be changed in order to align with the new values and desired culture. This may include a change to accountability systems, compensation, benefits and reward structures, and recruitment and retention programs to better align with the new values and to send a clear message to employees that the old system and culture are in the past.
- Select and socialize newcomers and terminate deviants. A way to implement a culture is to connect it to organizational membership, people can be selected and terminated in terms of their fit with the new culture. Encouraging employee motivation and loyalty to the company is key and will also result in a healthy culture. The company and change managers should be able to articulate the connections between the desired behavior and how it will affect and improve the company's success, to further encourage buy-in in the change process. Training should be provided to all employees to understand the new processes, expectations and systems.
- Develop ethical and legal sensitivity. Changes in culture can lead to tensions between organizational and individual interests, which can result in ethical and legal problems for practitioners. This is particularly relevant for changes in employee integrity, control, equitable treatment and job security. It is also beneficial, as part of the change process, to include an evaluation process, conducted periodically to monitor the change progress and identify areas that need further development. This step will also identify obstacles of change and resistant employees, and acknowledge and reward employee improvement, which will encourage continued change and evolvement. It may also be helpful and necessary to incorporate new change managers to refresh the process. Outside consultants may also be useful in facilitating the change process and providing employee training. Change of culture in organizations is very important and inevitable. Cultural innovation is bound to be more difficult than cultural maintenance because it entails introducing something new and substantially different from what prevails in existing cultures. People often resist changes, hence it is the duty of management to convince people that likely gain will outweigh the losses. Besides institutionalization, deification is another process that tends to occur in strongly developed organizational cultures. The organization itself may come to be regarded as precious in itself, as a source of pride, and in some sense unique. The organization's members begin to feel a strong bond with it that transcends material returns, and they begin to identify with it. The organization turns into a sort of clan.

## Mergers and Cultural Leadership

One of the biggest obstacles in the way of the merging of two organizations is organizational culture. Each organization has its own unique culture and most often, when brought together, these cultures clash. When mergers fail employees point to issues such as identity, communication problems, human resources problems, ego clashes, and inter-group conflicts, which all fall under the category of "cultural differences".

One way to combat such difficulties is through cultural leadership. Organizational leaders must also be cultural leaders and help facilitate the change from the two old cultures into the one new culture. This is done through cultural innovation followed by cultural maintenance.

- Cultural innovation includes:
    - Creating a new culture: recognizing past cultural differences and setting realistic expectations for change.
    - Changing the culture: weakening and replacing the old cultures.
- Cultural maintenance includes:
    - Integrating the new culture: reconciling the differences between the old cultures and the new one.
    - Embodying the new culture: Establishing, affirming, and keeping the new culture.

## Corporate Subcultures

Corporate culture is the total sum of the values, customs, traditions, and meanings that make a company unique. Corporate culture is often called "the character of an organization", since it embodies the vision of the company's founders. The values of a corporate culture influence the ethical standards within a corporation, as well as managerial behavior.

Senior management may try to determine a corporate culture. They may wish to impose corporate values and standards of behavior that specifically reflect the objectives of the organization. In addition, there will also be an extant internal culture within the workforce. Work-groups within the organization have their own behavioral quirks and interactions which, to an extent, affect the whole system. Roger Harrison's four-culture typology, and adapted by Charles Handy, suggests that unlike organizational culture, corporate culture can be 'imported'. For example, computer technicians will have expertise, language and behaviors gained independently of the organization, but their presence can influence the culture of the organization as a whole.

Criticism of the usage of the term by managers began already in its emergence in the early 80s. Most of the criticism comes from the writers in critical management studies who for example express skepticism about the functionalist and unitarist views about culture that are put forward by mainstream management writers. They stress the ways in which these cultural assumptions can stifle dissent towards management and reproduce propaganda and ideology. They suggest that organizations do not encompass a single culture, and cultural engineering may not reflect the interests of all stakeholders within an organization.

Parker has suggested that many of the assumptions of those putting forward theories of organizational culture are not new. They reflect a long-standing tension between cultural and structural (or informal and formal) versions of what organizations are. Further, it is reasonable to suggest that complex organizations might have many cultures, and that such sub-cultures might overlap and contradict each other. The neat typologies of cultural forms found in textbooks rarely acknowledge such complexities, or the various economic contradictions that exist in capitalist organizations.

Among the strongest and most widely recognized writers on corporate culture, with a long list of articles on leadership, culture, gender and their intersection, is Linda Smircich. As a part of the critical management studies, she criticizes theories that attempt to categorize or 'pigeonhole' organizational culture. She uses the metaphor of a plant root to represent culture, saying that it drives organizations rather than vice versa. Organizations are the product of organizational culture; we are unaware of how it shapes behavior and interaction (also implicit in Schein's underlying assumptions), which undermines attempts to categorize and define organizational culture.

## Models

Several methods have been used to classify organizational culture. While there is no single "type" of organizational culture and organizational cultures vary widely from one organization to the next, commonalities do exist and some researchers have developed models to describe different indicators of organizational cultures. Some are described below:

## Hofstede

Hofstede looked for differences between over 160 000 IBM employees in 50 different countries and three regions of the world, in an attempt to find aspects of culture that might influence business behavior. He suggested things about cultural differences existing in regions and nations, and the importance of international awareness and multiculturalism for their own cultural introspection. Cultural differences reflect differences in thinking and social action, and even in "mental programs", a term Hofstede uses for predictable behavior. Hofstede relates culture to ethnic and regional groups, but also organizations, professional, family, social and subcultural groups, national political systems and legislation, etc.

Hofstede suggests the need for changing "mental programs" with changing behavior first, which will lead to value change. Though certain groups like Jews and Gypsies have maintained their identity through centuries, their values show adaptation to the dominant cultural environment.

Hofstede demonstrated that there are national and regional cultural groupings that affect the behavior of organizations and identified four dimensions of culture (later five) in his study of national cultures:

- Power distance: Different societies find different solutions regarding social inequality. Although invisible, inside organizations power inequality of the "boss-subordinate relationships" is functional and according to Hofstede reflects the way inequality is addressed in the society. "According to Mulder's Power Distance Reduction theory subordinates will try to reduce the power distance between themselves and their bosses and bosses will try to maintain or enlarge it", but there is also a degree to which a society expects there to be differences in the levels of power. A high score suggests that there is an expectation that some individuals wield larger amounts of power than others. A low score reflects the view that all people should have equal rights.

- Uncertainty avoidance is the way of coping with uncertainty about the future. Society copes with it with technology, law and religion (though different societies have different ways of addressing it), and according to Hofstede organizations deal with it with technology, law and rituals, or in two ways – rational and non-rational, with rituals being the non-rational. Hofstede listed some of the rituals as the memos and reports, some parts of the accounting system, a large part of the planning and control systems, and the nomination of experts.
- Individualism vs. collectivism: Disharmony of interests on personal and collective goals. Hofstede raises the idea that society's expectations of Individualism/Collectivism will be reflected by the employee inside the organization. Collectivist societies will have more emotional dependence on members in their organizations; when in equilibrium an organization is expected to show responsibility to members. Extreme individualism is seen in the US. In fact, collectivism in the US is seen as "bad". Other cultures and societies than the US will therefore seek to resolve social and organizational problems in ways different from American ways. Hofstede says that a capitalist market economy fosters individualism and competition, and depends on it, but individualism is also related to the development of the middle class. Some people and cultures might have both high individualism and high collectivism. For example, someone who highly values duty to his or her group does not necessarily give a low priority to personal freedom and self-sufficiency.
- Masculinity vs. femininity: Reflects whether a certain society is predominantly male or female in terms of cultural values, gender roles and power relations.
- Long- Versus Short-Term Orientation which he describes as "The long-term orientation dimension can be interpreted as dealing with society's search for virtue. Societies with a short-term orientation generally have a strong concern with establishing the absolute Truth. They are normative in their thinking. They exhibit great respect for traditions, a relatively small propensity to save for the future, and a focus on achieving quick results. In societies with a long-term orientation, people believe that truth depends very much on situation, context and time. They show an ability to adapt traditions to changed conditions, a strong propensity to save and invest, thriftiness, and perseverance in achieving results."

These dimensions refer to the effect of national cultures on management, and can be used to adapt policies to local needs. In a follow up study, another model is suggested for organizational culture.

## O'Reilly, Chatman and Caldwell

Two common models and their associated measurement tools have been developed by O'Reilly et al. and Denison.

O'Reilly, Chatman & Caldwell developed a model based on the belief that cultures can be distinguished by values that are reinforced within organizations. Their Organizational Cultural Profile (OCP) is a self reporting tool which makes distinctions according eight categories – Innovation, Supportiveness, Stability, Respect for People, Outcome Orientation, Attention to Detail, Team

Orientation, and Aggressiveness. The model is also suited to measure how organizational culture affects organizational performance, as it measures most efficient persons suited to an organization and as such organizations can be termed as having good organizational culture. Employee values are measured against organizational values to predict employee intentions to stay, and turnover. This is done through an instrument like Organizational Culture Profile (OCP) to measure employee commitment.

## Daniel Denison

Daniel Denison's model asserts that organizational culture can be described by four general dimensions – Mission, Adaptability, Involvement and Consistency. Each of these general dimensions is further described by the following three sub-dimensions:

- Mission – Strategic Direction and Intent, Goals and Objectives and Vision.
- Adaptability – Creating Change, Customer Focus and Organizational Learning.
- Involvement – Empowerment, Team Orientation and Capability Development.
- Consistency – Core Values, Agreement, Coordination/Integration.

Denison's model also allows cultures to be described broadly as externally or internally focused as well as flexible versus stable. The model has been typically used to diagnose cultural problems in organizations.

## Deal and Kennedy

Deal and Kennedy defined organizational culture as the way things get done around here.

Deal and Kennedy created a model of culture that is based on 4 different types of organizations. They each focus on how quickly the organization receives feedback, the way members are rewarded, and the level of risks taken:

- Work-hard, play-hard culture: This has rapid feedback/reward and low risk resulting in: Stress coming from quantity of work rather than uncertainty. High-speed action leading to high-speed recreation. Examples: Restaurants, software companies.
- Tough-guy macho culture: This has rapid feedback/reward and high risk, resulting in the following: Stress coming from high risk and potential loss/gain of reward. Focus on the present rather than the longer-term future. Examples: police, surgeons, sports.
- Process culture: This has slow feedback/reward and low risk, resulting in the following: Low stress, plodding work, comfort and security. Stress that comes from internal politics and stupidity of the system. Development of bureaucracies and other ways of maintaining the status quo. Focus on security of the past and of the future. Examples: banks, insurance companies.
- Bet-the-company culture: This has slow feedback/reward and high risk, resulting in the following: Stress coming from high risk and delay before knowing if actions have paid off.

The long view is taken, but then much work is put into making sure things happen as planned. Examples: aircraft manufacturers, oil companies.

## Edgar Schein

According to Schein, culture is the most difficult organizational attribute to change, outlasting organizational products, services, founders and leadership and all other physical attributes of the organization. His organizational model illuminates culture from the standpoint of the observer, described at three levels: artifacts, espoused values and basic underlying assumptions.

At the first and most cursory level of Schein's model is organizational attributes that can be seen, felt and heard by the uninitiated observer – collectively known as artifacts. Included are the facilities, offices, furnishings, visible awards and recognition, the way that its members dress, how each person visibly interacts with each other and with organizational outsiders, and even company slogans, mission statements and other operational creeds.

Artifacts comprise the physical components of the organization that relay cultural meaning. Daniel Denison describes artifacts as the tangible aspects of culture shared by members of an organization. Verbal, behavioral and physical artifacts are the surface manifestations of organizational culture.

Rituals, the collective interpersonal behavior and values as demonstrated by that behavior, constitute the fabric of an organization's culture. The contents of myths, stories, and sagas reveal the history of an organization and influence how people understand what their organization values and believes. Language, stories, and myths are examples of verbal artifacts and are represented in rituals and ceremonies. Technology and art exhibited by members of an organization are examples of physical artifacts.

The next level deals with the professed culture of an organization's members – the values. Shared values are individuals' preferences regarding certain aspects of the organization's culture (e.g. loyalty, customer service). At this level, local and personal values are widely expressed within the organization. Basic beliefs and assumptions include individuals' impressions about the trustworthiness and supportiveness of an organization, and are often deeply ingrained within the organization's culture. Organizational behavior at this level usually can be studied by interviewing the organization's membership and using questionnaires to gather attitudes about organizational membership.

At the third and deepest level, the organization's tacit assumptions are found. These are the elements of culture that are unseen and not cognitively identified in everyday interactions between organizational members. Additionally, these are the elements of culture which are often taboo to discuss inside the organization. Many of these 'unspoken rules' exist without the conscious knowledge of the membership. Those with sufficient experience to understand this deepest level of organizational culture usually become acclimatized to its attributes over time, thus reinforcing the invisibility of their existence. Surveys and casual interviews with organizational members cannot draw out these attributes—rather much more in-depth means is required to first identify then understand organizational culture at this level. Notably, culture at this level is the underlying and driving element often missed by organizational behaviorists.

Using Schein's model, understanding paradoxical organizational behaviors becomes more apparent. For instance, an organization can profess highly aesthetic and moral standards at the second level of Schein's model while simultaneously displaying curiously opposing behavior at the third and deepest level of culture. Superficially, organizational rewards can imply one organizational norm but at the deepest level imply something completely different. This insight offers an understanding of the difficulty that organizational newcomers have in assimilating organizational culture and why it takes time to become acclimatized. It also explains why organizational change agents usually fail to achieve their goals: underlying tacit cultural norms are generally not understood before would-be change agents begin their actions. Merely understanding culture at the deepest level may be insufficient to institute cultural change because the dynamics of interpersonal relationships (often under threatening conditions) are added to the dynamics of organizational culture while attempts are made to institute desired change.

According to Schein, the two main reasons why cultures develop in organizations is due to external adaptation and internal integration. External adaptation reflects an evolutionary approach to organizational culture and suggests that cultures develop and persist because they help an organization to survive and flourish. If the culture is valuable, then it holds the potential for generating sustained competitive advantages. Additionally, internal integration is an important function since social structures are required for organizations to exist. Organizational practices are learned through socialization at the workplace. Work environments reinforce culture on a daily basis by encouraging employees to exercise cultural values. Organizational culture is shaped by multiple factors, including the following:

- External environment.
- Industry.
- Size and nature of the organization's workforce.
- Technologies the organization uses.
- The organization's history and ownership.

## Gerry Johnson

Gerry Johnson described a cultural web, identifying a number of elements that can be used to describe or influence organizational culture:

- The paradigm: What the organization is about, what it does, its mission, its values.
- Control systems: The processes in place to monitor what is going on. Role cultures would have vast rule-books. There would be more reliance on individualism in a power culture.
- Organizational structures: Reporting lines, hierarchies, and the way that work flows through the business.
- Power structures: Who makes the decisions, how widely spread is power, and on what is power based?

- Symbols: These include organizational logos and designs, but also extend to symbols of power such as parking spaces and executive washrooms.
- Rituals and routines: Management meetings, board reports and so on may become more habitual than necessary.
- Stories and myths: build up about people and events, and convey a message about what is valued within the organization.

These elements may overlap. Power structures may depend on control systems, which may exploit the very rituals that generate stories which may not be true.

## Stanley G. Harris

Schemata (plural of schema) are knowledge structures a person forms from past experiences, allowing the person to respond to similar events more efficiently in the future by guiding the processing of information. A person's schemata are created through interaction with others, and thus inherently involve communication.

Stanley G. Harris argues that five categories of in-organization schemata are necessary for organizational culture:

- Self-in-organization schemata: a person's concept of oneself within the context of the organization, including her/his personality, roles, and behavior.
- Person-in-organization schemata: a person's memories, impressions, and expectations of other individuals within the organization.
- Organization schemata: a subset of person schemata, a person's generalized perspective on others as a whole in the organization.
- Object/concept-in-organization schemata: knowledge an individual has of organization aspects other than of other persons.
- Event-in-organization schemata: a person's knowledge of social events within an organization.

All of these categories together represent a person's knowledge of an organization. Organizational culture is created when the schematas (schematic structures) of differing individuals across and within an organization come to resemble each other (when any one person's schemata come to resemble another person's schemata because of mutual organizational involvement), primarily done through organizational communication, as individuals directly or indirectly share knowledge and meanings.

## Charles Handy

Charles Handy, popularized Roger Harrison with linking organizational structure to organizational culture. The described four types of culture are:

- Power culture: concentrates power among a small group or a central figure and its control is radiating from its center like a web. Power cultures need only a few rules and little bureaucracy but swift in decisions can ensue.

- Role culture: authorities are delegated as such within a highly defined structure. These organizations form hierarchical bureaucracies, where power derives from the personal position and rarely from an expert power. Control is made by procedures (which are highly valued), strict roles descriptions and authority definitions. These organizations have consistent systems and are very predictable. This culture is often represented by a "Roman Building" having pillars. These pillars represent the functional departments.
- Task culture: teams are formed to solve particular problems. Power is derived from the team with the expertise to execute against a task. This culture uses a small team approach, where people are highly skilled and specialized in their own area of expertise. Additionally, these cultures often feature the multiple reporting lines seen in a matrix structure.
- Person culture: formed where all individuals believe themselves superior to the organization. It can become difficult for such organizations to continue to operate, since the concept of an organization suggests that a group of like-minded individuals pursue organizational goals. However some professional partnerships operate well as person cultures, because each partner brings a particular expertise and clientele to the firm.

## Kim Cameron and Robert Quinn

Kim Cameron and Robert Quinn conducted research on organizational effectiveness and success. Based on the Competing Values Framework, they developed the Organizational Culture Assessment Instrument that distinguishes four culture types.

Competing values produce polarities like flexibility vs. stability and internal vs. external focus – these two polarities were found to be most important in defining organizational success. The polarities construct a quadrant with four types of culture:

- Clan culture (internal focus and flexible): A friendly workplace where leaders act like father figures.
- Adhocracy culture (external focus and flexible): A dynamic workplace with leaders that stimulate innovation.
- Market culture (external focus and controlled): A competitive workplace with leaders like hard drivers.
- Hierarchy culture (internal focus and controlled): A structured and formalized workplace where leaders act like coordinators.

Cameron and Quinn designated six characteristics of organizational culture that can be assessed with the Organizational Culture Assessment Instrument (OCAI).

Clan cultures are most strongly associated with positive employee attitudes and product and service quality. Market cultures are most strongly related with innovation and financial effectiveness criteria. The primary belief in market cultures that clear goals and contingent rewards motivate employees to aggressively perform and meet stakeholders' expectations; a core belief in clan cultures is that the organization's trust in and commitment to employees facilitates open communication and employee involvement. These differing results suggest that it is important for executive leaders to consider the match between strategic initiatives and organizational culture when determining how to embed a culture that produces competitive advantage. By assessing the current organizational culture as well as the preferred situation, the gap and direction to change can be made visible as a first step to changing organizational culture.

## Robert A. Cooke

Robert A. Cooke defines culture as the behaviors that members believe are required to fit in and meet expectations within their organization. The Organizational Culture Inventory measures twelve behavioral norms that are grouped into three general types of cultures:

- Constructive cultures, in which members are encouraged to interact with people and approach tasks in ways that help them meet their higher-order satisfaction needs.
- Passive/defensive cultures, in which members believe they must interact with people in ways that will not threaten their own security.
- Aggressive/defensive cultures, in which members are expected to approach tasks in forceful ways to protect their status and security.

## Constructive Cultures

In constructive cultures, people are encouraged to be in communication with their co-workers, and work as teams, rather than only as individuals. In positions where people do a complex job, rather than something simple like a mechanical task, this culture is efficient.

- Achievement: Completing a task successfully, typically by effort, courage, or skill (pursue a standard of excellence) (explore alternatives before acting) – Based on the need to attain high-quality results on challenging projects, the belief that outcomes are linked to one's effort rather than chance and the tendency to personally set challenging yet realistic goals. People high in this style think ahead and plan, explore alternatives before acting and learn from their mistakes.
- Self-actualizing: Realization or fulfillment of one's talents and potentialities – considered as a drive or need present in everyone (think in unique and independent ways) (do even simple tasks well) – Based on needs for personal growth, self-fulfillment and the realization of one's potential. People with this style demonstrate a strong desire to learn and experience things, creative yet realistic thinking and a balanced concern for people and tasks.
- Humanistic-encouraging: Help others to grow and develop (resolve conflicts constructively) – Reflects an interest in the growth and development of people, a high positive regard for them and sensitivity to their needs. People high in this style devote energy to coaching and counselling others, are thoughtful and considerate and provide people with support and encouragement.
- Affiliative: Treat people as more valuable than things (cooperate with others) – Reflects an interest in developing and sustaining pleasant relationships. People high in this style share their thoughts and feelings, are friendly and cooperative and make others feel a part of things.

Organizations with constructive cultures encourage members to work to their full potential, resulting in high levels of motivation, satisfaction, teamwork, service quality, and sales growth. Constructive norms are evident in environments where quality is valued over quantity, creativity is valued over conformity, cooperation is believed to lead to better results than competition, and effectiveness is judged at the system level rather than the component level. These types of cultural norms are consistent with (and supportive of) the objectives behind empowerment, total quality management, transformational leadership, continuous improvement, re-engineering, and learning organizations.

## Passive/Defensive Cultures

Norms that reflect expectations for members to interact with people in ways that will not threaten their own security are in the Passive/Defensive Cluster.

The four Passive/Defensive cultural norms are:

- Approval
- Conventional
- Dependent
- Avoidance

In organizations with Passive/Defensive cultures, members feel pressured to think and behave in ways that are inconsistent with the way they believe they should in order to be effective. People are expected to please others (particularly superiors) and avoid interpersonal conflict. Rules, procedures, and orders are more important than personal beliefs, ideas, and judgment. Passive/Defensive cultures experience a lot of unresolved conflict and turnover, and organizational members report lower levels of motivation and satisfaction.

## Aggressive/Defensive Cultures

This style is characterized with more emphasis on task than people. Because of the very nature of this style, people tend to focus on their own individual needs at the expense of the success of the group. The aggressive/defensive style is very stressful, and people using this style tend to make decisions based on status as opposed to expertise.

- Oppositional: This cultural norm is based on the idea that a need for security that takes the form of being very critical and cynical at times. People who use this style are more likely to question others work; however, asking those tough question often leads to a better product. Nonetheless, those who use this style may be overly-critical toward others, using irrelevant or trivial flaws to put others down.
- Power: This cultural norm is based on the idea that there is a need for prestige and influence. Those who use this style often equate their own self-worth with controlling others. Those who use this style have a tendency to dictate others opposing to guiding others' actions.

- Competitive: This cultural norm is based on the idea of a need to protect one's status. Those who use this style protect their own status by comparing themselves to other individuals and outperforming them. Those who use this style are seekers of appraisal and recognition from others.
- Perfectionistic: This cultural norm is based on the need to attain flawless results. Those who often use this style equate their self-worth with the attainment of extremely high standards. Those who often use this style are always focused on details and place excessive demands on themselves and others.

Organizations with aggressive/defensive cultures encourage or require members to appear competent, controlled, and superior. Members who seek assistance, admit shortcomings, or concede their position are viewed as incompetent or weak. These organizations emphasize finding errors, weeding out "mistakes" and encouraging members to compete against each other rather than competitors. The short-term gains associated with these strategies are often at the expense of long-term growth.

## Adam Grant

Adam Grant, author of the book *Give and Take*, distinguishes organizational cultures into giver, taker and matcher cultures according to their norms of reciprocity. In a giver culture, employees operate by "helping others, sharing knowledge, offering mentoring, and making connections without expecting anything in return", whereas in a taker culture "the norm is to get as much as possible from others while contributing less in return" and winners are those who take the most and are able to build their power at the expense of others. The majority of organizations are mid-way, with a matcher culture, in which the norm is to match giving with taking, and favours are mostly traded in closed loops.

In a study by Harvard researchers on units of the US intelligence system, a giver culture turned out to be the strongest predictor of group effectiveness.

As Grant points out, Robert H. Frank argues that "many organizations are essentially winner-take-all markets, dominated by zero-sum competitions for rewards and promotions". In particular, when leaders implement forced ranking systems to reward individual performance, the organisational culture tends to change, with a giver culture giving way to a taker or matcher culture. Also awarding the highest-performing individual within each team encourages a taker culture.

## Stephen McGuire

Stephen McGuire defined and validated a model of organizational culture that predicts revenue from new sources. An Entrepreneurial Organizational Culture (EOC) is a system of shared values, beliefs and norms of members of an organization, including valuing creativity and tolerance of creative people, believing that innovating and seizing market opportunities are appropriate behaviors to deal with problems of survival and prosperity, environmental uncertainty, and competitors' threats, and expecting organizational members to behave accordingly.

## Elements

- People and empowerment focused.

- Value creation through innovation and change.
- Attention to the basics.
- Hands-on management.
- Doing the right thing.
- Freedom to grow and to fail.
- Commitment and personal responsibility.
- Emphasis on the future.

### Eric Flamholtz

Eric Flamholtz has identified and validated a model of organizational culture components that drive financial results. The model consist of five identified dimensions of corporate culture: 1) treatment of customers, 2) treatment of people, 3) performance standards and accountability, 4) innovation and change, and 5) process orientation. These five dimensions have been confirmed by factor analysis in addition, Flamholtz has published empirical research that show the impact of organizational culture on financial performance. Flamholtz has also proposed that organizational (corporate) culture is not just an asset in the economic sense; but is also an "asset" in the conventional accounting sense. Flamholtz and Randle have also examined the evolution of organizational culture at different stages of organizational growth.

### Ethical Frameworks and Evaluations of Corporate Culture

Four organizational cultures can be classified as apathetic, caring, exacting, and integrative.

- An apathetic culture shows minimal concern for either people or performance.
- A caring culture exhibits high concern for people but minimal concern for performance issues.
- An exacting culture shows little concern for people but a high concern for performance.
- An integrative culture combines a high concern for people and performance.

A cultural audit is an assessment of an organization's values.

## Organizational Architecture

Organizational architecture has two very different meanings. In one sense it literally refers to the organization's built environment and in another sense it refers to architecture metaphorically, as a structure which fleshes out the organizations. The various features of a business's organizational architecture has to be internally consistent in strategy, architecture and competitive environment.

- Organizational architecture or organizational space: the influence of the spatial environment on humans in and around organizations.
- Organizational architecture or organization design: the creation of roles, processes, and formal reporting relationships in an organization.

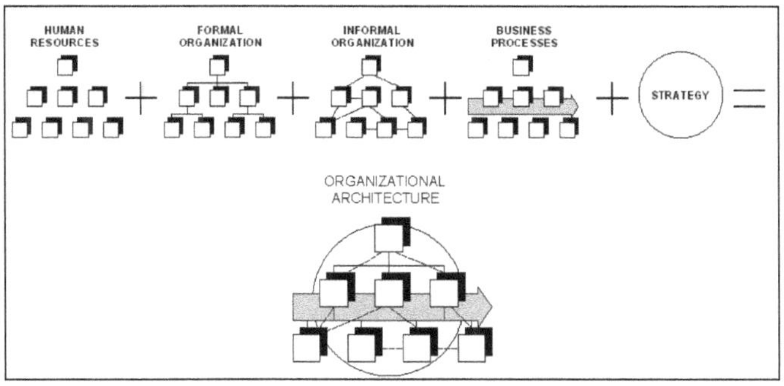


Simplified scheme of an organization.

Organizational space describes the influence of the spatial environment on the health, the mind, and the behavior of humans in and around organizations. It is an area of research in which interdisciplinarity is a central perspective. It draws from management, organization and architecture added with knowledge from, for instance, environmental psychology, social medicine, or spatial science. In essence, it may be regarded as a special field of expertise of organization studies and change management (people) applied to architecture. This perspective on organizational architecture is elaborated in organizational space.

Organization design or architecture of an organization as a metaphor provides the framework through which an organization aims to realize its core qualities as specified in its vision statement. It provides the infrastructure into which business processes are deployed and ensures that the organization's core qualities are realized across the business processes deployed within the organization. In this way, organizations aim to consistently realize their core qualities across the services they offer to their clients. This perspective on organizational architecture is elaborated below.

## Design

### Design Process and Approach

Although the process of organization design isn't necessarily linear, a five milestone process has been created to organize the approach. The five milestone design process is as follows:

- Business Case and Discovery:
    - Goal: Build a business case for the change; compare the current state to future state and implications that would be involved.
    - Milestone: at the end of this phase, the problem to be solved is clear.
- Strategic Grouping:
    - Goal: Determine what basic grouping of work will create the capabilities necessary to deliver the decided strategy.

- Milestone: Decided on a structure change which supports the strategy.

- Integration:
  - Goal: The boundaries created by grouping work must be breached to deliver results for customers, partners and shareholders.
  - Milestone: Pieces have been tied together and defined power relationships.
- Talent and Leadership:
  - Goal: Determine the number of positions, the profile of a candidate who will fill those positions, and who will report to the leader of the new structure(s).
  - Milestone: Critical roles have been designed and staffed and defined work for the executive team.
- Transition:
  - Goal: Set the transition plan to account for a logical implementation plan.
  - Milestone: The change is being executed and lead, and closely monitoring the changes to prepare for any adjustments.

## Reshaping Organization Structure

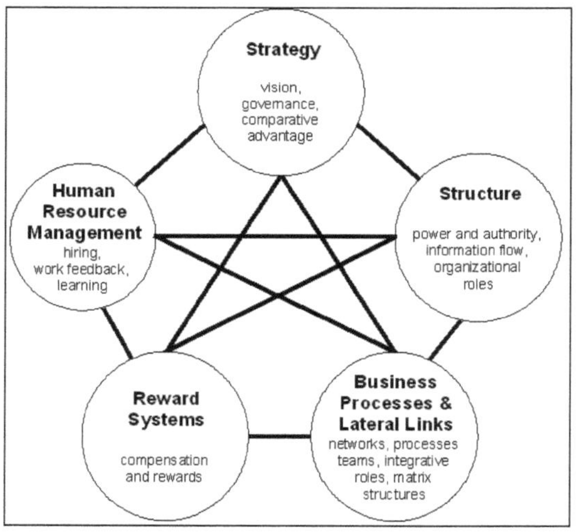


Galbraith's Star Model of organizational design.

Organization design can be defined, narrowly, as the process of reshaping organization structure and roles. It can also be more effectively defined as the alignment of structure, process, rewards, metrics, and talent with the strategy of the business. Jay Galbraith and Amy Kates have made the case persuasively (building on years of work by Galbraith) that attention to all of these organizational elements is necessary to create new capabilities to compete in a given market. This systemic view, often referred to as the "star model" approach, is more likely to lead to better performance.

Organization design may involve strategic decisions, but is properly viewed as a path to effective strategy execution. The design process nearly always entails making trade-offs of one set of structural benefits for another. Many companies fall into the trap of making repeated changes in organization structure, with little benefit to the business. This often occurs because changes in structure are relatively easy to execute while creating the impression that something substantial is happening. This often leads to cynicism and confusion within the organization. More powerful change happens when there are clear design objectives driven by a new business strategy or forces in the market require a different approach to organize resources.

The organization design process is often explained in phases. Phase one is the definition of a business case, including a clear picture of strategy and design objectives. This step is typically followed by "strategic grouping" decisions, which define the fundamental architecture of the organization - essentially deciding which major roles will report at the top of the organization. The classic options for strategic grouping are to organize by:

- Behavior
- Function
- Product or category
- Customer or market
- Geography
- Matrix

Each of the basic building block options for strategic grouping brings a set of benefits and drawbacks. However, such generic pros and cons are not the basis for choosing the best strategic grouping. An analysis must be completed relative to a specific business strategy.

Subsequent phases of organization design include operational design of processes, roles, measures, and reward systems, followed by staffing and other implementation tasks.

The field is somewhat specialized in nature and many large and small consulting firms offer organization design assistance to executives. Some companies attempt to establish internal staff resources aimed at supporting organization design initiatives. There is a substantial body of literature in the field, arguably starting with the work of Peter Drucker in his examination of General Motors decades ago. Other key thinkers built on Drucker's thinking, including Galbraith, Nadler, et al. and Lawrence & Lorsch.

Organization design can be considered a subset of the broader field of organization effectiveness and organization development, both of which may entail more behaviorally focused solutions to effectiveness, such as leadership behaviors, team effectiveness and other characteristics of that nature. Many organizational experts argue for an integrated approach to these disciplines, including effective talent management practices.

## Five Principles of Good Design

- Specialization Principle - the primary concern in the specialization principle how to group responsibilities into units. The unit boundaries should be defined to achieve the important benefits available.

- Coordination Principle - this principle links closely with the specialization principle, to ensure the links are established between the units.
- Knowledge and Competence Principle - the primary concern in this principle is determining which responsibilities to decentralize and what hierarchical levels to create.
- Control and Commitment Principle - the primary concern in this principle is insuring managers have a process to effectively discharge decentralized principles.
- Innovation and Adaptation Principle - the primary concern in this principle is insuring the organization can change and evolve in the future.

## Five Good Design Tests

- Specialist culture test (Specialization Principle).
- Difficult links test (Coordination Principle).
- Redundant hierarchy test (Knowledge and Competence Principle).
- Accountability test (Control and Commitment Principle).
- Flexibility test (Innovation and Adaptation Principle).

## Characteristics of Effective Organizational Design

Some systems are effective and efficient whereas others are not. Successful systems may be attributable to the skill exercised in designing the system or to the quality of management practised during operations, or both. Successful systems are characterized by their simplicity, flexibility, reliability, economy, and acceptability. Simplicity, flexibility, and reliability tend to be a function of design, whereas economy and acceptability pertain to both design and operations. Numerous relationships exist among these characteristics; for example, simplicity will affect economy and possibly reliability. Moreover, management must reach a compromise between economy and reliability, and between technical efficiency and organizational climate. The balance reached will determine whether short- or long-run objectives are optimized.

## Simplicity

An effective organizational system need not be complex. On the contrary, simplicity in design is a desirable quality. Consider the task of communicating information about the operation of a system and the allocation of its inputs. The task is not difficult when components are few and the relationships among them are straightforward. However, the problems of communication multiply with each successive stage of complexity.

The proper method for maintaining simplicity is to use precise definitions and to outline the specific task for each subsystem. Total systems often become complex because of the sheer size and nature of operations, but effectiveness and efficiency may still be achieved if each subsystem maintains its simplicity.

## Flexibility

Conditions change and managers should be prepared to adjust operations accordingly. There are two ways to adjust to a changing operating environment: to design new systems or to modify operating systems. An existing system should not be modified to accommodate a change in objectives, but every system should be sufficiently flexible to integrate changes that may occur either in the environment or in the nature of the inputs. For example, a company should not use the same system to build missiles as it uses to build airplanes, nor the same system to sell insurance as the one originally designed to sell magazines. However, it should be possible to modify an existing system to produce different sizes, varieties, or types of the same product or service.

A practical system must be well designed but it cannot be entirely rigid. There will always be minor variations from the general plan, and a system should be able to adapt to such changes without excessive confusion. The advantages associated with having a flexible system will become more apparent when we consider the difficulty of administering change.

## Reliability

System reliability is an important factor in organizations. Reliability is the consistency with which operations are maintained, and may vary from zero output (a complete breakdown or work stoppage) to a constant or predictable output. The typical system operates somewhere between these two extremes. The characteristics of reliability can be designed into the system by carefully selecting and arranging the operating components; the system is no more reliable than its weakest segment. When the requirements for a particular component — such as an operator having unique skills — are critical, it may be worthwhile to maintain a standby operator. In all situations, provisions should be made for quick repair or replacement when failure occurs. One valid approach to the reliability-maintenance relationship is to use a form of construction that permits repair by replacing a complete unit. In some television sets, for example, it is common practice to replace an entire section of the network rather than try to find the faulty component. Reliability is not as critical an issue when prompt repair and recovery can be instituted.

## Economy

An effective system is not necessarily an economical (efficient) system. For example, the postal service may keep on schedule with mail deliveries but only by hiring a large number of additional workers. In this case, the efficiency of the postal system would be reduced. In another example, inventories may be controlled by using a comprehensive system of storekeeping. However, if the cost of the storekeeping were greater than the potential savings from this degree of control, the system would not be efficient. It is often dysfunctional and expensive to develop much greater capacity for one segment of a system than for some other part. Building in redundancy or providing for every contingency usually neutralizes the operating efficiency of the system. When a system's objectives include achieving a particular task at the lowest possible cost, there must be some degree of trade-off between effectiveness and efficiency. When a system's objective is to perform a certain mission regardless of cost, there can be no trade-off.

## Acceptability

Any system, no matter how well designed, will not function properly unless it is accepted by the people who operate it. If the participants do not believe it will benefit them, are opposed to it, are pressured into using it, or think it is not a good system, it will not work properly. If a system is not accepted, two things can happen: (1) the system will be modified gradually by the people who are using it, or (2) the system will be used ineffectively and ultimately fail. Unplanned alterations in an elaborate system can nullify advantages associated with using the system.

## Differentiation and Integration

A basic consideration in the design of organizations is dividing work into reasonable tasks (differentiation) while giving simultaneous attention to coordinating these activities and unifying their results into a meaningful whole (integration). Two guidelines may be followed in grouping activities:

- Units that have similar orientations and tasks should be grouped together. (They can reinforce each other's common concern and the arrangement will simplify the coordinating task of a common manager).
- Units required to integrate their activities closely should be grouped together. (The common manager can coordinate them through the formal hierarchy).

When units neither have similar orientations nor share their activities, the task of grouping becomes more difficult. For example, when units are similar in nature and function but are also relatively independent, the manager must base his decision on the most appropriate way to group activities according to his past experience.

A difficult task associated with system-subsystem determination is to establish proper boundaries of operations. The more specific and distinct the goals of the operation, the easier it is to set boundaries. Other factors such as the influence of the environment, the availability of men and machines, the time schedule for design and operation, the cost of alternative designs, and the particular biases of the designers must be considered when establishing boundaries.

## The Role of Management

Designers with imagination have the best chance to group people and machines into workable combinations having the greatest efficiency and effectiveness within the recognized constraints. Certain characteristics should be designed into an effective and efficient system — simplicity, flexibility, reliability, economy, and acceptability.

At this point, the designer must determine what has to be done to achieve the stated objective(s) and how the total task can be divided into meaningful units. Of the many possible combinations, one must be selected as that which satisfies the decision criteria better than the other alternatives. Of course, the balance between technical efficiency and the human factors that determine organizational climate should be included in making this decision. The eventual success or failure of the project is somewhat predetermined by management's attitude and the relationship between the designers and those who must implement the process.

The systems approach suggests a new role for management. In the traditional view, the manager operated in a highly structured, rigid system having well-defined goals, clear-cut relationships, tight controls, and hierarchical information flows. In the flexible (or open) systems view, the organization is not static but is continually evolving to meet both external and internal changes. The manager's role is to develop a viable organization, cope with change, and help participants establish a dynamic equilibrium. Leonard Sayles has expressed the manager's problem as follows:

> "The one enduring objective is the effort to build and maintain a predictable, reciprocating system of relationships, the behavioral patterns of which stay within reasonable physical limits. But this is seeking a moving equilibrium, since the parameters of the system (the division of labor and the controls) are evolving and changing. Thus, the manager endeavors to introduce regularity in a world that will never allow him to achieve the ideal".

The systems approach does not offer a prescription for making a manager's difficult and complex job easier. Rather it helps him understand and operate more effectively within the reality of complex systems. The systems approach suggests that operations cannot be neatly departmentalized but must be viewed as overlapping subsystems. In addition, it suggests that leadership patterns must be modified, particularly when dealing with professionals and highly trained specialists, and motivation must take the form of active, willing participation rather than forceful subjugation.

Systems design involves establishing projects and facilitating subsystems to accomplish certain tasks or programs. In this approach, the network of human independence required to accomplish a given task is based on the shared responsibility of all members of the subsystem. In contrast, the traditional organization is geared to functional performance and the integrating force is authority. Instead of gearing participant activities to obedience to rules and closely structured behavior, the systems approach provides a basis for active cooperation in meeting task requirements. The manager is looked upon as a resource person who can help the group meet its goals and also as a source of authority and control. Thus, systems theory lends a structure by which the concepts of motivation, leadership, and participation can be applied effectively within the organization.

Implementation is, of course, implicit in the connotation of systems design; otherwise it would be nothing more than an empty exercise. It follows that the interface between managers and systems designers is critical, and mutual understanding must be fostered to maximize returns from design efforts. The system must be tailored to the needs of the organization and adapted continually as circumstances change. In a general sense, managers engage in systems design on a day-to-day basis when they plan activities and organize systems to accomplish objectives. Specialized staff groups have evolved to perform tasks such as long-range planning, organizational studies, and systems design. However, since managers are ultimately responsible for organizational endeavors, they should make a special effort to help ensure the development of useful systems and to make design activities an extension of the manager's role rather than a separate function.

Operating managers need to understand the organizational decision-making requirements and the information needed to support the system. Although the probability of success in implementation is enhanced considerably if management is vitally interested in the project, technical expertise and motivation for change are more likely to be found in staff groups. The solution to the apparent dichotomy would seem to be a team approach, with specialists supporting operating managers who are responsible for the project's success. A manager might devote either part-time to such an effort or full-time temporarily, if the task requires it.

A project involving an integrated system for the entire company might well require years to complete. If operating people are delegated responsibility and authority for such a project, particularly if they are delegated the authority to outline specifications, they should also maintain sufficient contact with the day-to-day operations and its attendant information flow to retain their expertise for decision making. If the environment is dynamic or internal capabilities undergo change, it might be wise to rotate people from operations to systems design periodically, so that operating expertise is updated continually.

## Organizational Diagnostics

In the field of corporate diagnosis is a process that involves the three steps of publicly entering a human system, collecting valid data about experiences, and feeding back to the system toward promoting corporate performance.

The effective diagnosis of organizational culture, and structural and operational strengths and weaknesses are fundamental to any successful organizational development intervention. As Beckhard said in the preface to his seminal work:

> "In our rapidly changing environment, new organization forms must be developed; more effective goal-setting and planning processes must be learned, and practiced teams of independent people must spend real time improving their methods of working, decision-making and communicating. Competing or conflicting groups must move towards a collaborative way of work. In order for these changes to occur and be maintained, a planned, managed change effort is necessary - a program of organizational development."

This was written in 1969 and while much has been learnt, it is just as true today.

Since the beginnings of organizational development as a profession, diagnosis has moved from the purely behavioral towards a strategic and holistic business diagnostic approach, and from looking at human interventions in isolation to exploring the interactions of people in the context in which they operate. As organizations are more collaborative in nature, the traditional silo approach to diagnostics is becoming increasingly rare. Organizational development and in particular the diagnostic phase of activities is spreading from the occupational psychologists towards mainstream business. This is important for OD practitioners as the role is increasingly holistic.

### The Organizational Diagnosis Models

The following models have been introduced for organizational diagnosis:

- Force Field Analysis.
- Leavitt's model.
- Likert system analysis.

- Weisbord's six-box model; defined by focusing on one major output, exploring the extent to which consumers of the output are satisfied with it, and tracing the reasons for any dissatisfaction.
- Congruence model for organization analysis.
- Mckinsey 7s framework.
- Tichy's technical political cultural (TPC) framework.
- High-performance programming.
- Diagnosing individual and group behavior.
- Burke–Litwin model of organizational performance and change.

All models are based on open system (Open System Theory, OST): From the General System Theory defined by Von Bertalaffy (a system complex of interacting elements), Katz and Kahn apply the concept of Open System Theory (OST), looking at the relationship between the organizations and the environment in which they are involved. This focus reflects on the organization's ability to adapt to changes in environment conditions (with or without the need for information processing).

- Falletta's organizational intelligence model.
- Semantic Network Analysis.

## The Consulting Process

The organizational diagnostic phase is often integrated within an overall OD process, commonly called 'a consulting process'. An example of such a process is:

Entry → Diagnosis → Action Planning → Implementation → Termination

As the second phase in the consulting cycle, it is also the first fully operational phase of the consulting process or cycle. The purpose of the diagnosis is to examine the problem faced by the organization in detail, to identify factors and forces that are causing the problem and to prepare the collected information to decide how to implement possible solutions to the identified problems.

The diagnosis of the problem is a separate phase from the solutions themselves.

## Models of Diagnosis

## Open Systems Theory

The premise of the theory is that organizations are social systems which are dependent upon the environment in which they exist for inputs. Open systems theory allows for repeated cycles of input, transformation (i.e., throughputs), output, and renewed input within organizations. A feedback loop connects organizational outputs with renewed inputs.

Traditional organizational theories have viewed organizations as "closed" systems which are independent of the environment in which they exist.

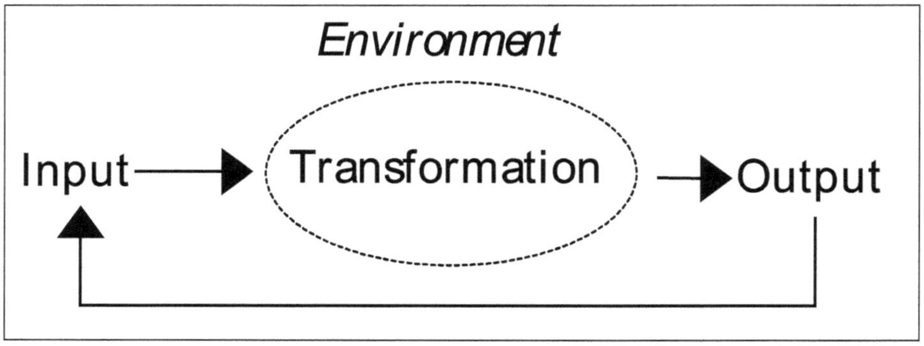


Open systems theory.

## Organizational Diagnostic Models

The 12 models selected for this review are presented in the chronological order:

- Lewin's Force Field Analysis.
- Leavitt's Model.
- Likert's System Analysis.
- Weisbord's Six-Box Model.
- Nadler and Tushman's Congruence Model for Organization Analysis.
- McKinsey 7S Framework.
- Galbrath's STAR Model.
- Tichy's Technical Political Cultural (TPC) Framework.
- Nelson and Burns' High-Performance Programming.
- Harrison's Diagnosing Individual and Group Behavior Model.
- Burke-Litwin Model of Organizational Performance & Change.
- Falletta's Organizational Intelligence Model.

## Lewin's Force Field Analysis

In 1951, Lewin developed a model for analyzing and managing organizational problems which he has termed Force Field Analysis. This model is relatively simple to understand and easy to visualize. A depiction of the model identifies both driving forces and restraining forces within an organization. These driving forces, such as environmental factors push for change within the organization while the restraining forces, such as organizational factors (e.g., limited resources or poor morale), act as barriers to change. To understand the problem within the organization, the driving forces and restraining forces are first identified and, hence, defined. Goals and strategies for moving the equilibrium of the organization toward the desired direction can then be planned.

The model relies upon the change process, with the social implications built into the model (e.g., disequilibrium is expected to occur until equilibrium is reestablished). The general goal of this model is to intentionally move to a desirable state of equilibrium by adding driving forces, where important, and eliminating restraining forces, where appropriate. These changes are thought to occur simultaneously within the dynamic organization.

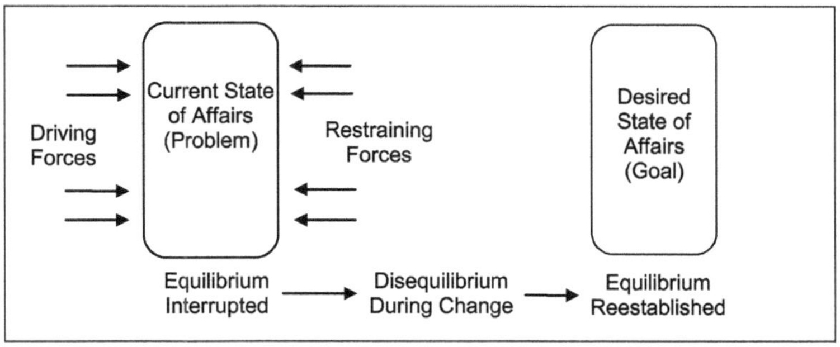


Lewin's force field analysis.

## Leavitt's Model

Sometime after Lewin conceptualized Force Field Analysis, Leavitt designed another relatively simple model. This model does specify particular variables within organizations, rather than driving forces; these variables include: task variables, structure variables, technological variables, and human variables.

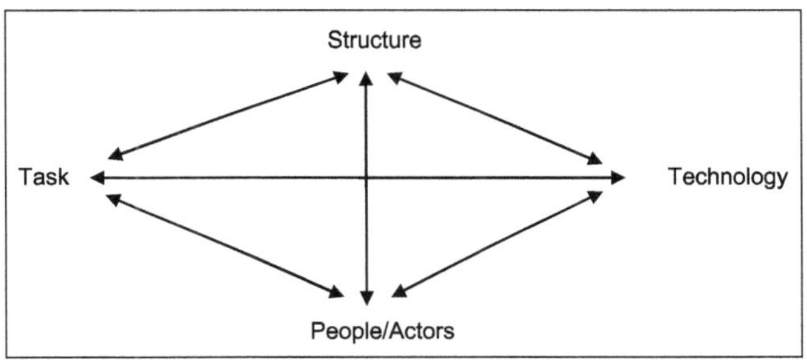


Leavitt's model.

The structure variable refers to the authority systems, communication systems, and work flow within the organization. The technological variable includes all the equipment and machinery required for the task variable; the task variable refers to all the tasks and subtasks involved in providing products and services. Finally, the human variable (i.e., people/actors) refers to those who carry out the tasks associated with organizational goals (i.e., products and services). The diamond shaped arrows in the model emphasize the interdependence among the four variables. Leavitt has postulated that a change in one variable will affect the other variables. For example, with a planned change in one variable (e.g., the introduction of advanced technology), one or more variables will be impacted. Such interventions are typically designed to affect the task variable (e.g., to affect positive changes in products or services). In this example, the other variables would also likely change, as morale (i.e., people) might increase and communication (i.e., structure) might be improved due to the new technology.

Although Leavitt describes the variables within his model as dynamic and interdependent, the model is too simple to make any direct causal statements regarding the four variables. Similar to the Force Field Analysis model, Leavitt suggests that a change in one variable may result in compensatory or retaliatory change in the other variables; this notion is similar to the opposing forces in Lewin's model. However, unlike Force Field Analysis, Leavitt does not address the role of the external environment in bringing about change in any of the variables.

## Likert System Analysis

The organizational dimensions Likert addresses in his normative framework include motivation, communication, interaction, decision making, goal setting, control, and performance (Likert, 1967). While Likert did not use an illustration to depict his framework, like the earlier models reviewed thus far, he describes four different types of management systems within organizations, which take into account the organizational dimensions he identifies.

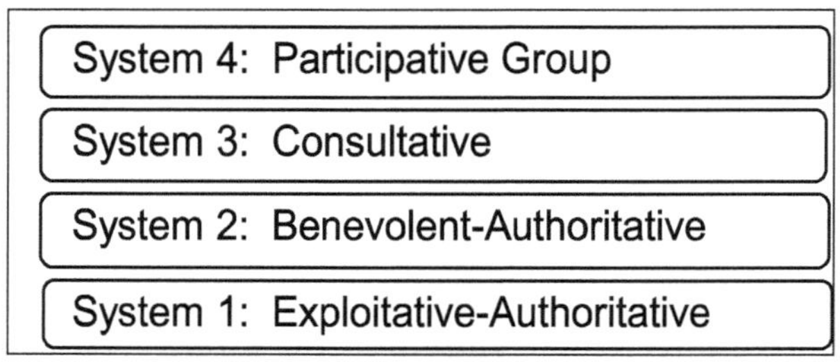


Likert's system analysis.

In order to determine the management system operating in any given organization, Likert developed a 43-item survey instrument with questions related to the seven organizational dimensions. The purpose of the instrument was to measure employees' perceptions (e.g., upper management, supervisors, and staff) of the organizational dimensions within the organization.

Interestingly and contrary to popular belief, Likert's original scale did not have standardized scale labels such as "strongly agree," "agree," "neither agree nor disagree," "disagree," and "strongly disagree." Instead, Likert provided customized scale labels for each item stem (i.e., for all 43 items). The first response alternative, in this case "provides minimum information," represents Likert's System 1: Exploitative-Authoritative. The second response alternative, "gives subordinates only information superior feels they need," represents System 2: Benevolent-Authoritative, and so forth. To determine the perceived functioning of the organization, the responses of various employee groups are averaged across items and dimensions. A profile is graphically plotted, indicating the current management system level for each of Likert's seven dimensions.

The terminology and system devised by Likert have been adapted and/or changed by other researchers over the years. For example, Nelson and Burns have introduced a version of Likert's framework with the following terminology: the reactive organization (System 1), the responsive organization (System 2), the proactive organization (System 3), and the highperforming organization (System 4). These changes have been made to reflect more modern terminology and contemporary theory.

## Weisbord's Six-Box Model

Weisbord proposes six broad categories in his model of organizational life, including purposes, structures, relationships, leadership, rewards, and helpful mechanisms. The purposes of an organization are the organization's mission and goals. Weisbord refers to structure as the way in which the organization is organized; this may be by function – where specialists work together – or by product, program, or project – where multi-skilled teams work together. The ways in which people and units interact is termed relationships. Also included in the box of relationships is the way in which people interact with technology in their work. Rewards are the intrinsic and extrinsic rewards people associate with their work. The leadership box refers to typical leadership tasks, including the balance between the other boxes. Finally, the helping mechanisms are the planning, controlling, budgeting, and information systems that serve to meet organizational goals. The external environment is also depicted in Weisbord's model, although it is not represented as a "box".

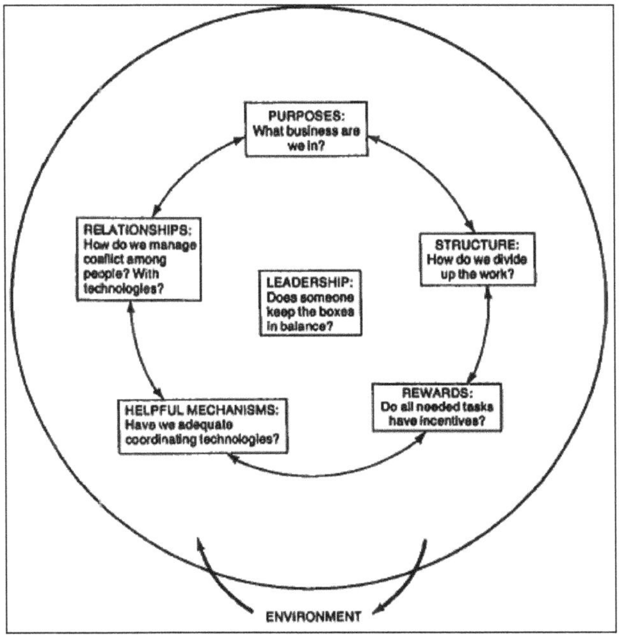


Conceptualization of weisbord's six-box model.

Weisbord identifies as inputs the money, people, ideas, and machinery which are used to fulfill the organization's mission. The outputs are products and services.

Two premises which are not apparent in Weisbord's model are crucial to understanding the boxes in the model. The first premise refers to formal versus informal systems. Formal systems are those policies and procedures the organization claims to do. In contrast, informal systems are those behaviors which actually occur. The bigger the gap between the formal and informal systems, the less effective the organization is consider to be. The second premise concerns the fit between the organization and the environment, that is, the discrepancy between the existing organization and the way the organization should function to meet external demands. Weisbord defines external demands or pressures as customers, government, and unions.

Weisbord poses diagnostic questions for each box of his model. For example, he suggests that OD consultants determine whether organizational members agree with and support the organization's mission and goals within the purposes box. This question refers to his premise regarding the nature of the formal and informal systems within the organization. A sample of some of the questions he poses is as follows in table.

Table: Sample Questions for Weisbord's Six-Box Model.

| | |
|---|---|
| Purposes | Do organizational members agree with and support the organization's mission and goals? |
| Structure | Is there a fit between the purpose and the internal structure of the organization? |
| Relationships | What types of relations exist between individuals, between departments, and between individuals and the nature of their jobs? Is their interdependence? What is the quality of relations? What are the modes of conflict? |
| Rewards | What does the organization formally reward, and for what do organizational members feel they are rewarded and punished? What does the organization need to do to fit with the environment? |
| Leadership | Do leaders define purposes? Do they embody purposes in their programs? What is the normative style of leadership? |
| Helpful Mechanisms | Do these mechanisms help or hinder the accomplishment of organizational objectives? |

In summary, Weisbord's model focuses on internal issues within an organization primarily by posing "diagnostic questions" which have to do with the fit between "what is" and "what should be." The questions he poses are not predicted by the model; rather, they appear to be based on his OD practice. These questions serve to convolute the model because they do not flow from the logic of the model. Moreover, Weisbord omits many interconnections between the boxes of the model. Finally, Weisbord only tangentially addresses the impact of the external environment in the model.

## Nadler and Tushman's Congruence Model for Organization Analysis

The Nadler-Tushman Congruence Model is a more comprehensive model, specifying inputs, throughputs, and outputs, which is consistent with open systems theory. This model is very similar to Leavitt's model; it also retains the formal and informal systems of the Weisbord six-box model.

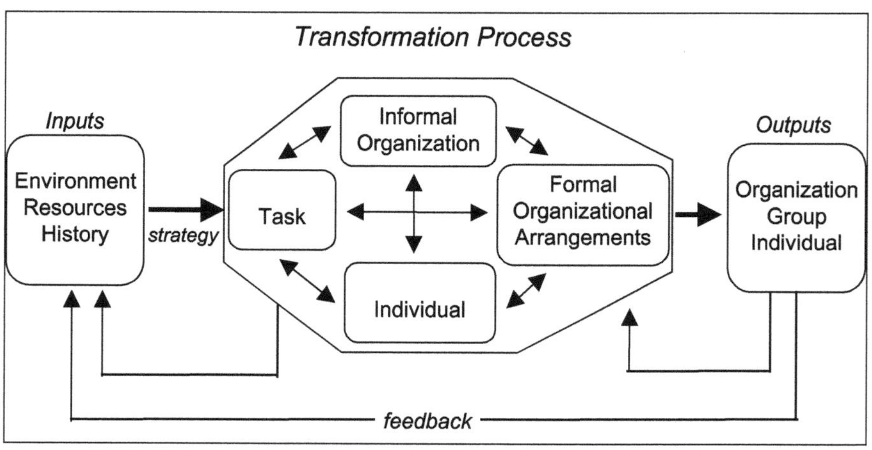


Nadler-tushman's congruence model.

The model is based on several assumptions which are common to modern organizational diagnostic models; these assumptions are as follows:

- Organizations are open social systems within a larger environment.

- Organizations are dynamic entities (i.e., change is possible and occurs).
- Organizational behavior occurs at the individual, the group, and the systems level.
- Interactions occur between the individual, group, and systems levels of organizational behavior.

These assumptions have been used in some of the previous models examined, although only implicitly.

The inputs within the Nadler-Tushman Congruence model include such factors as the environment, resources, history (i.e., patterns of past behavior), and organizational strategies. Nadler and Tushman are explicit in their conceptualization of each of the factors. For example, they describe the resources available to the organization as human resources, technology, capital, information, and other less tangible resources. While strategy is an input in the model, it is the single most important input to the organization and is depicted by the arrow from the input box to the organization.

The system components of the whole organizational transformation process are informal organizational arrangements, task, formal organizational arrangements, and individual components. Similarly, the outputs of the model include individual, group, and system outputs: products and services, performance, and effectiveness. While outputs such as products and services are generally understood, specific examples of organizational performance and effectiveness are identified by Nadler and Tushman in table.

Table: Inputs, system components, and outputs of the congruence model.

| Inputs | | | |
|---|---|---|---|
| Environment | Resources | History | Strategy |
| All factors, including institutions, groups, individuals, events, and so on, that are outside the organization being analyzed, but that have a potential impact on that organization. | Various assets to which the organization has access, including human resources, capital, information, and so on, as well as less tangible resources (recognition in the market, and so forth). | The patterns of past behavior, activity, and effectiveness that may affect current organizational functioning. | The stream of decisions about how organizational resources will be configured to meet demands, constraints, and opportunities within the context of the organization's history. |
| System Components (i.e., throughputs) | | | |
| Task | Individual | Formal Org. Arrangements | Informal Organization |
| The basic and inherent work to be done by the organization and its parts. | The characteristics of individuals in the organization. | The various structures, processes, methods, and so on that are formally created to get individuals to perform tasks. | The emerging arrangements, including structures, processes, relationships, and so forth. |
| Outputs (e.g., performance and effectiveness) | | | |
| Individual behavior and affect | Group and Intergroup Behavior | | System Functioning (i.e., organizational) |

| Absenteeism, lateness, turnover, levels of satisfaction, drug usage, and off-the-job activities which impact perfor-mance. | Intergroup conflict, collaboration, and quality of inter-group communication. | Attainment of desired goals of production, re-turn on investment, etc.; utilization of available resources; adaptability to external environmental demands. |
|---|---|---|

Nadler and Tushman apply the concept of congruence to their model. They describe congruence, or fit, as "the degree to which the needs, demands, goals, objectives, and/or structures of one component are consistent with the needs, demands, goals, objectives, and/or structures of another component" (i.e., how well pairs of components fit together). For example, a task demands a level of skill and knowledge and likewise, the individuals available to perform the task possess varying levels of skill and knowledge. Nadler and Tushman explain that the greater the skill and knowledge match between the task and the individual, the more effective the performance will be. Six paired comparisons within the system are possible based on the four components. Through analysis of the congruence between the system parts, the whole organization is diagnosed.

## McKinsey 7S Framework

The McKinsey 7S Framework was named after a consulting company, McKinsey and Company, and first introduced in 1980. The McKinsey 7S Framework was created as a recognizable model for business and industry and largely popularized through two best-selling books namely, The Art of Japanese Management, and In Search of Excellence. The seven variables, which the authors term "levers," all begin with the letter "S".

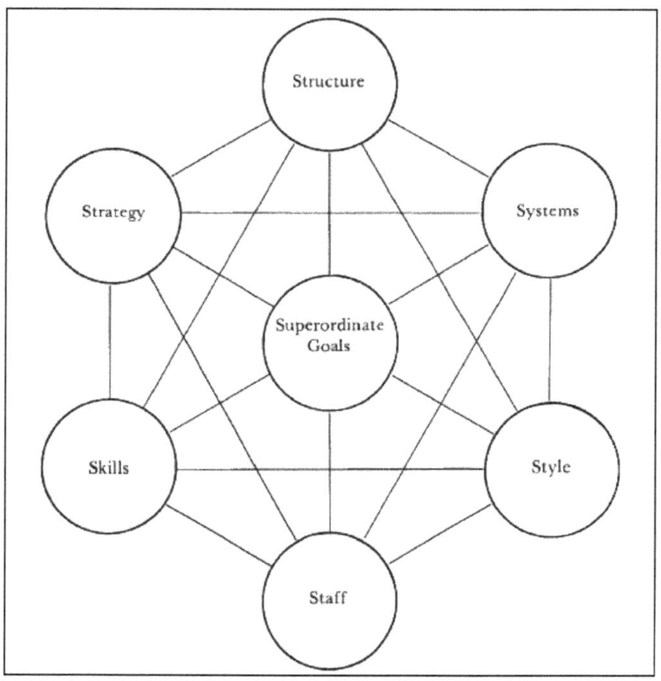


Mckinsey 7s framework.

The shape of the model was also designed to illustrate the interdependency of the variables; the illustration of the model has been termed the "Managerial Molecule." While Waterman, Peters, and Phillips thought that other variables existed within complex organizations, the variables represented in the model were considered to be of crucial importance to managers and practitioners.

The seven variables include structure, strategy, systems, skills, style, staff, and superordinate goals (i.e., share values). Structure is defined as the skeleton of the organization or the organizational chart. Strategy is described as the plan or course of action in allocating resources to achieve identified goals over time. The systems are the routinized processes and procedures followed within the organization. Staff are described in terms of personnel categories within the organization (e.g., engineers), whereas the skills variable refers to the capabilities of the staff within the organization as a whole. The way in which key managers behave in achieving organizational goals is considered to be the style variable; this variable is thought to encompass the cultural style of the organization. The shared values variable, originally termed superordinate goals, refers to the significant meanings or guiding concepts that organizational members share.

Peters and Waterman have concluded that American companies tend to focus on those variables which they feel they can change (e.g., structure, strategy, and systems) while neglecting the other variables. These other variables (e.g., skills, style, staff, and shared values) are considered to be "soft" variables. The original creators of the model have concluded that a company cannot merely change one or two variables to change the whole organization. For long-term benefit, they feel that the variables should be changed to become more congruent as a system.

The external environment is not mentioned in the McKinsey 7S Framework, although Waterman, Peters, and Phillips do acknowledge that other variables exist and that they depict only the most crucial variables in the model. While alluded to in their discussion of the model, the notion of performance or effectiveness is not made explicit in the model.

## Galbraith's STAR Model

Introduced in 1982, Galbraith's Star Model is one of the most widely-used organizational design frameworks. According to Galbraith, the Star Model is a framework for making design choices and decisions on organizational strategy and execution. The model includes five design elements or variables that leaders can use to influence behavior and performance outcomes in an organization. The Star Model is depicted in figure below.

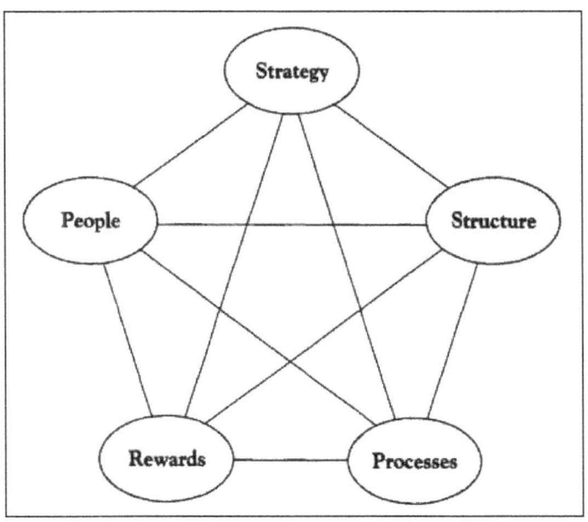


Galbraith's star model.

The model depicts five design elements: strategy, structure, processes, rewards, and people. These design elements affect the overall direction of the organization, the nature of leadership, the flow of information, and the competencies and motivation workers. Strategy is a multi-dimensional concept which can be defined in a number of different ways. In general, strategy is the means by which an organization intends on achieving its objectives and goals with respect to improving or innovating for competitive advantage. Leaders, in turn, develop and reinforce the organizational capabilities need for strategy attainment. Questions related to each of the variables in the model are shown in table.

Table: Sample Questions for Galbraith's Star Model.

| | |
|---|---|
| Strategy | What is the formula for success? How do we differentiate ourselves from our competitors? |
| Structur | How are we organized? What are the key leadership roles? How is the work managed? Who has power and authority? |
| Processes | How are decisions made? How does work flow between roles? What are the mechanisms for authority? |
| Rewards | How is behavior shaped by the goals? How do we assess progress? |
| People | What skills are needed? How do we best develop our talent? |

The Star Model does not specify a specific performance outcome (e.g., organizational culture, performance, or effectiveness). However, Kates and Galbraith explain that the model is merely a framework for decision making on crucial design elements that can be directly controlled by upper management. Culture, for example, is vitally important for any organization, but cannot be directly controlled by management. Rather, culture is a manifestation or outcome of the specific design choices made in an organization. Likewise, individual, group, and organizational effectiveness and performance are considered a byproduct of the variables in the model. In short, the Star Model depicts the organizational design variables that can be directly controlled by the leadership in an organization.

Kates and Galbraith emphasize the importance of alignment among the variables in the Star Model. They recommend conducting an assessment to determine whether the variables are aligned to support the overall strategy and execution.

The Star Model and the notion of alignment suggest interdependencies among the design elements in the model. However, there are no implied causal relationships or directionality among the variables in the model. Rather, the variables are complimentary in that a change in one design element may affect another variable in the model.

## Tichy's Technical Political Cultural (TPC) Framework

Similar to some of the previous models, Tichy's model includes inputs, throughputs, and outputs, which is consistent with the open systems perspective discussed earlier. Tichy identifies key variables in the model which are important to the change management process. The environment and history, broadly construed, are two major categories of input to the organization whereas resources are a third category of input. The throughput variables, or change levers, identified in the model include mission/strategy, tasks, prescribed networks, people, organizational processes, and emergent networks.

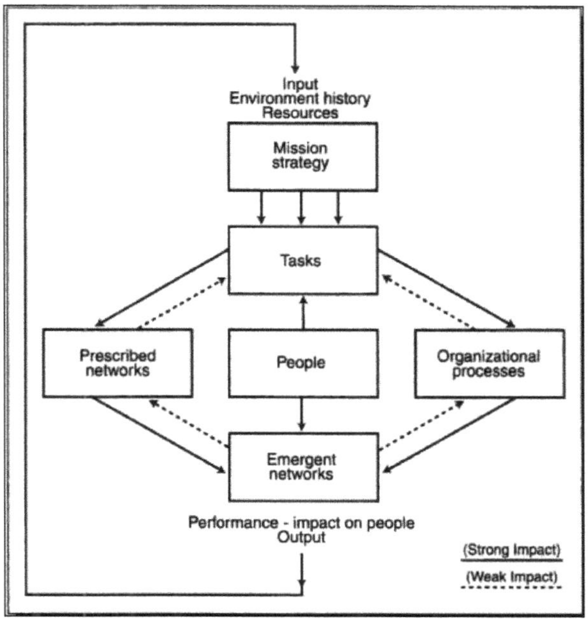


Tichy's technical, political, cultural framework.

Tichy defines the mission/strategy variable as the organization's approach to carrying out its mission and strategy and criteria for effectiveness (i.e., the organization's purpose). The tasks variable refers to the technology by which the organization's work is accomplished. The prescribed networks (i.e., the formal organization) have to do with the designed social structure of the organization, such as the organization of departments and the communication and authority networks. The people variable refers to the characteristics of organizational members, including their background, motivation, and managerial style. The mechanisms which enable the formal organization to carry out the work are termed the organizational processes; these include organizational communication, decision-making, conflict management, control, and reward systems. The final throughput variable, emergent networks, refers to the structures and processes in the organization, which emerge informally.

The focal point of Tichy's model is the output variable, which he terms organizational effectiveness. Of course, the output is dependent upon the input and throughput variables. All of the variables, including the input and output categories, are considered to be interrelated in the model. While some variables have a strong influence on other variables, other variables have a weaker, or reciprocal, relationship on other variables – as denoted by the straight and dashed lines.

In considering the variables in the model, Tichy applies an overlay which is vital to his theorizing. This overlay concerns the technical, political, and cultural dynamics going on within the variables of the model (abbreviated as TPC). The TPC overlay raises four questions which are vital to organizational diagnosis. These questions address the technical, political, and cultural dynamics of the organization. These questions follow:

- How well are the parts of the organization aligned with each other for solving the organization's technical problems?

- How well are the parts of the organization aligned with each other for solving the organization's political problems?
- How well are the parts of the organization aligned with each other for solving the organization's cultural problems?
- How well aligned are the three subsystems of the organization, the technical, political, and cultural?

The technical dynamics are those aspects of the organization which are knowable, such as production processes or available resources. The political dynamics are the views of dominant groups, including bargaining by powerful organizational groups. The cultural dynamics constitute the shared symbols and values which make up the organizational culture. As depicted in the illustration of the model, Tichy uses a rope metaphor to emphasize the strategic importance of the three strands (i.e., technical, political, and cultural) in the change process. The three strands must be managed together, or realigned, for effective change.

According to Tichy's model, organizational diagnosis is quite complex. An OD consultant would begin by collecting data relevant to the four questions for each variable represented in the model. The data may be collected by document analysis, interviews, questionnaires, and interviews. In order to determine where alignment is needed, summary data would be included in a matrix and analyzed for alignment and action planning.

## Nelson and Burns' High-performance Programming

Nelson and Burns' high-performance programming framework assesses the current level of performance of an organization in order to plan interventions to transform the organization into a high performing system. Similar to Likert System Analysis, Nelson and Burns describe four organizational systems which are more or less effective. These systems, or frames, as Nelson and Burns call them, include the high-performing organization (level 4), the proactive organization (level 3), the responsive organization (level 2), and the reactive organization (level 1). Each of these levels is conceptualized in table. To diagnose an organization, a survey instrument is used with questions related to Nelson and Burns' eleven dimensions or variables. These eleven variables are time frame, focus, planning, change mode, management, structure, perspective, motivation, development, communication, and leadership. The variables are measured on a standard Likert-type scale such as "strongly disagree," "disagree," "neither agree nor disagree," "agree," and "strongly agree".

Table: Nelson and Burns' High-Performance Programming.

| | |
|---|---|
| The HighPerforming Organization (Level 4) | Leaders in the high-performing organization are fully invested in empowering organizational members. There is a common focus on organizational excellence. Communication throughout the organization is relatively unrestrictive. The organization is in a constant state of evolution guided by a common vision. Organizational members prize highly their identity with the organization, and opportunities for self actualization are substantial. |

| | |
|---|---|
| The Proactive Organization (Level 3) | The proactive organization focuses on the future. Leadership has become focused on developing purpose for the organization. Members focus on the quality of their contribution to organizational successes. The organization is actively involved in planning and development strategies. |
| The Responsive Organization (Level 2) | The responsive organization is more functional, having achieved some clarity of purpose and goals. The organization has some capability to adapt to changing environmental circumstances. Leaders actively coach members in the direction of organizational goals, and some cohesion has developed among work teams. |
| The Reactive Organization (Level 1) | The reactive organization is one badly in need of renewal. The organization lacks shared focus, and management is preoccupied with assigning blame for poor outcomes. Members spend a disproportionate amount of time avoiding aversive consequences, and leaders spend much of their time enforcing policies that often lack relevance to any common purpose. |

The leadership activities associated with the four levels of performance in the high-performance programming framework is as follows: the high-performing organization is associated with "empowering" leadership, the proactive organization is associated with "purposing" leadership, the responsive organization is associated with "coaching" leadership, and the reactive organization is associated with "enforcing" leadership. To clarify, "purposing" leadership activity refers to leadership behavior which maintains an integrated, focused purpose for the organization. Nelson and Burns describe these leadership behaviors to emphasize the importance of empowerment and support for individuals' growth and development within the organization.

## Diagnosing Individual and Group Behavior

Harrison has devised a model for diagnosing individual and group behavior within organizations. The model which was later refined as a framework for diagnosing group behavior is somewhat unique in that it focuses on outputs such as organizational effectiveness, quality of work life (QWL), and individual well-being. The model represents an open systems perspective with minimal boundaries between the organization and external environment. However, the external environment is not represented by anything other than resources and feedback loops.

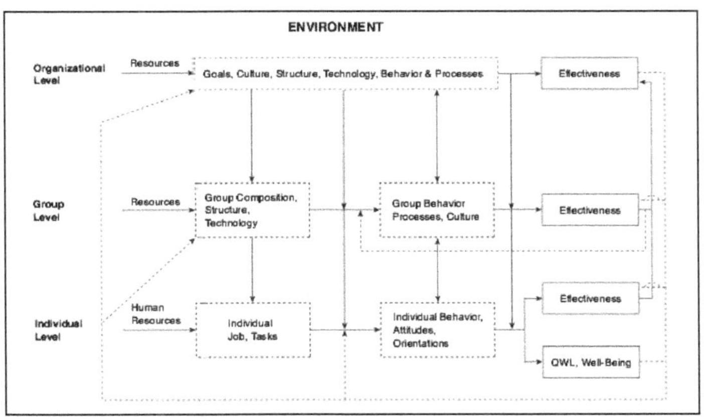


Harrison's model for diagnosing individual and group behaviour.

The variables accounted for in the model are conceptualized at the organizational, group, and individual levels. The organizational level of effectiveness appears to represent a more abstract level of effectiveness, which is a function of the outputs associated with organizational goals, culture, structure, technology, behavior, and processes. Whereas, the variables which influence group level effectiveness are the group composition, structure, and technology of the organization, as well as group behavior, processes, and culture. Notice that these variables are very broad. In contrast, the variables which affect the individual level of effectiveness including QWL and individual well-being are the individual, job, and tasks as well as individual behavior, attitudes, and orientation.

The inputs to the model are the resources, including human resources, which are available to the organization and feedback loops from prior organizational outcomes. Since there is no definitive boundary around the organization, it is not clear whether all the resources are derived from the external environment, the organization itself, or a combination of the two. The outputs at the organizational level are the products and services the organization produces. The outcomes associated with group performance within the organization are the solutions, plans, and tactics devised during operations. At the individual level, outcomes include the quality of individual members' work efforts, their initiative, cooperation with others, and commitment to their work; negative outcomes are related to absenteeism and tardiness at the individual level. Lastly, perceptions of job security, working conditions, the meaningfulness and challenge of work, and the degree to which work contributes to the psychological well-being of members are all related to QWL outcomes.

Harrison denotes the lines of influence in the model as either main lines of influence or feedback loops. However, not all of these relationships are reciprocal, as some of the other models have suggested. The extensive number of lines of influence and feedback loops in the model makes it difficult to determine the relationships among variables.

## The Burke-Litwin Causal Model

The Burke-Litwin Causal Model of Organizational Performance and Change (B-L model) was developed by Litwin and others and later refined by Burke in the late 1980's. This model includes several key features which go beyond the models discussed earlier. First, the B-L model includes 12 theoretical constructs (i.e., organizational variables or factors). Second, it distinguishes between the culture and the climate of an organization. Third, the B-L model distinguishes between transformational and transactional dynamics in organizations. Lastly and of significance, the B-L model specifies the nature and direction of influence of organizational variables.

The 12 organizational variables in the B-L model are external environment, mission and strategy, leadership, organizational culture, structure, management practices, systems, work unit climate, task requirements and individual skills, motivation, individual needs and values, and individual and organizational performance. With the representation of the external environment as a variable, it is evident that open systems theory underlies the B-L model. The external environment variable is considered to be the input to the system with the individual and organizational performance variable representing the output.

The feedback loops on the right and left sides of the model go in both directions. For example, the performance variable affects the external environment through its products and services, and likewise, the individual and organizational performance is affected by demands from the external environment. The remaining variables represent throughputs in open systems theory.

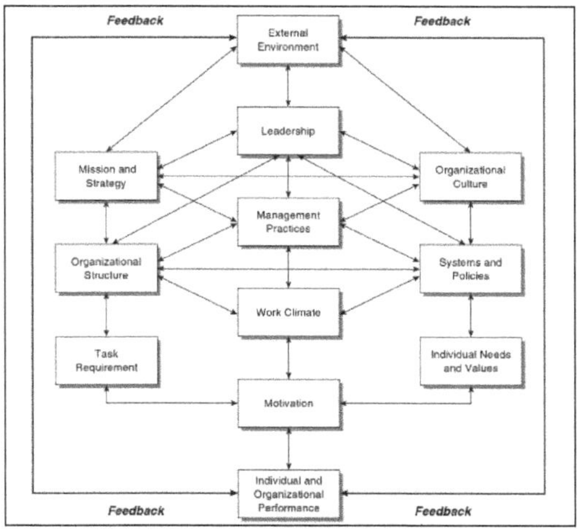


The Burke-Litwin causal model.

As is evident through the climate and culture variables, Burke and Litwin make a distinction between organizational climate and culture. Climate is defined as individuals' perceptions of how their work unit is managed and how effectively they and their colleagues work together. People are much more cognizant of organizational climate than culture (i.e., climate is in the foreground, whereas culture is in the background). In contrast, culture has been defined as the relatively enduring set of values, norms, and beliefs that underlie the social system of the workplace. These values, norms, and beliefs related to organizational culture are not entirely available to one's consciousness.

In addition to the distinction between culture and climate, the B-L model distinguishes between transformational and transactional dynamics within organizations. Burke and Litwin's consideration of transformational and transactional dynamics is rooted in leadership theory and specifically, in the differences between leaders and managers. In the model, transformational change is associated more with leadership, while transactional change is associated more with management. Hence, transformational dynamics represent fundamental changes in behaviors and values that are required for genuine change in organizational culture. In terms of management, transactional dynamics are the everyday interactions and exchanges in work life related to organizational climate.

As mentioned, the model has been revised over time by Burke and his colleagues in a series of organizational studies. Burke and Litwin have welcomed further empirical investigation of the validity of the organizational model. To date, however, only a handful of applied research studies have been conducted on the model. These studies largely focused on assessing the B-L model's predictive or statistical conclusion validity, reliability and internal consistency (e.g., Cronbach's alpha), and/or usefulness in terms of facilitating organizational diagnosis, development, and change.

## Organizational Intelligence Model

The final organizational diagnostic model is a relatively new model, the Organizational Intelligence Model (OI Model) that was originally developed by Falletta in 2004 and later refined and published. The OI model is a diagnostic framework for OD purposes as well as an analysis framework in the design and interpretation of employee and organizational survey efforts.

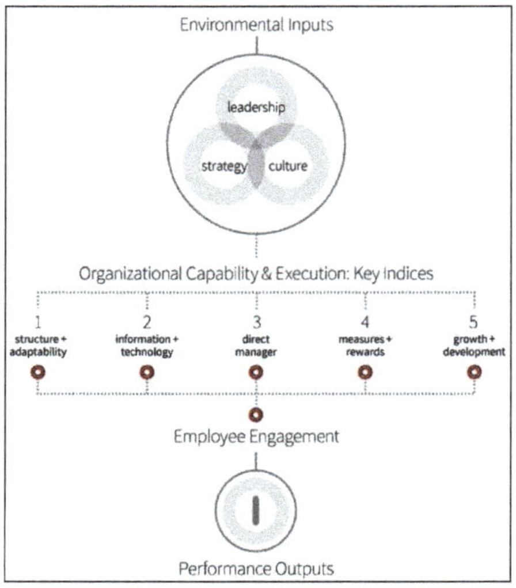


Falletta's organizational intelligence model.

The OI model includes 11 variables. The model includes several elements that are similar to the B-L model. For example, it depicts a top-down causal chain, making some tentative assertions with respect to cause and effect. The variables in the upper part of the model, such as environmental inputs, affect the organization from the outside. Within the organization, the strategic drivers (i.e., leadership, strategy, and culture) affect key indices which represent organizational capability and execution. These include the organization's structure and adaptability, information and technology, quality of direct managers, measures and rewards, and growth and development opportunities.

Table: Factor Descriptions of the Organizational Intelligence Model.

| Factor | Description |
|---|---|
| Environmental Inputs | The outside conditions or situations that affect the organization (e.g., government policy, competitive intelligence, customer feedback, the economy). |
| Strategy | The means by which an organization intends on achieving its objectives and goals with respect to improving or innovating for competitive advantage. |
| Leadership | The most senior level of executives (VP and above) in the organization. |
| Culture | The underlying values, beliefs and norms that drive team and organizational behaviour. |
| Structure & Adaptability | The structure is how the organization is designed (i.e., levels, roles, decision rights, responsibilities and accountabilities) to execute on the strategy. Whereas, adaptability refers to the extent to which the organization is ready and able to change. |
| Information & Technology | The business systems, practices, and capabilities that facilitate and reinforce people's work (e.g., communication, IT infrastructure, knowledge sharing). |
| Direct Manager | The relative quality and effectiveness of an employee's direct manager or supervisor. |

| | |
|---|---|
| Measures & Rewards | Measures refer to the ways in which individual and team performance and accomplishments are measured and managed. Rewards are the monetary and non-monetary incentives that reinforce people's behavior and actions, including advancement and promotion. |
| Growth & Development | The practices, resources, and opportunities available for employee skill development and enhancement, including development planning, training and learning, and stretch assignments. |
| Employee Engagement | Employee engagement involves the cognitive, emotional and behavioral relationship employees have with their jobs and organizations, and effort and enthusiasm they put into their daily work (i.e., the extent to which employees contribute their discretionary energy and effort on behalf of the organizations they serve). |
| Performance Outputs | The outcomes and indicators of individual and organizational achievement and results. |

The five key indices directly influence employee engagement and in turn the performance outputs variable (i.e., the key indices serve as the primary drivers of employee engagement and performance). Lastly, the performance outputs variable influences the environmental inputs variable and vice versa (i.e., there is a reciprocal relationship between these variables) which serves as a feedback loop with respect to open systems theory.

Unlike the other models presented, the OI model squarely depicts the emerging construct of employee engagement despite the healthy debate that is underway about how it differs from other well-research constructs such as employee satisfaction, involvement, commitment, and motivation. The use of employee engagement as a key variable in organizational research is gaining momentum.

Table: Hypothesized Relationships among the Variables in the OI Model.

| Strategic Drivers |
|---|
| External Inputs influences Leadership, Strategy, and Culture |
| Leadership and Strategy (reciprocal relationship) |
| Leadership and Culture (reciprocal relationship) |
| Strategy and Culture (reciprocal relationship) |
| Leadership influences →Key Indices of Employee Engagement and Performance |
| Strategy influences →Key Indices of Employee Engagement and Performance |
| Culture influences →Key Indices of Employee Engagement and Performance |
| Organizational Capability & Execution: Key Indices (i.e., Primary Drivers) |
| Structure & Adaptability influences → Employee Engagement |
| Information & Technology influences → Employee Engagement |
| Direct Manager influences → Employee Engagement |
| Measures & Rewards influences → Employee Engagement |

| Growth & Development influences → Employee Engagement |
|---|
| Employee Engagement influences → Performance Outputs |
| Performance Outputs and Environmental Inputs (i.e., a reciprocal relationship and feedback loop) |

While the Organizational Intelligence Model is similar in some respects to other top-down, causal models (e.g., the B-L model), it differs in the following ways:

- The Organizational Intelligence Model includes the emerging construct of employee engagement which is gaining momentum.
- The Organizational Intelligence Model depicts and emphasizes growth and development (i.e., Human Resource Development) as a key factor for nurturing, engaging, and retaining talent.
- The Organizational Intelligence Model has been tested in a number of organizational settings with respect to statistical conclusion validity (e.g., multiple regression) and reliability and internal consistency (e.g., Cronbach's alpha).

## References


- What-is-organizational-communication, introductiontocommunication: courses.lumenlearning.com, Retrieved 14 February, 2019
- Zarei, B., Chaghouee, Y. and Ghapanchi, F. (2014) - Organizational Diagnosis in Project-Based Companies: Challenges and Directions, Sage open,4(2), pp. 1–7, doi:10.1177/2158244014537498
- Organizational-diagnostic-models- 1571785: brainmass.com,
- Ravasi, D.; Schultz, M. (2006). "Responding to organizational identity threats: Exploring the role of organizational culture". Academy of Management Journal. 49 (3): 433–458. CiteSeerX 10.1.1.472.2754
- Kesler, Gregory, 1952- (2011). Leading organization design : how to make organization design decisions to drive the results you want. Kates, Amy. (1st ed.). San Francisco, CA: Jossey-Bass. pp. 9–10. ISBN 9780470912836. OCLC 693772818

# 3

# Organizational Behavior and Ethics

Organizational behavior studies human behavior in a work environment including job structure, performance, communication, leadership, etc. Organizational ethics refers to the principles, values and rules by which businesses operate. This chapter has been carefully written to provide an easy understanding of organizational behavior and ethics.

Organizational behavior (OB) is the academic study of the ways people act within groups. Its principles are applied primarily in attempts to make businesses operate more effectively.

The study of organizational behavior includes areas of research dedicated to improving job performance, increasing job satisfaction, promoting innovation, and encouraging leadership. Each has its own recommended actions, such as reorganizing groups, modifying compensation structures, or changing methods of performance evaluation.

The study of organizational behavior has its roots in the late 1920s, when the Western Electric Company launched a now-famous series of studies of the behavior of workers at its Hawthorne Works plant in Cicero, Illinois.

Researchers there set out to determine whether workers could be made to be more productive if their environment was upgraded with better lighting and other design improvements. To their surprise, the researchers found that the environment was less important than social factors. It was more important, for example, that people got along with their co-workers and felt their bosses appreciated them.

Those initial findings inspired a series of wide-ranging studies between 1924 and 1933. They included the effects on productivity of work breaks, isolation, and lighting, among many other factors.

The best known of the results is called the Hawthorne Effect, which describes the way test subjects' behavior may change when they know they are being observed. Researchers are taught to consider whether and to what degree the Hawthorne Effect is skewing their findings on human behavior.

Organizational behavior was not fully recognized by the American Psychological Association as a field of academic study until the 1970s. However, the Hawthorne research is credited for validating organizational behavior as a legitimate field of study, and it's the foundation of the human resources profession as we now know it.

## Goals of Organizational Behavior Study

The leaders of the Hawthorne study had a couple of radical notions. They thought they could use the techniques of scientific observation to increase an employee's amount and quality of work. And they did not look at workers as interchangeable resources. Workers, they thought, were unique in terms of their psychology and potential fit within a company.

Over the following years, the concept of organizational behavior widened. Beginning with World War II, researchers began focusing on logistics and management science. Studies by the Carnegie School of Home Economics in the 1950s and 1960s solidified these rationalist approaches to decision-making.

Today, those and other studies have evolved into modern theories of business structure and decision-making.

The new frontiers of organizational behavior are the cultural components of organizations, such as how race, class, and gender roles affect group building and productivity. These studies take into account the ways in which identity and background inform decision-making.

## Real World Examples of Organizational Behavior

Findings from organizational behavior research are used by executives and human relations professionals to better understand a business's culture, how that culture helps or hinders productivity and employee retention, and how to evaluate candidates' skills and personality during the hiring process.

Organizational behavior theories inform real-world evaluation and management of groups of people. There are a number of components:

- Personality plays a large role in the way a person interacts with groups and produces work. Understanding a candidate's personality, either through tests or through conversation, helps determine whether they are a good fit for an organization.
- Leadership, what it looks like and where it comes from, is a rich topic of debate and study within the field of organizational behavior. Leadership can be broad, focused, centralized or de-centralized, decision-oriented, intrinsic in a person's personality, or simply a result of a position of authority.
- Power, authority, and politics all operate inter-dependently in a workplace. Understanding the appropriate ways these elements are exhibited and used, as agreed upon by workplace rules and ethical guidelines, are key components to running a cohesive business.

# Characteristics and Nature of Organizational Behavior

## Behavioral Approach to Management

Organisational behavior is that part of whole management which represents the behavioral approach to management. Organisational behavior has emerged as a distinct field of study because of the importance of human behavior in organisations.

## Cause and Effect Relationship

Human behavior is generally taken in terms of cause and effect relationship and not in philosophical terms. It helps in predicting the behavior of individuals. It provides generalizations that managers can use to anticipate the effect of certain activities on human behavior.

## Organisational Behavior is a Branch of Social Sciences

Organisational behavior is heavily influenced by several other social sciences viz. psychology, sociology and anthropology. It draws a rich array of research from these disciplines.

## Three Levels of Analysis

Organisational behavior encompasses the study of three levels of analysis namely individual behavior, inter-individual behavior and the behavior of organisations themselves. The field of organisational behavior embraces all these levels as being complementary to each other.

## A Science as well as an Art

Organisational behavior is a science as well as an art. The systematic knowledge about human behavior is a science and the application of behavioral knowledge and skills is an art. Organisational behavior is not an exact science because it cannot exactly predict the behavior of people in organisations. At best a manager can generalize to a limited extent and in many cases, he has to act on the basis of partial information.

## A Body of Theory, Research and Application

Organisational behavior consists of a body of theory, research and application which helps in understanding the human behavior in organisation. All these techniques help the managers to solve human problems in organisations.

## Beneficial to both Organisation and Individuals

Organisational behavior creates an atmosphere whereby both organisation and individuals are benefitted by each other. A reasonable climate is created so that employees may get much needed satisfaction and the organisation may attain its objectives.

### Rational Thinking

Organisational behavior provides a rational thinking about people and their behavior. The major objective of organisational behavior is to explain and predict human behavior in organisations, so that result yielding situations can be created.

### Nature of Organisational Behavior

Organisational behavior in the study of human behavior in the organisations. Whenever an individual joins an organisation he brings with him unique set of personal characteristics, experiences from other organisations and a personal background. At the first stage organisational behavior must look at the unique perspective that each individual brings to the work setting.

The second stage of organisational behavior is to study the dynamics of how the incoming individuals interact with the broader organisation. No individual can work in isolation. He comes into contact with other individuals and the organisation in a variety of ways. The individual who joins a new organisation has to come into contact with the co-workers, managers, formal policies and procedures of the organisation etc.

Over the time, he is affected by his work experience and the organisation as well as his personal experiences and maturity. On the other hand, the organisation is also affected by the presence or absence of the individual. Thus, it is essential that OB must study the ways in which the individuals and organisation interact with each other.

The organisational behavior must be studied from the perspective of the organisation itself because an organisation exists before a particular individual joins in and continues to exist after he or she has left the organisation. Thus, OB is the study of human behavior in the organisation, the individual-organisation interaction and the organisation itself. And these factors are influenced by the external environment in which the individuals and the organisation exist.

Thus, we can say that we cannot study individual behavior completely without learning something about the organisation. On the other hand, we cannot study the organisations without studying the behavior of the individuals working in it. This is because the organisation influences and is influenced by the people working in it. Moreover, both the individuals and the organisation are influenced by the external environment. Thus, the field of organisational behavior is a complex field. It seeks to throw light on the entire canvas of human factor in the organisations which will include the causes and effects of such behavior.

## Importance of Organizational Behavior

Organizational behavior (OB) can help employees navigate a business's culture as well as help managers better understand how that culture helps or hinders employee productivity and retention. OB can also help managers evaluate a potential job candidate's skills and personality during the hiring process, allowing human resources to find the best fit for departments within the company. While there is never one exact way to assess these things, OB theory offers a set of guidelines to help organizations create a positive and vibrant internal culture.

One of the main goals of OB is to understand what motivates employees. How organizations measure job satisfaction varies, but most common metrics include a fair and equitable reward system, compelling work, enjoyable working conditions and good supervisors. By understanding what motivates employees, managers can adjust their policies to increase job satisfaction, thereby increasing productivity.

OB not only helps employees understand themselves better, it also offers a roadmap for managers to improve all aspects of their organizations:

- Improve job performance,
- Increase job satisfaction,
- Promote innovation,
- Encourage leadership,
- Improve customer service,
- Encourage ethical behavior,
- Create a positive work environment.

Depending on the challenges and desired outcomes, managers may use different tactics such as reorganizing workgroups, changing performance evaluations or modifying compensation structures. Understanding what motivates employees also plays a large part in how managers adjust company procedures or policies.

Not only does organizational behavior provide a roadmap for human resources and supervisors to manage more effectively, it also helps employees navigate an organization's culture.

When a strong model of OB is in place, employees can understand themselves better and know how they can best flourish inside an organization. And managers are better able to predict how employees might react under differing circumstances and adjust accordingly.

Creating a culture where relationships are cooperative, employees feel valued and companies flourish is at the heart of organizational behavior.

## Attributes of Individual Behavior in an Organization

The main and most important problem that managers are facing today is the management of people. This is the most challenging issues in each organization in daily life. Organizational behavior is studing individual, group andorganization in general to examine the effectof organizational structure, organizational culture and performance.

Human behavior which is very different from one to another, and knowing that each individual is different from others, the challenge that we have in order to have an effective organization is based on the amounts you attunesuccess, managers and the rest of the organization. The behavior of an individual in the organization is thecombination between the individual and environmental characteristics. In reality, the manager should use existing resources to a certain task, and should be able to understand the difference between the behavior of different individuals, and use them in the appropriate way to achieve team collaboration in the organization.

In the world of the individual, there is a general sample of human behavior which explains the process of differentiation between individuals. Knowledge or perception is a man thought process that describes how we transform taken information, store and use as knowledge in decision-making in the future. This includes things such as visual images, language, problem solving, decision making etc. In order to understand individuals behavior and their personalities, it is important to understand the basis of thinking of a person.

## Factors which Affect the Individual Behavior in Organization

Basic element and initiator of an organization is individual. With his initiative and organization, organization is created and continuously renewed, and as a reward for the effort she takes money from it. This means that the organization depends on the commitment of the individual, and the individual depends on the tools that are implemented in the organization. Every individual in another way, contributes to the success of the organization, so there is no need to analyze the impact of his behavior on the results of the organization.

Communication skills are some of the most important skills of organizational behavior of individual. How much we are communicable to others it shows how successful will be our careers. In order to achieve this we should be familiar with the concept of organizational behavior, to know how to gather force, to intertwine in politics and to manage conflicts and stress. Have you ever thought why people behave in a certain way in their work place? Organizational Behavior presents the studying of actions that influence people's behavior in the place where they work.

The purpose of the theoreticians of "Organizational Behavior" is to explain and predict people's actions and how they affect in their behavior. Organizational behavior as study field is based on three levels: individual, group and organization. Thus, organizational behavior is an applied knowledge which implements gained knowledge from individual, groups and organizations in order to make the organization work effectively.

There are many factors that determine this behavior:

- Values: Built system of individual's values is a basic belief of a person, that a certain way or someone's personal behavior is acceptable in aspect of some other behaviors. This is an assessment about what is good and bad. The system of values according to which is the individual leaded, is important because of the way in which a report is determined toward people, from which depends human relations in the organization. Also, value system to the individuals contributes in the way of decision making and problem solving, as well as the method of determining what is right and what is inappropriate for the organization.
- Attitudes: Attitudes are a system of beliefs and opinions that people have about what surrounds them in daily life. Actually, attitudes are statements of individuals to contain assessment, favorable or unfavorable to the things, events or people. Individual may have

attitudes about many things. But what more important is for any organization is which is the attitude for working duties, for the relation towards work, work conditions, for managers, for equipment for work, etc.

- Personality: Every individual has a unique style of behavior and their attitudes. They determine the identity of the individual personality. People can be described as calm, aggressive, ambitious etc. All these characteristics are caused by environmental effects or inherited characteristics. Personality characteristics are reflected to the organization on how individual is engaged in work.
- Motivation: Motivation of individual has a big impact on his behavior in the organization. Motives encourage workers to finish their duties. From this it depends the approach that individual will have toward work. The level of motivation depends largely on managers, so from their ability in certain ways to enable individuals to make more efforts.
- Learning: People learn different things every day, thus they adapt their behavior to the environment. The willingness of the individual to accept requests and suggestions of managers, to overcome and respect procedures in work processes and so on, can positively influence his behavior in the organization.
- Skills and Abilities: Ability is preparation and knowledge to complete certain physical or mental activities. Skill is the ability that quickly, correctly and precisely to fulfill or to complete a particular task. Skills and abilities through learning and work can change and can be improved. All this affects directly the behavior and contribution of individual to the organization.

The individual is the basic element and the initiator of the organization, because with his initiative organization is created and continually renewed. Groups are an unavoidable element of any organization, despite of size, interest, their establishment etc. Needs of people become reasons or essential factors due to which groups are established.

Requirements and new market challenges more rarely can enjoy the skills and capabilities of best individuals in the organization. They seek solutions to which there is only the formation of teams and practicing teamwork.

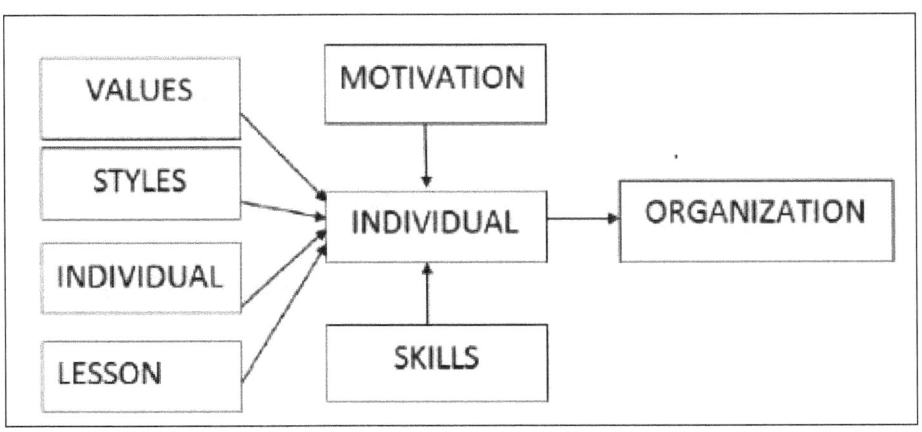


Factors that Determine Individual Behavior in the Organization.

## Individual Skills in a Working Environment

Person's skills are natural features or learned. Skills can be classified as mental skills and physical abilities, so different tasks require different levels for both skills. Mental abilities represent intelligence, reasoning, memory, analytics and communication. While physical abilities represent muscle strength, sustainability, physical strength, and other physical skills. Awareness of an individual can determine which skills a person needs in a given task, while manager perception based on skills of individual determine the type of assignment.

Individual represents the basic unit of any ambition (enterprise) organized. Individuals dream the organization, represent it, and change it. Through organized forms individuals realize their needs, by investing their effort or work and by being rewarded.

Both individual and organizations serve each other. Perception includes the selection process and the emotion's organization in general, special entity or experience. With selection individual in a way opposes to admit some sensations because it is not able to get everything at once.

Selective perception means accepting or denying something because we want to believe or we accept it because it fulfills our needs. Organization of experiences or stimulating sensations also affects the individual's behavior, respectively in the case of perception is done their mobilization so that the parts constitutes entirety. An important element of perception is the completion or fulfillment of integrity with new elements (that may be lacking). However, during the completing process or giving new elements can bes crated situations when we distort an individual appearance to the entirety. E.g. than when we create the stereotype impression about entirety or phenomenon, respectively when creating presuppositions about people by ranking in several categories based on similar features.

Recently, for people as a source it is said that they are not only one of the factors of production, but they are the most important factor of production. The reasons for this are numerous: the rapid developments of technology, economic and demographic changes, productivity reduce and alienation of workers etc. Therefore, today many enterprises place human resources at their long- term strategic plans. Skills in the work environment are the skills that enable that allow people to perform a job. They constitute knowledge base that is necessary to perform at work, to agree with customers and managers, as well as to compete with colleagues. These skills are necessary for each employee who will be part of a company.

## Age in the Working Environment

Age has a role in behavior, productivity and satisfaction of an individual in an organization. It is believed by almost all that the performance decreases with the increase of age. Whether this is true or not, many people believe and act based on this belief. Age has major roles to individual and based in some research it is said that man as older it is, the less it tends to leave work. As proof of this conclusion is that as many people grow older, the opportunity for employment is lower. Factors that determine the status in informal groups appear: education, age, ability or experience.

According to international conventions, the minimum age for acceptance to any work, which by its nature or the conditions of work damages health or morals of young person shall not be lower than 18 years. Legislation or the competent authorities may authorize the employment since the age of

16, only if the welfare of the young will be protected and in the cases when young people possess adequate information and professional preparations in the respective branches.

Also is believed that in general productivity decreases with the increase of age of employee. According to some surveys done to some individual is assumed that individual skills specifically extends the speed, strength and coordination fall over the years and the continuous upset that work gives and lack of intellectual simulation, contribute to the reduction of productivity.

## Gender in Work Environment

Although numerous studies have concluded that men and women are equal in their mental ability and performance at work, often different societies emphasize some differences. According to the records, the results are that there are few significant differences between men and women affecting their performance at work. For example, there are no differences between men and women in the ability to solve problems in analytical skills, on motivation, leadership or ability to learn. Psychological studies have shown that women are more likely to undergo authority and men are more aggressive in this direction.

Regarding absence, women have higher rates because it is a known fact in society whim of family responsibility is entirely on women. Based on legal provisions approved by state, which prohibits discrimination of any kind, employer may not prefer candidates according to criteria which are not related to work such as, gender, physical look, religious or ethnic affiliation.

People in the organization perform numerous activities (job duties), realize their interests, by working with others and trying to influence others in the organization, face with stress and frustration in the workplace, bringing decisions, etc. When this behavior is important to the organization, it is about organizational behavior.

It is important to understand today's complex work, and with this to improve individual and overall effect of work and at the same time increase employee satisfaction. Organizational behavior should help in, explaining the behavior of individuals and groups, in predicting the future behavior as well as control and management of employees.

Gender is a factor of duties separation, hard physical work and activities which are done by men, while women are engaged in easier physical work. It is a result from, physical-biological and sociological differences between genders. Men were given higher positions with greater authority and better prices, while women are concentrated in lower levels. Characteristic also for developed countries and with the same work position men and women are paid in different ways. This stems from the role of women at home and non-payment for housework – which women do without payment, duty household, the myth of romantic love and so on.

In a wider sense, gender discrimination at work, happens when a person or group of persons are treated unequally in work context because of gender. Unequal treatment can affect the level of payment, for example when a woman is paid less for a same work with a man. Gender discrimination can occur also in terms of opportunities, as well as the way of handling the job. A study done in Harvard showed that professional yields of women are better than those of male colleagues. In fact the only banks that are not included in the credit crisis are those that have women in leadership positions, explains Heather McGregor, a finance specialist at the bank.

## Race and Culture in the Working Environment

Culture shows the values that employees should accept to act in accordance with the organization's goals. This affects the way in which employees and managers are approaching with problems, serve customers, collaborate with suppliers, react with competitors and lead activities in the present and the future. Each organization is distinguished by a unique culture. It has its history, the way of access to his to problems and finishing its activities, management styles, working methods, his heroes, experiences embedded in changing etc. In other words, the atmosphere of its folklore, and personality.

Although all organizations have a unique culture, however, all cultures do not have equal impact for employees. According to the type of culture, organizations can monitor as organizations with weak culture and strong. Poor culture is characterized by the lack of a deep feeling for the purpose of organizing to the majority of workers. They see their work as a way to get money and who share their loyal department, colleagues, unions or boss. Strong culture is characterized by cohesion; employees understand the organization's goals and strategy, they know their individual roles and work to fulfill their part. Strong culture is a powerful tool for channeling the behavior of employees in ways that will support the strategy, as follows:

- Knowing exactly what is expected from them, employed in organizations with a strong culture must not lose time to understand what and how to do - culture provides informal system rules and tension of submissions, in order to determine a behavior in most of the time. In an organization with a weak culture, the lack of a strong organizational identity and work climate full of proposals creates considerable confusion among employees and unnecessary expenditure of effort.
- Strong culture makes work a way of life, provides the structure, standards and value systems that need to operate and to promote strong identification of employees in the organization. As a result, employees feel better and often engage in work to help the organization to be successful.

Race and culture have always played an important role in the behavior of various individuals, both in the workplace and in society, there has been considerable diversity. In these cases, this would create a contemporary culture and the most appropriate in an organization and at the same time will eliminate wrong perceptions and offensive. Mainly, management recruitment and career development regarding employment equity, equal opportunities and diversity aspects (e.g. gender, sexual orientation, disability, age, race and religion.

# Organizational Behavior Management

Organizational behavior management (OBM) applies behavioral principles to individuals and groups in business, industry, government and human service settings, a publication from the American Psychological Association. OBM can be seen as the intersection between behavioral science and improvement in organizational environments.

OBM is rooted in the field of applied behavior analysis (ABA), which develops techniques to produce socially significant behavior in a wide range of areas and behavioral problems. ABA is one of three disciplines of behavior analysis, or the science of behavior, which includes:

- Applied wing of the discipline of behavior analysis (ABA),
- Experimental analysis of behavior, focusing on basic principles of behavior,
- Branch of behavior analysis that focuses on the conceptual and philosophical underpinnings of the science of behavior (behaviorism).

Like ABA, OBM is focused almost exclusively on practical strategies that can be used to change behavior. For instance, instead of focusing on personality traits that are most predictive of high performers, ABA and OBM are more concerned about investigating methods to improve performance.

The growth of OBM has resulted in three primary specialty areas:

- Performance management applies behavioral principles to manage the performance of employees. This used to be synonymous with the term "OBM," but it is now its own field, contrasted by specialty areas geared toward other levels of the organization.
- Systems analysis refers to the analysis and modification of organizational processes to benefit the organization. This field focuses on how individuals or groups of workers can complete interdependent tasks that lead to created products or services important to the entire organization.
- Behavior-based safety is a fast-growing specialty that analyzes and modifies work environments to reduce injuries and promote safe behavior. Instead of other disciplines' approach to safety from the standpoint of mechanical or structural engineering, behavior-based safety concentrates on changing employees' behavior to reduce injuries and make safe performance more common.

## Workings of Organizational Behavior Management

Organizational behavior management (OBM) applications isolate, analyze and modify environment events that most directly affect performance. Specific interventions allow practitioners to effectively modify behavior in organizational environments.

## Sample Interventions

There are two categories of OBM interventions: antecedent-based interventions and consequence-based interventions.

Antecedent-based interventions include: task clarification, equipment modification, goal setting, prompting and training.

- Task clarification involves clearly defining employees' tasks.
- Equipment modification involves altering equipment used for tasks.

- Goal setting involves setting performance goals and then access to rewards.
- Prompting involves prompts to perform or continue performing an activity.
- Training involves identifying and modifying inadequate employee knowledge, skills or capacity.

Consequence-based interventions include feedback, praise and monetary and nonmonetary incentives.

- Feedback involves delivering information about past performance to the employee, which can vary according to format (verbal, written, graphic) and delivery agent (manager-supervisor, consultant-researcher or fellow employee). It is by far the most common intervention used in OBM.
- Monetary and nonmonetary incentives involve money, benefits or tangible items contingent on performance; in practice and research, they are often combined.

## Steps in an OBM Consultation

Here are some common steps that take place during an OBM consultation, regardless of problem, setting and intervention.

- Determine key results: Typically, the practitioner or researcher works with managers and executives to identify desired results.
- Find the pinpoints: The practitioner works with managers and executives to determine important behaviors and immediate results required to accomplish the key results. These behaviors and results are often referred to as "pinpoints" or "targets."
- Develop a measurement system: The practitioner helps the target audience develop an accurate and reliable way to measure the pinpointed behavior and results. This method often involves tracking costs associated with the pinpoints. Measurements will provide information about the current levels of the behavior and results, as well as providing a baseline comparison that can be used to evaluate the effects of solutions.
- Diagnose the problem: The practitioner teaches managers to ask questions and conduct observations of the work environment and completed tasks to help determine the cause of performance deficiencies. Asking questions and collecting data typically involves four broad areas of potential causes: antecedents, knowledge and skills, equipment and processes (including a systems analysis), and consequences.
- Develop and implement a solution: After the results of the assessment, the practitioner then works with managers to develop and implement solutions that address identified deficiencies.
- Evaluate the effects: Typically, results are measured before, during and after solution implementation. There are at least three types of results that are of interest to the OBM practitioner: behavior change results, treatment acceptability and cost-benefit results. Behavior

change results help verify whether the solution changed the intended behavior and produced the intended outcomes. Treatment acceptability is important in OBM because the solution will not be maintained if employees and managers deem it unpalatable. Cost-benefit results help the practitioner calculate return-on-investment figures.

# Organizational Citizenship Behavior

Organizational citizenship behavior (OCB) is a person's voluntary commitment within an organization or company that is not part of his or her contractual tasks.

Organizational citizenship behavior has been studied since the late 1970s. Over the past three decades, interest in these behaviors has increased substantially. Organizational behavior has been linked to overall organizational effectiveness, thus these types of employee behaviors have important consequences in the workplace.

Organ defines OCB as "individual behavior that is discretionary, not directly or explicitly recognized by the formal reward system, and that in the aggregate promotes the effective functioning of the organization". Organ's definition of OCB includes three critical aspects that are central to this construct:

- First, OCBs are thought of as discretionary behaviors, which are not part of the job description, and are performed by the employee as a result of personal choice.
- Second, OCBs go above and beyond that which is an enforceable requirement of the job description.
- Finally, OCBs contribute positively to overall organizational effectiveness.

At the same time, Organ's definition of OCB has generated a great deal of criticism. The very nature of the construct makes it difficult to operationally define. Critics started questioning whether or not OCBs, as defined by Organ, were discretionary in nature. Organ, in response to criticisms, notes that since his original definition, jobs have moved away from a clearly defined set of tasks and responsibilities and have evolved into much more ambiguous roles. Without a defined role, it quickly becomes difficult to define what is discretionary.

## Similar Constructs

### Contextual Performance

OCB has often been compared to contextual performance. Similarly to OCB, this concept emerged in response to the realization that only looking at job specific work behaviors ignored a significant portion of the job domain. Originally, experts in this field focused only on activities that directly supported the output of the organization. As the job market became more aggressive, it became necessary for employees to go above and beyond that which is formally required by the job description in order to remain competitive. Contextual performance is defined as non-task related work behaviors and activities that contribute to the social and psychological aspects of the organization.

Contextual performance consists of four elements: persistence of enthusiasm, assistance to others, rule and proscribed procedure following, and openly defending the organizations objectives. OCB and contextual performance share their defining attributes as they both consist of behaviors other than those needed to perform the routine functions of the job. Both also require that these behaviors contribute to the overall success of the organization. Additionally, they also agree on the theme that these behaviors are discretionary and each employee chooses the amount and degree to which they will perform them. However, while contextual performance and OCB share a good part of their content domain, there are some important differences between the two constructs. One of the main requirements of OCBs is that they are not formally rewarded, which is not the case for contextual performance. Organ contends that OCBs may at some point encourage some sort of reward, but that these rewards would be indirect and uncertain. Also, contextual performance does not require that the behavior be extra-role, only that it be non-task. The differences between contextual performance and OCB are slight and easy to miss, however, they do exist.

## Prosocial Organizational Behavior

OCB has also been compared to prosocial organizational behavior (POB). POB is defined as behavior within an organization that is aimed at improving the welfare of an individual, a group or an organization. The important distinction here is that this type of behavior, unlike OCB, can be unrelated to the organization. Thus, someone exhibiting prosocial behavior could be helping a coworker with personal matter.

## Extra-role Behavior

Extra-role behavior (ERB), first defined by Van Dyne, Cummings and Mclean-Parks, is another construct similar to OCB. ERB is defined as "behavior that attempts to benefit the organization and that goes beyond existing role expectations". While similar in many aspects, there do exist some important differences between OCB and ERB. Two concepts are a part of ERB that are not included in OCB: whistle blowing and principled organizational dissent. Whistle blowing involves the reporting of one employee by another so that unethical and or illegal practices are brought to the attention of authorities. Principled organizational dissent is when employees protest the organization because of some kind of injustice. Both of these ideas contribute to ERB in the sense that their purpose is to further the good of the organization and that they are not included in the formal job description. This again, is a construct very similar to OCB.

## Altruism and General Compliance

Smith, Organ, and Near first proposed that OCB is composed of altruism and general compliance. These two dimensions serve to improve organizational effectiveness in different ways. Altruism in the workplace consists essentially of helping behaviors. These behaviors can both be directed within or outside of the organization. There is no direct link, or one-to-one relationship, between every instance of helping behavior and a specific gain for the organization. The idea is that over time, the compilation of employees helping behavior will eventually be advantageous for the organization.

General compliance behavior serves to benefit the organization in several ways. Low rates of absenteeism and rule following help to keep the organization running efficiently. A compliant employee does not engage in behaviors such as taking excessive breaks or using work time for personal matters. When these types of behaviors are minimized the workforce is naturally more productive.

Later, Organ deconstructed the dimension of general compliance and added additional dimensions of OCB. This deconstruction resulted in a five-factor model consisting of altruism, courtesy, conscientiousness, civic virtue, and sportsmanship. The definition of altruism remained much as it was, defined by discretionary behaviors that have the effect of helping a specific work colleague with an organizationally relevant task or problem. Conscientiousness consists of behaviors that go well beyond the minimum role requirements of the organization. These behaviors indicate that employees accept and adhere to the rules, regulations, and procedures of the organization.

Civic virtue is characterized by behaviors that indicate the employee's deep concerns and interest in the life of the organization. This dimension also encompasses positive involvement in the concerns of the organization. Examples of civic virtue can be seen in daily affairs such as attending meetings and keeping up with what is going on with the organization in general. Civic virtue can also be demonstrated on a larger scale by defending the organization's policies and practices when they are challenged by an outside source.

Courtesy has been defined as discretionary behaviors that aim at preventing work-related conflicts with others. This dimension is a form of helping behavior, but one that works to prevent problems from arising. It also includes the word's literal definition of being polite and considerate of others. Examples of courteous behaviors are asking fellow employees if they would like a cup of coffee while you are getting one for yourself, making extra copies of the meeting agenda for your teammates, and giving a colleague ample notice when you alter something that will affect them.

Finally, sportsmanship has been defined as a willingness on the part of the employee that signifies the employee's tolerance of less-than-ideal organizational circumstances without complaining and blowing problems out of proportion. Organ et al. further define sportsmanship as an employee's "ability to roll with the punches" even if they do not like or agree with the changes that are occurring within the organization. By reducing the number of complaints from employees that administrators have to deal with, sportsmanship conserves time and energy.

It has been proven empirically that the factors listed above are the most robust and distinct factors in assessing OCB. However, in a meta-analysis of the OCB literature, LePine, Erez, and Johnson found that these five dimensions are very highly correlated and do not have much differentiation among antecedents, indicating some overlap in the dimensions.

## Behaviors Directed at the Individual and the Organization

A different way of organizing the OCB construct was proposed by Williams and Anderson. They divided up the dimensions of OCB into two different types of OCB based on whom the behaviors were directed at. Organizational citizenship behavior – individuals (OCBI) include behaviors that are aimed at other individuals in the workplace while organizational citizenship behavior-organizational (OCBO) include behaviors directed at the organization as a whole. Altruism and courtesy are actions aimed at other employees and thus fall under the umbrella of OCBIs. Conscientiousness, civic virtue, and sportsmanship are behaviors intended for the benefit of the organization and can subsequently be considered OCBOs.

## Gender Differences

Research on gender-role stereotypes has gone on for decades. It is widely accepted that certain behaviors are considered more feminine and certain behaviors are considered more masculine. Feminine behaviors have been characterized as interpersonal in orientation and focused on a concern for others. Masculine behaviors, on the other hand, are typically more aggressive and independent. In line with these ideas, the OCB dimensions of altruism, courtesy, civic virtue and sportsmanship can be divided by gender role. Altruism and courtesy, are considered in-role behavior for women, while civic virtue and sportsmanship, previously mentioned as OCBOs, are regarded as more in-role for men. The dimension of conscientiousness, which includes attention to detail and adherence to organizational rules, is excluded, as this dimension does not seem to adhere to any particular gender norm.

## Antecedents

Early research regarding the antecedents of OCB focused on employee attitudes, dispositions, and leader supportiveness. More recently, many different variables have been examined in the effort to determine the antecedents of OCB. Commonly studied antecedents of OCB are job satisfaction, perceptions of organizational justice, organizational commitment, personality characteristics, task characteristics, and leadership behavior. These antecedents have been analyzed at both the overall and individual OCB levels.

One of the most intuitive antecedents of OCB is job satisfaction. Organ and Ryan conducted a meta-analysis of 28 studies and found a modest relationship between job satisfaction and OCB. This relationship was stronger than the relationship between job satisfaction and in-role performance. Other attitudinal measures, perceived fairness, organizational commitment, and leader supportiveness are found to correlate with OCB at about the same rate as satisfaction.

In terms of personality characteristics, conscientiousness, agreeableness, and positive and negative affectivity garner the most support as antecedents of OCB. Conscientiousness, in particular, has been found to have a strong relationship with the general compliance component of OCB. However, it has also been reported that personality measures are weaker predictors of OCB when compared to attitudinal predictors.

Task characteristics such as feedback, routinization, and intrinsic satisfaction are found to be significantly related to altruism, courtesy, conscientiousness, sportsmanship, and civic virtue. Positive relationships were found between both task feedback and intrinsic satisfaction and OCB, while a negative relationship was found between task routinization and OCB. Even though task characteristics have been found to predict OCB, some debate exists as to whether this is a direct effect or a relationship mediated by job satisfaction.

Leadership behaviors have also been found to be an important predictor of OCB. These behaviors fall into four categories: transformational leadership behavior, transactional leadership behavior, behaviors having to do with the path-goal theory of leadership, and behaviors having to do with the leader-member exchange theory. Transformational leadership behaviors, including articulating a vision, providing an appropriate model, fostering the acceptance of group goals, high performance expectations, and intellectual stimulation, have significant positive relationships with Organ's dimensions of OCB. Two types of behaviors representative of transactional leadership style, contingent reward behavior and non-contingent punishment behavior, have significant relationships with Organ's dimensions of OCB. Additionally, both the supportive leadership and leader role clarification aspects of the path-goal theory of leadership are positively related to OCB. Podsakoff et al. found that leader-member exchange was positively related to altruism and an overall composite measure of OCB.

## Consequences

During the early 1990s, scholars gained real momentum in the area of OCB with regard to empirical research. Empirical research regarding the consequences of OCBs has focused on two main areas: organizational performance and success and managerial evaluations of performance and reward allocation. Some evidence also exists on the impacts of OCB on the employees themselves.

## Organizational Performance and Success

Multiple studies and meta-analyses have been conducted to look at the relationship between OCBs and organizational performance and success. Podsakoff and MacKenzie looked at an insurance agency and found that the OCBs civic virtue and sportsmanship were both significantly related to indices of sales performance. Podsakoff, Ahearne, and MacKenzie examined paper mill workers and found that helping behavior was significantly related to product quality. MacKenzie, Podsakoff, and Ahearne found that civic virtue and helping behavior were significantly related to the percent of team quota sales. Walz and Niehoff examined 30 different restaurants and found that helping behavior was significantly related to operating efficiency, customer satisfaction, and quality of performance. Researchers found that helping behavior was also negatively correlated with wasted food. Koys used a combination of OCB dimensions to form a composite measure of OCB. Results from this study indicated that the composite measure of OCB was positively correlated with restaurant profits.

More recently, Podsakoff, Blume, Whiting, and Podsakoff found that OCBs were positively related to unit-level performance and customer satisfaction. Nielsen, Hrivnak, and Shaw, in their meta-analytic review of the existing group literature, examined the relationship between OCBs and performance at the group level. These researchers found a positive and significant relationship between overall OCB and performance at the group level. In addition, Nielsen et al. found that similar patterns of relationships existed for each dimension of OCB: civic virtue, sportsmanship, altruism, conscientiousness, and courtesy.

## Managerial Evaluations and Reward Allocations

With regard to the relationship between OBs and managerial evaluations, Podsakoff and colleagues found, in a summary of empirical evidence, that OCBs uniquely accounted for 42.9% of the variance in managerial performance evaluations. Results from this study also indicated that altruism or helping was significantly related to performance evaluations in eight out of the ten studies it was included in; sportsmanship was significantly related to performance evaluations in five out of the eight studies it was included in; conscientiousness was significantly related to performance evaluations in all three of the studies it was included in; and civic virtue was significantly related to performance evaluations in six out of the eight studies it was included in.

More recently, Podsakoff et al. found that OCBs have a positive relationship with performance ratings and reward allocations. Podsakoff, Whiting, Podsakoff, and Mishra examined the effects of job candidates' tendency to exhibit OCBs on selection decisions made in the context of a job interview. These researchers found that candidates whose interview responses indicated a tendency to engage in helping others, challenge the status quo by voicing their opinions, and support and defend an organization were generally viewed as more competent, received higher overall evaluations, and received higher recommended starting salaries than those who did not.

Research has also looked at the relationship between task-performance, CWB, and OCB with overall managerial evaluations. When compared with task-performance and CWB, OCB is found to contribute least to overall managerial evaluations. This somewhat inconsistent pattern of results across the OCB literature with regard to antecedents exemplifies the need for more research in this area.

## The Effects of OCB on Employees

There is some tension visible in existing literature on the effects of OCB on the employees who perform these citizenship behaviors. Allowing employees some scope to work outside their formal roles is thought to enhance the employee experience and lower turnover intentions and actual turnover. However, these benefits of OCB appear to come at a cost. Emotional exhaustion and conflict between home life and work are both higher for conscientious employees, and these effects are stronger amongst employees exhibiting high in-role performance.

## Measures

Researchers have developed a variety of measures for OCB. However before being able to measure a construct it must be defined. As discussed earlier, this is not a cut and dried task. Thus, the conceptual definitions of OCB used by researches differ from study to study.

Bateman and Organ's study was one of the first to tackle the measurement of OCB. Their definition of OCB "includes any of those gestures (often taken for granted) that lubricate the social machinery of the organization but that do not directly inhere in the usual notion of task performance". Based on this definition, they constructed a 30-item OCB scale that measured cooperation, altruism, compliance, punctuality, housecleaning, protecting company property, conscientiously following company rules, and dependability. The scale asked each participant to rate their agreement or disagreement with each of the 30 items using a 7-point scale that ranged from negative 3 to positive 3.

Another important early study was Smith et al., which took a slightly more complicated measurement approach by developing a scale in stages. In order to develop their 16-item scale, these researchers interviewed managers in manufacturing organizations and asked them to "identify instances of helpful, but not absolutely required behavior". The researchers created a 20-item scale based on the interviews in addition to the scale items used in the Bateman and Organ study. The third step involved administering the scale to a group of 67 students who had managerial experience. The students were asked to complete the scale while thinking of someone who currently, or had in the past, worked for them. Students then described the person's work behavior and their responses to the scale items. After factor analysis, four items were dropped resulting in the 16-item scale. It is with this scale that the authors found results indicating the first two distinct dimensions of OCB: altruism and generalized compliance. Examples of items in Smith et al.'s scale include:

- Helps others who have been absent.
- Gives advance notice if unable to come to work.
- Assists supervisor with his or her work.
- Attend functions not required but that help company image.

In 1990, Podsakoff, MacKenzie, Moorman, and Fetter conducted an important study using the five dimensions of OCB: altruism, conscientiousness, sportsmanship, courtesy, and civic virtue. These researchers developed a 24-item scale by having 10 of their colleagues sort each of the 24 items into one of the five OCB dimensions or an "other" category if they felt the item did not fit any of the five defined conceptual dimensions. Participants were asked to indicate their level of agreement using a 7-point scale ranging from "strongly disagree" to "strongly agree." This five-factor structure has served as the building block for a substantial amount of OCB research. Examples of items in Podsakoff et al.'s scale include:

- Obeys company rules and regulations even when no one is watching.
- Attends meetings that are not mandatory, but are considered important.
- Mindful of how his/her behavior affects other people's jobs.
- Willingly helps others who have work related problems.

## Counterproductive Work Behavior

Counterproductive work behavior (CWB) is employee behavior that goes against the legitimate interests of an organization. These behaviors can harm organizations or people in organizations including employees and clients, customers, or patients. It has been proposed that a person-by-environment interaction can be utilized to explain a variety of counterproductive behaviors. For instance, an employee who is high on trait anger (tendency to experience anger) is more likely to respond to a stressful incident at work (e.g., being treated rudely by a supervisor) with CWB.

Some researchers use the CWB term to subsume related constructs that are distinct. Workplace deviance is behavior at work that violates norms for appropriate behavior. Retaliation consists of harmful behaviors done by employees to get back at someone who has treated them unfairly. Workplace revenge are behaviors by employees intended to hurt another person who has done something harmful to them. Workplace aggression consists of harmful acts that harm others in organizations.

### Dimensional Models

Several typologies of CWB exist.

Using the term deviance (behavior that violates accepted norms), Robinson and Bennett created a four-class typology of CWBs, dividing them into the following dimensions:

- Production deviance, involving behaviors like leaving early, intentionally working slowly, or taking long breaks,
- Property deviance, involving sabotage of equipment, theft of property, and taking kick-backs,
- Political deviance, involving showing favoritism, revenge, gossiping, or blaming others,
- Personal aggression, involving harassment, verbal abuse, and endangerment.

A five dimension typology of CWB:

- Abuse against others,
- Production deviance,
- Sabotage,
- Theft,
- Withdrawal.

An 11-dimension typology of CWB:

- Theft of property,
- Destruction of property,
- Misuse of information,
- Misuse of time and resources,
- Unsafe behavior,
- Poor attendance,
- Poor quality of work,
- Alcohol use,
- Drug use,
- Inappropriate verbal action,
- Inappropriate physical action.

A two-dimensional model of CWBs distinguished by organizational versus person target has gained considerable acceptance. Additional dimensions have been proposed for research purposes, including a legal v. illegal dimension, a hostile v. instrumental aggression dimension, and a task-related v. a non-task-related dimension. CWBs that violate criminal law may have different antecedents than milder forms of CWBs. Similarly, instrumental aggression (i.e., aggression with a deliberate goal in mind) may have different antecedents than those CWBs caused by anger.

## Dimensions

### Absenteeism

Absenteeism is typically measured by time lost (number of days absent) measures and frequency (number of absence episodes) measures. It is weakly linked to affective predictors such as job satisfaction and commitment. Absences fit into two types of categories. Excused absences are those due to personal or family illness; unexcused absences include an employee who does not come to work in order to do another preferred activity or neglects to call in to a supervisor. Absence can be linked to job dissatisfaction. Major determinants of employee absence include employee affect, demographic characteristics, organizational absence culture, and organization absence policies. Absence due to non-work obligations is related to external features of a job with respect to dissatisfaction with role conflict, role ambiguity, and feelings of tension. Absences due to stress and illness are related to internal and external features of the job, fatigue and gender. Research has found that women are more likely to be absent than men, and that the absence-control policies and culture of an organization will predict absenteeism.

### Abuse against Others

Physical acts of aggression by members of an organization, committed in organizational settings are considered as workplace violence. While most researchers examine overall workplace aggression, there is a line of research that separates workplace aggression according to its targets, whether interpersonal or organizational. In this model of workplace aggression, trait anger and interpersonal conflict have been found to be significant predictors of interpersonal aggression, while interpersonal conflict, situational constraints, and organizational constraints have been found to be predictors of organizational aggression. Other factors significantly linked to aggression are sex and trait anger, with men and individuals with higher levels of trait anger showing more aggressive behaviors.

### Cyber Loafing

Cyber loafing can be defined as surfing the web in any form of non-job-related tasks performed by the employee. Cyber loafing has emerged as more and more people use computers at work. One survey showed that 64% of US workers use the internet for personal tasks at work. It has been suggested that cyber-loafing is responsible for a 30–40% decrease in employee productivity and was estimated to have cost US businesses $5.3 billion in 1999.

### Incivility

Workplace incivility is disrespectful and rude behavior in violation of workplace norms for respect." The effects of incivility include increased competitiveness, increases in sadistic behavior, and inattentiveness. A study of cyber incivility showed that higher levels of incivility are associated with lower job satisfaction, lower organizational commitment, and higher turnover rates. Two factors that seem to be associated with becoming a victim of incivility are low levels of agreeableness and high levels of neuroticism. The affective events theory suggests that individuals who experience more incidents of incivility may be more sensitive to these behaviors and therefore more likely to report them.

## Knowledge Hiding, Knowledge Hoarding and Knowledge Sabotage

Counterproductive knowledge behavior refers to employees' actions impeding organizational knowledge flows. Examples include knowledge hiding defined as the intentional attempts of employees to conceal their knowledge when their colleagues request it, knowledge hoarding which is the accumulation of knowledge by employees while concealing the fact that they possess this knowledge, and knowledge sabotage which is an incident when an employee (i.e., the saboteur) intentionally provides wrong knowledge (information, advice, a document, or a recommendation) to another employee (the target).

## Lateness

Lateness is described as arriving at work later or leaving earlier than required. Problems associated with lateness include compromised organizational efficiency. Tardy and late employees responsible for critical tasks can negatively affect organizational production. Other workers may experience psychological effects of the tardy employee including morale and motivational problems as they attempt to "pick up the slack." Other employees may begin to imitate the example set by the behavior of tardy employees. Lateness costs US business more than $3 billion annually.

## Production Deviance

Production deviance is ineffective job performance that is done on purpose, such as doing tasks incorrectly or withholding of effort. Such behaviors can be seen in disciplinary actions and safety violations.

## Sabotage

Employee sabotage are behaviors that can "damage or disrupt the organization's production, damaging property, the destruction of relationships, or the harming of employees or customers." Research has shown that often acts of sabotage or acts of retaliation are motivated by perceptions of organizational injustice and performed with the intention of causing harm to the target.

## Service

Service sabotage originated from counter-productive behavior literature. Lloyd C. Harris and Emmanuel Ogbonna from Cardiff University drew from employee deviance and dysfunctional behaviors studies to conceptualize service sabotage as a disturbing phenomenon in the work place. Service sabotage refer to organizational member behaviors that are intentionally designed negatively to affect service. Empirical evidence suggested that more than 90% employees accept that service sabotage is an everyday occurrence in their organization.

## Sexual Harassment

Sexual harassment is defined as "unwelcome sexual advances, requests for sexual favors, and other verbal or physical contact when: (a) submission to the conduct by the employee is either explicitly or implicitly a term or condition of an individual's employment, (b) submission to or rejection of such conduct by an individual is used as a basis for employment decisions affecting the individual and/or (c) such conduct [that] has the purpose or effect of unreasonably interfering with work performance, or creating an intimidating, hostile or offensive working environment".

## Substance Abuse

Substance abuse by employees at work is a problem that can have an effect on work attendance, performance, and safety and can lead to other injuries outside of work and health problems.

## Theft

Employee theft is defined as employees taking things not belonging to them from an organization. Employee theft is estimated to account for billions of dollars of loss globally each year, with employees accounting for more theft than customers. This may include large embezzlements or the pilfering of pencils and paperclips, but the losses in the aggregate are substantial. At least one study suggests that 45% of companies experience financial fraud, with average losses of $1.7 million. Factors such as Conscientiousness have been shown to be negatively related to theft behaviors. Many organizations use integrity tests during the initial screening process for new employees in an effort to eliminate those considered most likely to commit theft. Causes of employee theft include characteristics of the individual and environmental conditions such as frustrating and unfair working conditions.

## Turnover

Turnover is when employees leave the organization, either voluntarily (quitting) or involuntarily (being fired or laid off). Research on voluntary employee job turnover has attempted to understand the causes of individual decisions to leave an organization. It has been found that lower performance, lack of reward contingencies for performance, and better external job opportunities are the main causes. Other variables related to turnover are conditions in the external job market and the availability of other job opportunities, and length of employee tenure. Turnover can be optimal as when a poorly performing employee decides to leave an organization, or dysfunctional when the high turnover rates increase the costs associated with recruitment and training of new employees, or if good employees consistently decide to leave. Avoidable turnover is when the organization could have prevented it and unavoidable turnover is when the employee's decision to leave could not be prevented. The satisfaction-turnover relationship is affected by alternative job prospects. If an employee accepts an unsolicited job offer, job dissatisfaction was less predictive of turnover because the employee more likely left in response to "pull" (the lure of the other job) than "push" (the unattractiveness of the current job). Similarly, job dissatisfaction is more likely to translate into turnover when other employment opportunities are plentiful.

## Withdrawal

Employee withdrawal consists of behaviors such as absence, lateness, and ultimately job turnover. Absence and lateness has attracted research as they disrupt organizational production, deliveries and services. Unsatisfied employees withdraw in order to avoid work tasks or pain, and remove themselves from their jobs. Withdrawal behavior may be explained as employee retaliation against inequity in the work setting. Withdrawal may also be part of a progressive model and relate to job dissatisfaction, job involvement, and organizational commitment.

## Notable Behavior Exclusions

CWBs are "active and volitional acts engaged in by individuals, as opposed to accidental or unintentional actions." CWBs, therefore do not include acts that lack volition, such as the inability to successfully complete a task. Nor do CWBs include involvement in an accident, although purposeful avoidance of the safety rules that may have led to the accident would represent a CWB.

The U.S. Department of Health and Human Services (2002) estimates the cost of accidents to organizations to be $145 million annually. Most research on this topic has attempted to evaluate characteristics of the workplace environment that lead to accidents and determination of ways to avoid accidents. There has also been some research on the characteristics of accident-prone employees that has found they are typically younger, more distractible, and less socially adjusted than other employees. Recent research has shown that an organization's safety climate has been associated with lower accident involvement, compliance with safety procedures, and increased proactive safety behaviors.

Another set of behaviors that do not fit easily into the accepted definition of CWBs, are those described as unethical pro-organizational behaviors (UPBs). UPBs represent illegitimate means intended to further the legitimate interests of an organization. UPBs are not necessarily intended to harm the organization, although the UPBs may result in adverse consequences to the organization, such as a loss of trust and goodwill, or in criminal charges against the organization. In law enforcement, UPBs are exhibited in a form of misconduct called noble cause corruption. Noble cause corruption occurs when a police officer violates the law or ethical rules in order to reduce crime or the fear of crime. An example of this is testilying, in which a police officer commits perjury to obtain the conviction of a defendant. UPBs have not received the same attention from researchers that CWBs have received.

## Organizational Citizenship Behavior

Counterproductive work behavior and organizational citizenship behavior (OCB), which consists of behaviors that help organizations but go beyond required tasks, have been studied together and are generally found to be related in that individuals who do one are unlikely to do the other.

## Correlates, Predictors, Moderators and Mediators

### Affect

Affect or emotion at work, especially the experience of negative emotions like anger or anxiety, predict the likelihood of counterproductive work behaviors occurring. Affective personality traits, the tendency for individuals to experience emotions, can also predict CWB. For example, employees with high negative affectivity, the tendency to experience negative emotions, typically display more counterproductive work behaviors than those with positive affectivity, the tendency to experience positive emotions.

## Age

Age appears to be an important factor in predicting CWBs. While age does not appear to be strongly related to core task performance, creativity, or performance in training, it does appear to be positively related to organizational citizenship behaviors and negatively related to CWBs. Older employees seem to exhibit less aggression, tardiness, substance abuse, and voluntary absenteeism (although sickness related absenteeism is somewhat higher than younger employees). Some researchers argue that the lower rate of CWBs may be due to better self-regulation and self-control.

## Cognitive Ability

Research into the relationship between cognitive ability and CWBs is contradictory. When CWBs are operationalized as disciplinary records of detected CWBs, a strong negative relationship between cognitive ability has been found. This relationship did not hold, however, when cognitive ability was operationalized as educational attainment. A longitudinal study of adolescents through young adulthood found that, among those individuals who exhibited conduct disorders as youths, high levels of cognitive ability were associated with higher levels of CWBs, a positive relationship. Other research has found that general mental ability is largely unrelated to self-reports of CWBs including theft (although a weak link to incidents of lateness was detected). In the same study, grade point average showed a stronger relationship to CWBs. Contradictions in the findings may be explained in the differential effects between measures of cognitive ability and self-reported versus detected incidents of CWBs.

## Emotional Intelligence

Emotional intelligence (EI) has been defined as the ability to identify and manage emotional information in oneself and others and focus energy on required behaviors. The factors making up EI include:

- Appraisal and expression of emotion in self,
- Appraisal and recognition of emotions in others,
- Regulation of emotions,
- Use of emotions.

To the extent that EI includes the ability to manage emotions, it can be expected that it will have an influence on CWBs similar to that found for self-control. Research in this area is limited, however, one study looking for the moderating effects of EI on the relationships between distributive justice, procedural justice, and interactional justice failed to find a significant moderating effect in any of these relationships.

## Interpersonal Conflict

Interpersonal conflict in the workplace can also lead to counterproductive work behaviors. Interpersonal conflict with the supervisor can lead to counterproductive work behaviors such as defiance, undermining, and colluding with coworkers to engage in deviant behavior. Interpersonal conflict with peers can lead to counterproductive work behaviors such as harassment, bullying, and physical altercations.

### Organizational Constraints

Organizational constraints, the extent to which conditions at work interfere with job tasks, has been shown to relate to CWB so that jobs with high constraints have employees who engage in CWB. Not only do constraints lead to CWB, but CWB can lead to constraints. Employees who engage in CWB can find that constraints increase over time.

### Organizational Justice

Organizational justice or fairness perceptions have been shown to influence the display of counterproductive work behaviors. Distributive justice, procedural justice, and interactional justice have all been shown to include both counterproductive work behaviors aimed at individuals, such as political deviance and personal aggression; and counterproductive work behaviors aimed at the organization, such as production slowdown and property deviance.

Overall perceptions of unfairness may particularly elicit interpersonal counterproductive work behaviors such as political deviance and personal aggressions. Interpersonal justice and informational justice may also predict counterproductive work behaviors aimed at the supervisor, such as neglecting to follow supervisory instructions, acting rudely toward one's supervisor, spreading unconfirmed rumors about a supervisor, intentionally doing something to get one's supervisor in trouble, and encouraging coworkers to get back at one's supervisor.

### Personality

Personality is a predictor of an employee's proclivity toward counterproductive work behaviors. With regard to the Big Five personality traits: conscientiousness, agreeableness, extroversion and openness to experience all predict counterproductive behaviors. When an employee is low in conscientiousness, counterproductive work behaviors related to the organization are more likely to occur. Employees who are low in agreeableness will exhibit counterproductive work behaviors related to interpersonal deviant behaviors. Furthermore, in terms of greater specificity, for employees low in conscientiousness, sabotage and withdrawal are more likely to occur. For employees low in extraversion, theft is likely to occur. Finally, for employees high in openness to experience, production deviance is likely to occur.

### Narcissisism

Employees with narcissistic personalities tend to exhibit more counterproductive work behaviors, especially when the workplace is stressful.

### Psychopathy

According to Boddy, because of abusive supervision by corporate psychopaths, large amounts of anti-corporate feeling will be generated among the employees of the organisations that corporate psychopaths work in. This should result in high levels of counterproductive behavior as employees give vent to their anger with the corporation, which they perceive to be acting through its corporate psychopathic managers in a way that is eminently unfair to them.

## Self-control

Self-control has been evaluated as a significant explanation of CWBs. Like, conscientiousness, self-control, or internal control, is seen as a stable individual difference that tends to inhibit deviant behaviors. The identification of self-control as a factor in deviant behaviors flows from work in criminology, where self-control is seen as the strength of one's ability to avoid short-term gain for long-term costs. Using multiple regression analysis, one study compared the effects of 25 characteristics (including self-control, justicial factors, equity factors, positive affect, levels of autonomy, and a variety of other individual characteristics) on CWBs. The study showed that self-control was the best predictor of CWBs and that most of the other factors had negligible predictive value. Cognitive ability and age were among the remaining factors that showed some effect. These additional findings are consistent with research that tends to show older employees exercise a greater level of self-control.

## Target Personality

One line of research in CWBs looks not at the instigators of CWBs, but the victims' provocative target behavior, or the behaviors of the victims of CWBs, which are seen as potential mediating factors in the frequency and intensity of CWBs originated against them. This line of research suggests that low levels of agreeableness and conscientiousness, and high levels of neuroticism, in the victims of CWBs may lead to more incidents of CWBs, like incivility. The affective events theory has been used to explain that some individuals report being the victim of incivility more often because they are more sensitive to it than other workers.

## Peer Reporting

Normative behavior within organizations tends to discourage workers from reporting the observed CWBs of their peers, although this tendency can be reduced when a group is punished for the CWBs of individual members. There are three factors that seem to be most influential on peer reporting of CWBs: the emotional closeness between the person exhibiting the CWBs and the person observing the CWBs; the severity of the misconduct observed, and the presence of witness. Peers are more likely to report the CWBs of colleagues when the conduct is severe, or when there are other witnesses present, and less likely to report CWBs when they are emotionally close to the person committing the CWBs. A key problem in the use of peer reports of CWBs instead of self-reports of CWBs is that peer reports only capture observed behaviors and are not able to identify CWBs committed secretly.

## Managing Strategies

A substantial body of research has demonstrated that stable characteristics of individuals are associated with the likelihood of CWBs. Some examples of stable characteristics that have been demonstrated to have relationships with CWBs include conscientiousness and agreeability, motivation avoidance, cognitive ability, and self-control. To the extent that these stable conditions predict CWBs, reduction of CWBs in an organization can begin at the recruitment and selection phase of new employees.

Integrity screening is one common form of screening used by organizations as is cognitive ability screening. Personality testing is also common in screening out individuals who may have a higher incidence of CWBs. Work samples have been found to be a more effective screening tool than integrity testing alone, but integrity testing and cognitive testing together are even better screening tools. While the use of screening instruments may be an imperfect decision-making tool, the question often facing the recruitment officer is not whether the instrument is perfect, but whether, relative to other available screening tools, the screening tool is functional.

However, organizations must do more than screen employees in order to successfully manage CWBs. Substantial research has demonstrated that CWBs arise out of situational factors that occur in the day-to-day operations of an organization, including organizational constraints, lack of rewards, illegitimate tasks, interpersonal conflicts, and lack of organizational justice. Research has shown that individuals who are treated unfairly are more likely to engage in CWBs. One major step that organizations can take to reduce the impetus for CWBs is therefore to enhance organizational justice. Maintaining communications and feedback, allowing participation of employees, and supervisory training are other suggestions for mitigating CWBs. Organizations must also pay close attention to employees for signs and sources of interpersonal conflicts so that they can be identified and tended to as necessary.

Combating CWBs comes with some costs, including the costs of selection, monitoring, and implementing preventive measures to reduce triggers for CWBs. Before undertaking costly measures to reduce CWBs, it may be worthwhile for an organization to identify the costs of CWBs. If the cost-benefit analysis does not show a savings, then the organization must decide whether the battle against CWBs is worth fighting. There is at least one set of researchers that suggest that production deviance (withholding effort) and withdrawal can be a benefit to employees by allowing them to relieve tension in certain circumstances.

# Abusive Supervision

Abusive supervision is most commonly studied in the context of the workplace, although can arise in other areas such as in the household and at school. “Abusive supervision has been investigated as an antecedent to negative subordinate workplace outcome.” “Workplace violence has combination of situational and personal factors”. The study that was conducted looked at the link between abusive supervision and different workplace events.

## Workplace Bullying

Abusive supervision overlaps with workplace bullying in the workplace context. Research suggests that 75% of workplace bullying incidents are perpetrated by hierarchically superior agents. Abusive supervision differs from related constructs such as supervisor bullying and undermining in that it does not describe the intentions or objectives of the supervisor.

## Workplace Deviance

Workplace deviance is closely related to abusive supervision. Abusive supervision is defined as the "subordinates' perceptions of the extent to which their supervisors engage in the sustained display of hostile verbal and nonverbal behaviors". This could be when supervisors ridicule their employees, give them the silent treatment, remind them of past failures, fail to give proper credit, wrongfully assign blame or blow up in fits of temper. It may seem like employees who are abused by their supervisor will either directly retaliate or withdraw by quitting the job but in reality many strike out against their employer by engaging in organizational deviant behaviors. Since employees control many of the organization's resources, they often use, or abuse anything they can. This abuse of resources may come in the form of time, office supplies, raw materials, finished products or the services that they provide. This usually occurs in two steps. First step is that commitment is destroyed and employees stop caring about the welfare of the employer. The second step is that the abused employee will get approval (normally implied) of their coworkers to commit deviant acts.

Workplace experiences may fuel the worker to act out. Research has been conducted demonstrating that the perception of not being respected is one of the main causes for workplace deviance; workplace dissatisfaction is also a factor. According to Bolin and Heatherly, "dissatisfaction results in a higher incidence of minor offenses, but does not necessarily lead to severe offense". An employee who is less satisfied with his or her work may become less productive as their needs are not met. In the workplace, "frustration, injustices and threats to self are primary antecedents to employee deviance". Although workplace deviance does occur, the behavior is not universal. There are two preventive measures that business owners can use to protect themselves. The first is strengthening the employee's commitment by reacting strongly to abusive supervision so that the employee knows that the behavior is not accepted. Holding the employee at high esteem by reminding them of their importance, or setting up programs that communicate concern for the employee may also strengthen employee commitment. Providing a positive ethical climate can also help. Employers can do this by having a clear code of conduct that is applied to both managers and employees alike.

## Social Undermining

Social undermining can arise from abusive supervision, such as when a supervisor uses negative actions and it leads to "flow downhill"; a supervisor is perceived as abusive.

Research has shown that "abusive supervision is a subjective assessment made by subordinates regarding their supervisors" behavior towards them over a period of time. For example, abusive supervision includes a "boss demeaning, belittling, or invading privacy of the subordinate.

Hostile attribution bias is an extra punitive mentality where individuals tend to project blame on others. Researchers wanted to see how hostile attribution bias can moderate the relationship between perceptions of psychological contract violation and subordinates' perceptions of abusive supervision. Undermining does arise with abusive supervision, which affects families and aggression; they believe that there is a stronger positive relationship between experiences of psychological contract violation and subordinates' reports of abuse. It suggests that when someone has a negative work environment, it will affect their emotional training ground where this would result in negative home encounters. The findings from this study show that abused subordinates' family members reported a higher incidence of undermining in their home. When this occurs, complications arise at both home and work. Workplace abuse may be spawning negative interpersonal relations in the home, which may contribution to a downward spiral of relationships in both spheres.

When a subordinate is being abused, it can lead to negative affect towards their family where the subordinate starts undermining their family members. The undermining can arise from displaced aggression which is "redirection of a harm doing behavior from a primary to a secondary target". Family undermining arises from a negative work environment: when someone above you puts you down, one starts to think that one should be put down by one's family members.

### Machiavellianism

In research, the presence of Machiavellianism was positively associated with subordinate perceptions of abusive supervision.

### Context and Outcome Correlates

Abusive supervision has been investigated primarily in corporate and education contexts. In the corporate context, abusive supervision has been found to be negatively related to followers' attitudes towards the leader, job satisfaction, job-related attitudes, justice, commitment, positive self-evaluation, and well-being. In addition, such corporate abusive supervision is positively associated with undesirable consequences such as follower resistance, turnover intention, counterproductive work behavior, negative affectivity, and stress. In the education context, abusive supervision has been investigated in instructor-student relationships, and these studies found that such supervision is adversely related to anxiety and psychological well-being. Moreover, instructors' use of abusive supervision is associated with a range of affective, behavioral, and cognitive reactions from students.

## Workplace Bullying

Workplace bullying is a persistent pattern of mistreatment from others in the workplace that causes either physical or emotional harm. It can include such tactics as verbal, nonverbal, psychological, physical abuse and humiliation. This type of workplace aggression is particularly difficult because, unlike the typical school bully, workplace bullies often operate within the established rules and policies of their organization and their society. In the majority of cases, bullying in the workplace is reported as having been done by someone who has authority over the victim. However, bullies can also be peers, and occasionally subordinates.

Research has also investigated the impact of the larger organizational context on bullying as well as the group-level processes that impact on the incidence and maintenance of bullying behavior. Bullying can be covert or overt. It may be missed by superiors; it may be known by many throughout the organization. Negative effects are not limited to the targeted individuals, and may lead to a decline in employee morale and a change in organizational culture. It can also take place as overbearing supervision, constant criticism, and blocking promotions.

While there is no universally accepted formal definition of workplace bullying, and some researchers even question whether a uniform definition is possible due to its complex and multifaceted forms, but several researchers have endeavoured to define it:

- According to the widely used definition from Olweus, "Workplace bullying is a situation in which one or more persons systematically and over a long period of time perceive themselves to be on the receiving end of negative treatment on the part of one or more persons, in a situation in which the person(s) exposed to the treatment has difficulty in defending themselves against this treatment".
- According to Einarsen, Hoel, Zapf and Cooper, "Bullying at work means harassing, offending, socially excluding someone or negatively affecting someone's work tasks. In order for the label bullying (or mobbing) to be applied to a particular activity, interaction or process it has to occur repeatedly and regularly (e.g. weekly) and over a period of time (e.g. about six months). Bullying is an escalated process in the course of which the person confronted ends up in an inferior position and becomes the target of systematic negative social acts".
- According to Tracy, Lutgen-Sandvik, and Alberts, researchers associated with the Arizona State University's Project for Wellness and Work-Life, workplace bullying is most often "a combination of tactics in which numerous types of hostile communication and behaviour are used".
- Gary and Ruth Namie define workplace bullying as "repeated, health-harming mistreatment, verbal abuse, or conduct which is threatening, humiliating, intimidating, or sabotage that interferes with work or some combination of the three".
- Pamela Lutgen-Sandvik expands this definition, stating that workplace bullying is "persistent verbal and nonverbal aggression at work, that includes personal attacks, social ostracism, and a multitude of other painful messages and hostile interactions".
- Catherine Mattice and Karen Garman define workplace bullying as "systematic aggressive communication, manipulation of work, and acts aimed at humiliating or degrading one or more individual that create an unhealthy and unprofessional power imbalance between bully and target(s), result in psychological consequences for targets and co-workers, and cost enormous monetary damage to an organization's bottom line".
- The most common type of complaint filed with the U.S. Equal Employment Opportunity Commission involves retaliation, where an employer harasses or bullies an employee for objecting to illegal discrimination. Patricia Barnes, author of Surviving Bullies, Queen Bees & Psychopaths in the Workplace, argues that employers that bully are a critical but often overlooked aspect of the problem in the United States.

Because it can occur in a variety of contexts and forms, it is also useful to define workplace bullying by the key features that these behaviours possess. Bullying is characterized by:

- Repetition (occurs regularly),
- Duration (is enduring),

- Escalation (increasing aggression),
- Power disparity (the target lacks the power to successfully defend themselves),
- Attributed intent.

This distinguishes bullying from isolated behaviours and other forms of job stress and allows the term workplace bullying to be applied in various contexts and to behaviours that meet these characteristics. Many observers agree that bullying is often a repetitive behaviour. However, some experts who have dealt with a great many people who report abuse also categorize some once-only events as bullying, for example with cases where there appear to be severe sequelae. Expanding the common understanding of bullying to include single, severe episodes also parallels the legal definitions of sexual harassment in the US.

According to Pamela Lutgin-Sandvik, the lack of unifying language to name the phenomenon of workplace bullying is a problem because without a unifying term or phrase, individuals have difficulty naming their experiences of abuse, and therefore have trouble pursuing justice against the bully. Unlike sexual harassment, which named a specific problem and is now recognized in law of many countries (including U.S.), workplace bullying is still being established as a relevant social problem and is in need of a specific vernacular.

Euphemisms intended to trivialize bullying and its impact on bullied people include: incivility, disrespect, difficult people, personality conflict, negative conduct, and ill treatment. Bullied people are labelled as insubordinate when they resist the bullying treatment.

There is no exact definition for bullying behaviours in workplace, which is why different terms and definitions are common. For example, mobbing is a commonly used term in France and Germany, where it refers to a "mob" of bullies, rather than a single bully; this phenomenon is not often seen in other countries. In the United States, aggression and emotional abuse are frequently used terms, whereas harassment is the term preferred in Finland. Workplace bullying is primarily used in Australia, UK, and Northern Europe. While the terms "harassment" and "mobbing" are often used to describe bullying behaviors, "workplace bullying" tends to be the most commonly used term by the research community.

## Profiling

Researchers Caitlin Buon and Tony Buon have suggested that attempts to profile 'the bully' have been damaging. They state that the "bully" profile is that 'the bully' is always aware of what they are doing, deliberately sets out to harm their 'victims', targets a particular individual or type of person and has some kind of underlying personality flaw, insecurity or disorder. But this is unproven and lacks evidence. The researchers suggest referring to workplace bullying as generic harassment along with other forms of non-specific harassment and this would enable employees to use less emotionally charged language and start a dialogue about their experiences rather than being repelled by the spectre of being labelled as a pathological predator or having to define their experiences as the victims of such a person. Tony Buon and Caitlin Buon also suggest that the perception and profile of the workplace bully is not facilitating interventions with the problem. They suggest that to make significant progress and achieve behavior change over the long term then, organisations and individuals need to embrace the notion that everyone must all potentially house 'the bully' within them and their organisations. It exists in workplace cultures, belief systems, interactions and emotional competencies and cannot be transformed if externalization and demonization continue the problem by profiling 'the bully' rather than talking about behaviors and interpersonal interactions.

## Relationship among Participants

Based on research by H. Hoel and C.L. Cooper, most the perpetrators are supervisors. The second most common group is peers, followed by subordinates and customers. The three main relationships among the participants in workplace bullying:

- Between supervisor and subordinate,
- Among co-workers,
- Employees and customers.

Bullying may also occur between an organization and its employees.

Bullying behavior by supervisors toward subordinates typically manifests as an abuse of power by the supervisor in the workplace. Bullying behaviors by supervisors may be associated with a culture of bullying and the management style of the supervisors. An authoritative management style, specifically, often includes bullying behaviors, which can make subordinates fearful and allow supervisors to bolster their authority over others.

If an organization wishes to discourage bullying in the workplace, strategies and policies must be put into place to dissuade and counter bullying behavior. Lack of monitoring or of punishment/corrective action will result in an organizational culture that supports/tolerates bullying.

In addition to supervisor – subordinate bullying, bullying behaviors also occur between colleagues. Peers can be either the target or perpetrator. If workplace bullying happens among the co-workers, witnesses will typically choose sides, either with the target or the perpetrator. Perpetrators usually "win" since witnesses do not want to be the next target. This outcome encourages perpetrators to continue their bullying behavior. In addition, the sense of the injustice experienced by a target might lead that person to become another perpetrator who bullies other colleagues who have less power than they do, thereby proliferating bullying in the organization.

Maarit Varitia, a workplace bullying researcher, found that 20% of interviewees who experienced workplace bullying attributed their being targeted to their differences from others.

The third relationship in the workplace is between employees and customers. Although less frequent, such cases play a significant role in the efficiency of the organization. Overly stressed or distressed employees may be less able to perform optimally and can impact the quality of service overall.

The fourth relationship in the workplace is between the organization or system and its employees.

These cases, the issue is not simply an organizational culture or environmental factors facilitating bullying, but bullying-like behavior by an employer against an employee. Tremendous power imbalances between an organization and its employees enables the employer to "legitimately exercise" power (e.g., by monitoring and controlling employees) in a manner consistent with bullying.

Although the terminology of bullying traditionally implies an interpersonal relationship between the perpetrator and target, organizations' or other collectives' actions can constitute bullying both by definition and in their impacts on targets. However, while defining bullying as an interpersonal phenomenon is considered legitimate, classifying incidences of employer exploitation, retaliation, or other abuses of power against an employee as a form of bullying is often not taken as seriously.

## Organizational Culture

Bullying is seen to be prevalent in organizations where employees and managers feel that they have the support, or at least the implicit blessing of senior managers to carry on their abusive and bullying behavior. Furthermore, new managers will quickly come to view this form of behavior as acceptable and normal if they see others get away with it and are even rewarded for it.

When bullying happens at the highest levels, the effects may be far reaching. People may be bullied irrespective of their organizational status or rank, including senior managers, which indicates the possibility of a negative domino effect, where bullying may cascade downwards, as the targeted supervisors might offload their own aggression onto their subordinates. In such situations, a bullying scenario in the boardroom may actually threaten the productivity of the entire organisation.

## Geographical Culture

Research investigating the acceptability of the bullying behavior across different cultures clearly shows that culture affects the perception of the acceptable behavior. National background also influences the prevalence of workplace bullying.

Humane orientation is negatively associated with the acceptability of work-related bullying. Performance orientation is positively associated with the acceptance of bullying. Future orientation is negatively associated with the acceptability of bullying. A culture of femininity suggests that individuals who live and work in this kind of culture tend to value interpersonal relationships to a greater degree.

Three broad dimensions have been mentioned in relation to workplace bullying: power distance; masculinity versus femininity; and individualism versus collectivism.

In Confucian Asia, which has a higher performance orientation than Latin America and Sub-Saharan Africa, bullying may be seen as an acceptable price to pay for performance. The value Latin America holds for personal connections with employees and the higher humane orientation of Sub-Saharan Africa may help to explain their distaste for bullying. A culture of individualism in the US implies competition, which may increase the likelihood of workplace bullying situations.

## Culture of Fear

Ashforth discussed potentially destructive sides of leadership and identified what he referred to as petty tyrants, i.e., leaders who exercise a tyrannical style of management, resulting in a climate of fear in the workplace. Partial or intermittent negative reinforcement can create an effective climate of fear and doubt. When employees get the sense that bullies "get away with it," a climate of fear may be the result. Several studies have confirmed a relationship between bullying, on the one hand, and an autocratic leadership and an authoritarian way of settling conflicts or dealing with disagreements, on the other. An authoritarian style of leadership may create a climate of fear, where there is little or no room for dialogue and where complaining may be considered futile.

In a study of public-sector union members, approximately one in five workers reported having considered leaving the workplace as a result of witnessing bullying taking place. Rayner explained these figures by pointing to the presence of a climate of fear in which employees considered reporting to be unsafe, where bullies had "got away with it" previously despite management knowing of the presence of bullying.

## Kiss Up Kick Down

The workplace bully is often expert at knowing how to work the system. They can spout all the current management buzzwords about supportive management but use it as a cover. By keeping their abusive behavior hidden, any charges made by individuals about his or her bullying will always come down to your word against his. They may have a kiss up kick down personality, wherein they are always highly cooperative, respectful, and caring when talking to upper management but the opposite when it comes to their relationship with those whom they supervise. Bullies tend to ingratiate themselves to their bosses while intimidating subordinates. They may be socially popular with others in management, including those who will determine their fate. Often, a workplace bully will have mastered kiss up kick down tactics that hide their abusive side from superiors who review their performance.

As a consequence of this kiss up kick down strategy:

- A bully's mistakes are always concealed or blamed on underlings or circumstances beyond their control.
- A bully keeps the target under constant stress.
- A bully's power base is fear, not respect.
- A bully withholds information from subordinates and keeps the information flow top-down only.
- A bully blames conflicts and problems on subordinate's lack of competence, poor attitude, or character flaws.
- A bully creates an unnatural work environment where people constantly walk on eggshells and are compelled to behave in ways they normally would not.

The flow of blame in an organization may be a primary indicator of that organization's robustness and integrity. Blame flowing downwards, from management to staff, or laterally between professionals or partner organizations, indicates organizational failure. In a blame culture, problem-solving is replaced by blame-avoidance. Confused roles and responsibilities also contribute to a blame culture. Blame culture reduces the capacity of an organization to take adequate measures to prevent minor problems from escalating into uncontrollable situations. Several issues identified in organizations with a blame culture contradicts high reliability organizations best practices. Blame culture is considered a serious issue in healthcare organizations by the World Health Organization, which recommends to promote a no-blame culture, or just culture, a means to increase patients safety.

## Fight or Flight

The most typical reactions to workplace bullying are to do with the survival instinct – "fight or flight" – and these are probably a victim's healthier responses to bullying. Flight is often a response to bullying. It is very common, especially in organizations in which upper management cannot or will not deal with the bullying. In hard economic times, however, flight may not be an option, and fighting may be the only choice.

Fighting the bullying can require near heroic action, especially if the bullying targets just one or two individuals. It can also be a difficult challenge. There are some times when confrontation is called for. First, there is always a chance that the bully boss is labouring under the impression that this is the way to get things done and does not recognize the havoc being wrought on subordinates.

## Typology of Bullying Behaviors

With some variations, the following typology of workplace bullying behaviors has been adopted by a number of academic researchers. The typology uses five different categories.

- Threat to professional status: Including belittling opinions, public professional humiliation, accusations regarding lack of effort, intimidating use of discipline or competence procedures.
- Threat to personal standing: Including undermining personal integrity, destructive innuendo and sarcasm, making inappropriate jokes about the target, persistent teasing, name calling, insults, intimidation.
- Isolation: Including preventing access to opportunities, physical or social isolation, withholding necessary information, keeping the target out of the loop, ignoring or excluding.
- Overwork: Including undue pressure, impossible deadlines, unnecessary disruptions.
- Destabilisation: Including failure to acknowledge good work, allocation of meaningless tasks, removal of responsibility, repeated reminders of blunders, setting target up to fail, shifting goal posts without telling the target.

## Tactics

Research by the Workplace Bullying Institute, suggests that the following are the 25 most common workplace bullying tactics:

- Falsely accused someone of "errors" not actually made (71%).

- Stared, glared, was nonverbally intimidating and was clearly showing hostility (68%).
- Unjustly discounted the person's thoughts or feelings ("oh, that's silly") in meetings (64%).
- Used the "silent treatment" to "ice out" and separate from others (64%).
- Exhibited presumably uncontrollable mood swings in front of the group (61%).
- Made-up rules on the fly that even they did not follow (61%).
- Disregarded satisfactory or exemplary quality of completed work despite evidence (discrediting) (58%).
- Harshly and constantly criticized, having a different standard for the target (57%).
- Started, or failed to stop, destructive rumours or gossip about the person (56%).
- Encouraged people to turn against the person being tormented (55%).
- Singled out and isolated one person from other co-workers, either socially or physically (54%).
- Publicly displayed gross, undignified, but not illegal, behavior (53%).
- Yelled, screamed, threw tantrums in front of others to humiliate a person (53%).
- Stole credit for work done by others (plagiarism) (47%).
- Abused the evaluation process by lying about the person's performance (46%).
- Declared target "insubordinate" for failing to follow arbitrary commands (46%).
- Used confidential information about a person to humiliate privately or publicly (45%).
- Retaliated against the person after a complaint was filed (45%).
- Made verbal put-downs/insults based on gender, race, accent, age or language, disability (44%).
- Assigned undesirable work as punishment (44%).
- Created unrealistic demands (workload, deadlines, duties) for person singled out (44%).
- Launched a baseless campaign to oust the person; effort not stopped by the employer (43%).
- Encouraged the person to quit or transfer rather than to face more mistreatment (43%).
- Sabotaged the person's contribution to a team goal and reward (41%).
- Ensured failure of person's project by not performing required tasks, such as sign-offs, taking calls, working with collaborators (40%).

## Abusive Workplace Behaviors

According to Bassman, common abusive workplace behaviors are:

- Disrespecting and devaluing the individual, often through disrespectful and devaluing language or verbal abuse.
- Overwork and devaluation of personal life (particularly salaried workers who are not compensated).
- Harassment through micromanagement of tasks and time.
- Over evaluation and manipulating information (for example concentration on negative characteristics and failures, setting up subordinate for failure).
- Managing by threat and intimidation.
- Stealing credit and taking unfair advantage.
- Preventing access to opportunities.
- Downgrading an employee's capabilities to justify downsizing.
- Impulsive destructive behavior.

According to Hoel and Cooper, common abusive workplace behaviors are:

- Having opinions and views ignored.
- Withholding information which affects the target's performance.
- Being exposed to an unmanageable workload.
- Being given tasks with unreasonable or impossible targets or deadlines.
- Being ordered to do work below competence.
- Being ignored or facing hostility when the target approaches.
- Being humiliated or ridiculed in connection with work.
- Excessive monitoring of a person's work.
- Spreading gossip.
- Insulting or offensive remarks made about the target's person (i.e. habits and background), attitudes or private life.
- Having key areas of responsibility removed or replaced with more trivial or unpleasant tasks.

Abusive cyberbullying in the workplace can have serious socioeconomic and psychological consequences on the victim. Workplace cyberbullying can lead to sick leave due to depression which in turn can lead to loss of profits for the organisation.

## In Specific Professions

### Academia

Several aspects of academia, such as the generally decentralized nature of academic institutions and the particular recruitment and career procedures, lend themselves to the practice of bullying and discourage its reporting and mitigation.

### Blue-collar Jobs

Bullying has been identified as prominent in blue-collar jobs including on the oil rigs, and in mechanical areas and machine shops, warehouses and factories. It is thought that intimidation and fear of retribution cause decreased incident reports, which, in the socioeconomic and cultural milieu of such industries, would likely lead to a vicious circle. This is often used in combination with manipulation and coercion of facts to gain favour among higher ranking administrators. For example, an investigation that was conducted following a hazing incident at Portland Bureau of Transportation within the city government of Portland, Oregon, United States found a ritual of hazing and was kept under the cover for years under the cover of "no snitching" where snitches were punished and loyalty was praised. Two thirds of the interviewed employees in this investigation declared they deemed the best way they found to deal with the workplace's bad behaviors was "not to get involved", as they "feared retaliation if they did intervene or report the problems".

### Information Technology

A culture of bullying is common in information technology (IT), leading to high sickness rates, low morale, poor productivity and high staff turnover. Deadline-driven project work and stressed-out managers take their toll on IT workers.

### Legal Profession

Bullying in the legal profession is believed to be more common than in some other professions. It is believed that its adversarial, hierarchical tradition contributes towards this. Women, trainees and solicitors who have been qualified for five years or less are more impacted, as are ethnic minority lawyers and lesbian, gay and bisexual lawyers.

### Medicine

Bullying in the medical profession is common, particularly of student or trainee doctors. It is thought that this is at least in part an outcome of conservative traditional hierarchical structures and teaching methods in the medical profession which may result in a bullying cycle.

### Military

Bullying exists to varying degrees in the military of some countries, often involving various forms of hazing or abuse by higher members of the military hierarchy.

## Nursing

Bullying has been identified as being particularly prevalent in the nursing profession although the reasons are not clear. It is thought that relational aggression (psychological aspects of bullying such as gossiping and intimidation) are relevant. Relational aggression has been studied amongst girls but not so much amongst adult women.

## Teaching

School teachers are commonly the subject of bullying but they are also sometimes the originators of bullying within a school environment.

## Volunteering

Bullying can be common in volunteering settings. For example, one study found bullying to be the most significant factor of complaints amongst volunteers. Volunteers often do not have access to protections available to paid employees, so while laws may indicate that bullying is a violation of rights, volunteers may have no means to address it.

## Forms

Tim Field suggested that workplace bullying takes these forms:

- Serial bullying: The source of all dysfunction can be traced to one individual, who picks on one employee after another and destroys them, then moves on. Probably the most common type of bullying.
- Secondary bullying: The pressure of having to deal with a serial bully causes the general behavior to decline and sink to the lowest level.
- Pair bullying: This takes place with two people, one active and verbal, the other often watching and listening.
- Gang bullying or group bullying: Is a serial bully with colleagues. Gangs can occur anywhere, but flourish in corporate bullying climates. It is often called mobbing and usually involves scapegoating and victimisation.
- Vicarious bullying: Two parties are encouraged to fight. This is the typical "triangulation" where the aggression gets passed around.
- Regulation bullying: Where a serial bully forces their target to comply with rules, regulations, procedures or laws regardless of their appropriateness, applicability or necessity.
- Residual bullying: After the serial bully has left or been fired, the behavior continues. It can go on for years.
- Legal bullying: The bringing of a vexatious legal action to control and punish a person.
- Pressure bullying or unwitting bullying: Having to work to unrealistic time scales or inadequate resources.

- Corporate bullying: Where an employer abuses an employee with impunity, knowing the law is weak and the job market is soft.
- Organizational bullying: A combination of pressure bullying and corporate bullying. Occurs when an organization struggles to adapt to changing markets, reduced income, cuts in budgets, imposed expectations and other extreme pressures.
- Institutional bullying: Entrenched and is accepted as part of the culture.
- Client bullying: An employee is bullied by those they serve, for instance subway attendants or public servants.
- Cyberbullying: The use of information and communication technologies to support deliberate, repeated, and hostile behavior by an individual or group, that is intended to harm others.

Adult bullying can come in an assortment of forms. There are about five distinctive types of adult bullies. A narcissistic bully is described as a self-centred person whose egotism is frail and possesses the need to put others down. An impulsive bully is someone who acts on bullying based on stress or being upset at the moment. A physical bully uses physical injury and the threat of harm to abuse their victims, while a verbal bully uses demeaning and cynicism to debase their victims. Lastly, a secondary adult bully is portrayed as a person that did not start the initial bullying but participates in afterwards to avoid being bullied themselves ("Adult Bullying").

## Emotional Intelligence

Workplace bullying is reported to be far more prevalent than perhaps commonly thought. For some reason, workplace bullying seems to be particularly widespread in healthcare organizations; 80% of nurses report experiencing workplace bullying. Similar to the school environment for children, the work environment typically places groups of adult peers together in a shared space on a regular basis. In such a situation, social interactions and relationships are of great importance to the function of the organizational structure and in pursuing goals. The emotional consequences of bullying put an organization at risk of losing victimized employees. Bullying also contributes to a negative work environment, is not conducive to necessary cooperation and can lessen productivity at various levels. Bullying in the workplace is associated with negative responses to stress. The ability to manage emotions, especially emotional stress, seems to be a consistently important factor in different types of bullying. The workplace in general can be a stressful environment, so a negative way of coping with stress or an inability to do so can be particularly damning. Workplace bullies may have high social intelligence and low emotional intelligence (EI). In this context, bullies tend to rank high on the social ladder and are adept at influencing others. The combination of high social intelligence and low empathy is conducive to manipulative behavior, such that Hutchinson describes workplace bullying to be. In working groups where employees have low EI, workers can be persuaded to engage in unethical behavior. With the bullies' persuasion, the work group is socialized in a way that rationalizes the behavior, and makes the group tolerant or supportive of the bullying. Hutchinson & Hurley make the case that EI and leadership skills are both necessary to bullying intervention in the workplace, and illustrates the relationship between EI, leadership and reductions in bullying. EI and ethical behavior among other members of the work team have been shown to have a significant impact on ethical behavior of nursing teams. Higher EI is linked to improvements in the work environment and is an important moderator between conflict and reactions to conflict in the workplace. The self-awareness and self-management dimensions of EI have both been illustrated to have strong positive correlations with effective leadership and the specific leadership ability to build healthy work environments and work culture.

## Related Concepts

### Abusive Supervision

Abusive supervision overlaps with workplace bullying in the workplace context. Research suggests that 75% of workplace bullying incidents are perpetrated by hierarchically superior agents. Abusive supervision differs from related constructs such as supervisor bullying and undermining in that it does not describe the intentions or objectives of the supervisor.

### Power and Control

A power and control model has been developed for the workplace, divided into the following categories:

- Overt actions,
- Covert actions,
- Emotional control,
- Isolation,
- Economic control,
- Tactics,
- Restrictions,
- Management privilege.

### Workplace Mobbing

Workplace mobbing overlaps with workplace bullying. The concept originated from the study of animal behavior. It concentrates on bullying by a group.

### Workplace Incivility

Workplace bullying overlaps to some degree with workplace incivility but tends to encompass more intense and typically repeated acts of disregard and rudeness. Negative spirals of increasing incivility between organizational members can result in bullying, but isolated acts of incivility are not conceptually bullying despite the apparent similarity in their form and content. In case of bullying, the intent of harm is less ambiguous, an unequal balance of power (both formal and informal) is more salient, and the target of bullying feels threatened, vulnerable and unable to defend himself or herself against negative recurring actions.

## Personality Disorders and Dysfunctional Personality Characteristics

### Executives

In 2005, psychologists Belinda Board and Katarina Fritzon at the University of Surrey, UK, interviewed and gave personality tests to high-level British executives and compared their profiles with those of criminal psychiatric patients at Broadmoor Hospital in the UK. They found that three out of eleven personality disorders were actually more common in executives than in the disturbed criminals. They were:

- Histrionic personality disorder: including superficial charm, insincerity, egocentricity and manipulation.
- Narcissistic personality disorder: including grandiosity, self-focused lack of empathy for others, exploitativeness and independence.
- Obsessive-compulsive personality disorder: including perfectionism, excessive devotion to work, rigidity, stubbornness and dictatorial tendencies.

They described these business people as successful psychopaths and the criminals as unsuccessful psychopaths.

According to leading leadership academic Manfred F.R. Kets de Vries, it seems almost inevitable these days that there will be some personality disorders in a senior management team.

Industrial/organizational psychology research has also examined the types of bullying that exist among business professionals and the prevalence of this form of bullying in the workplace as well as ways to measure bullying empirically.

### Psychopathy

Narcissism, lack of self-regulation, lack of remorse and lack of conscience have been identified as traits displayed by bullies. These traits are shared with psychopaths, indicating that there is some theoretical cross-over between bullies and psychopaths. Bullying is used by corporate psychopaths as a tactic to humiliate subordinates. Bullying is also used as a tactic to scare, confuse and disorient those who may be a threat to the activities of the corporate psychopath. Using meta data analysis on hundreds of UK research papers, Boddy concluded that 36% of bullying incidents were caused by the presence of corporate psychopaths. According to Boddy there are two types of bullying:

- Predatory bullying: The bully just enjoys bullying and tormenting vulnerable people for the sake of it.
- Instrumental bullying: The bullying is for a purpose, helping the bully achieve their goals.

A corporate psychopath uses instrumental bullying to further their goals of promotion and power as the result of causing confusion and divide and rule.

People with high scores on a psychopathy rating scale are more likely to engage in bullying, crime and drug use than other people. Hare and Babiak noted that about 29% of corporate psychopaths are also bullies. Other research has also shown that people with high scores on a psychopathy rating scale were more likely to engage in bullying, again indicating that psychopaths tend to be bullies in the workplace.

A workplace bully or abuser will often have issues with social functioning. These types of people often have psychopathic traits that are difficult to identify in the hiring and promotion process. These individuals often lack anger management skills and have a distorted sense of reality. Consequently, when confronted with the accusation of abuse, the abuser is not aware that any harm was done.

## Narcissism

In 2007, researchers Catherine Mattice and Brian Spitzberg at San Diego State University, USA, found that narcissism revealed a positive relationship with bullying. Narcissists were found to prefer indirect bullying tactics (such as withholding information that affects others' performance, ignoring others, spreading gossip, constantly reminding others of mistakes, ordering others to do work below their competence level, and excessively monitoring others' work) rather than direct tactics (such as making threats, shouting, persistently criticizing, or making false allegations). The research also revealed that narcissists are highly motivated to bully, and that to some extent, they are left with feelings of satisfaction after a bullying incident occurs.

## Machiavellianism

According to Namie, Machiavellians manipulate and exploit others to advance their perceived personal agendas. In his view, Machiavellianism represents one of the core components of workplace bullying.

## Health Effects

According to Gary and Ruth Namie, as well as Tracy, et al., workplace bullying can harm the health of the targets of bullying. Organizations are beginning to take note of workplace bullying because of the costs to the organization in terms of the health of their employees.

According to scholars at The Project for Wellness and Work-Life at Arizona State University, "workplace bullying is linked to a host of physical, psychological, organizational, and social costs." Stress is the most predominant health effect associated with bullying in the workplace. Research indicates that workplace stress has significant negative effects that are correlated to poor mental health and poor physical health, resulting in an increase in the use of "sick days" or time off from work.

The negative effects of bullying are so severe that posttraumatic stress disorder (PTSD) and even suicide are not uncommon. Tehrani found that one in 10 targets experience PTSD, and that 44% of her respondents experienced PTSD similar to that of battered women and victims of child abuse. Matthiesen and Einarsen found that up to 77% of targets experience PTSD.

In addition, co-workers who witness workplace bullying can also have negative effects, such as fear, stress, and emotional exhaustion. Those who witness repetitive workplace abuse often choose to leave the place of employment where the abuse took place. Workplace bullying can also hinder the organizational dynamics such as group cohesion, peer communication, and overall performance.

According to the 2012 survey conducted by Workplace Bullying Institute (516 respondents), Anticipation of next negative event is the most common psychological symptom of workplace bullying reported by 80%. Panic attacks afflict 52%. Half (49%) of targets reported being diagnosed with clinical depression. Sleep disruption, loss of concentration, mood swings, and pervasive sadness and insomnia were more common (ranging from 77% to 50%). Nearly three-quarters (71%) of targets sought treatment from a physician. Over half (63%) saw a mental health professional for their work-related symptoms. Respondents reported other symptoms that can be exacerbated by stress: migraine headaches (48%), irritable bowel disorder (37%), chronic fatigue syndrome (33%) and sexual dysfunction (27%).

### Depression

Workplace depression can occur in many companies of various size and profession, and can have negative effects on positive profit growth. Stress factors that are unique to one's working environment, such as bullying from co-workers or superiors and poor social support for high pressure occupations, can build over time and create an inefficient work behavior in a depressed individual. In addition, inadequate or negative communication techniques can further drive an employee towards feeling of being disconnected from the company's mission and goals. One way that companies can combat the destructive consequences associated with employee depression is to offer more support for counseling and consider bringing in experts to educate staff on the consequences of bullying. Ignoring the problem of depression and decreased workplace performance is creating an unsustainable path towards intergroup conflict and lasting feelings of disillusionment.

## Workplace Incivility

Workplace incivility has been defined as low-intensity deviant behavior with ambiguous intent to harm the target. Uncivil behaviors are characteristically rude and discourteous, displaying a lack of regard for others. The authors hypothesize there is an "incivility spiral" in the workplace made worse by "asymmetric global interaction".

Incivility is distinct from aggression. The reduction of workplace incivility is a fertile area for applied psychology research.

### Subtle/Covert Examples

Examples at the more subtle end of the spectrum include:

- Asking for input and then ignoring it,
- "Forgetting" to share credit for a collaborative work,
- Giving someone a "dirty look",
- Interrupting others,
- Not listening,

- Side conversations during a formal business meeting/presentation,
- Speaking with a condescending tone,
- Waiting impatiently over someone's desk to gain their attention.

## Overt Examples

Somewhere between the extremes are numerous everyday examples of workplace rudeness and impropriety including:

- Disrespecting workers by comments, gestures or proven behaviors (hostility) based on characteristics such as their race, religion, gender, etc. This is considered workplace discrimination.
- Disrupting meetings,
- Emotional put-downs,
- Giving dirty looks or other negative eye contact (i.e. "hawk eyes" considered to be threatening in the culture of the United States),
- Giving public reprimands,
- Giving the silent treatment,
- Insulting others,
- Making accusations about professional competence,
- Not giving credit where credit is due,
- Overruling decisions without giving a reason,
- Sending a nasty and demeaning note (hate mail),
- Talking about someone behind his or her back,
- Undermining credibility in front of others.

Other overt forms of incivility might include emotional tirades and losing one's temper.

## Corporate Symptoms of Long Term Incivility

- Higher than normal employee turnover,
- A large number of employee grievances and complaints,
- Lost work time by employees calling in sick,
- Increased consumer complaints,
- Diminished productivity in terms of quality and quantity of work,

- Cultural and communications barriers,
- Lack of confidence in leadership,
- Inability to adapt effectively to change,
- Lack of individual accountability,
- Lack of respect.

### Predicting

### Gender

A number of studies have shown that women are more likely than men to experience workplace incivility and its associated negative outcomes. Research also shows that employees who witness incivility directed toward female coworkers have lower psychological wellbeing, physical health, and job satisfaction, which in turn relates lowered commitment toward the organization and higher job burnout and turnover intentions. Miner-Rubino and Cortina found that observing incivility toward women related to increased work withdrawal for both male and female employees, especially in work contexts where there were more men.

Other research shows that incivility directed toward same-gender coworkers tends to lead to more negative emotionality for observers. While both men and women felt anger, fear, and anxiety arising from same-gender incivility, women additionally reported higher levels of demoralization after witnessing such mistreatment. Furthermore, the negative effects of same-gender incivility were more pronounced for men observing men mistreating other men than for women observing women mistreating other women. Miner and Eischeid suggest this disparity reflects men perceiving uncivil behavior as a "clear affront to the power and status they have learned to expect for their group in interpersonal interactions".

Motherhood status has also been examined as a possible predictor of being targeted for incivility in the workplace. This research shows that mothers with three or more children report more incivility than women with two, one, or zero children. Fathers, on the other hand, report more incivility than men without children, but still less than mothers. While motherhood appears to predict increases in workplace incivility, results also showed that the negative outcomes associated with incivility were mitigated by motherhood status. Fatherhood status, on the other hand, did not mitigate the relationship between incivility and outcomes. Childless women reported more workplace incivility than childless men, and showed a stronger relationship between incivility and negative outcomes than childless men, mothers, and fathers.

## Organizational Commitment

Organizational commitment is an individual's psychological attachment to the organization. The basis behind many of these studies was to find ways to improve how workers feel about their jobs so that these workers would become more committed to their organizations. Organizational commitment predicts work variables such as turnover, organizational citizenship behavior, and job performance. Some of the factors such as role stress, empowerment, job insecurity and employability, and distribution of leadership have been shown to be connected to a worker's sense of organizational commitment.

Organizational scientists have also developed many nuanced definitions of organizational commitment, and numerous scales to measure them. Exemplary of this work is Meyer and Allen's model of commitment, which was developed to integrate numerous definitions of commitment that had been proliferated in the literature. Meyer and Allen's model has also been critiqued because the model is not consistent with empirical findings. It may also not be fully applicable in domains such as customer behavior. There has also been debate surrounding what Meyers and Allen's model was trying to achieve.

## Model of Commitment

Meyer and Allen's three-component model of commitment was created to argue that commitment has three different components that correspond with different psychological states. Meyer and Allen created this model for two reasons: first "aid in the interpretation of existing research" and second "to serve as a framework for future research". Their study was based mainly around previous studies of organizational commitment. Meyer and Allen's research indicated that there are three "mind sets" which can characterize an employee's commitment to the organization. Mercurio extended this model by reviewing the empirical and theoretical studies on organizational commitment. Mercurio posits that emotional, or affective commitment is the core essence of organizational commitment.

## Affective Commitment

AC is defined as the employee's positive emotional attachment to the organization. Meyer and Allen pegged AC as the "desire" component of organizational commitment. An employee who is affectively committed strongly identifies with the goals of the organization and desires to remain a part of the organization. This employee commits to the organization because he/she "wants to". This commitment can be influenced by many different demographic characteristics: age, tenure, sex, and education but these influences are neither strong nor consistent. The problem with these characteristics is that while they can be seen, they cannot be clearly defined. Meyer and Allen gave this example that "positive relationships between tenure and commitment maybe due to tenure-related differences in job status and quality". In developing this concept, Meyer and Allen drew largely on Mowday, Porter, and Steers's concept of commitment, which in turn drew on earlier work by Kanter. Mercurio stated that"affective commitment was found to be an enduring, demonstrably indispensable, and central characteristic of organizational commitment".

## Continuance Commitment

Continuance commitment is the "need" component or the gains versus losses of working in an organization. "Side bets", or investments, are the gains and losses that may occur should an individual stay or leave an organization. An individual may commit to the organization because he/she perceives a high cost of losing organizational membership. Things like economic costs (such as pension accruals) and social costs (friendship ties with co-workers) would be costs of losing organizational membership. But an individual doesn't see the positive costs as enough to stay with an organization they must also take into account the availability of alternatives (such as another organization), disrupt personal relationships, and other "side bets" that would be incurred from leaving their organization. The problem with this is that these "side bets" don't occur at once but that they "accumulate with age and tenure".

## Normative Commitment

The individual commits to and remains with an organization because of feelings of obligation, the last component of organizational commitment. These feelings may derive from a strain on an individual before and after joining an organization. For example, the organization may have invested resources in training an employee who then feels a 'moral' obligation to put forth effort on the job and stay with the organization to 'repay the debt.' It may also reflect an internalized norm, developed before the person joins the organization through family or other socialization processes, that one should be loyal to one's organization. The employee stays with the organization because he/she "ought to". But generally if an individual invest a great deal they will receive "advanced rewards". Normative commitment is higher in organizations that value loyalty and systematically communicate the fact to employees with rewards, incentives and other strategies. Normative commitment in employees is also high where employees regularly see visible examples of the employer being committed to employee well-being. An employee with greater organizational commitment has a greater chance of contributing to organizational success and will also experience higher levels of job satisfaction. High levels of job satisfaction, in turn, reduces employee turnover and increases the organization's ability to recruit and retain talent. Meyer and Allen based their research in this area more on theoretical evidence rather than empirical, which may explain the lack of depth. They drew off Wiener's research for this commitment component.

## Critique to the Three-component Model

Since the model was made, there has been conceptual critique to what the model is trying to achieve. Specifically from three psychologists, Omar Solinger, Woody Olffen, and Robert Roe. To date, the three-component conceptual model has been regarded as the leading model for organizational commitment because it ties together three aspects of earlier commitment research. However, a collection of studies have shown that the model is not consistent with empirical findings. Solinger, Olffen, and Roe use a later model by Alice Eagly and Shelly Chaiken, Attitude-behavior Model, to present that TCM combines different attitude phenomena. They have come to the conclusion that TCM is a model for predicting turnover. In a sense the model describes why people should stay with the organization whether it is because they want to, need to, or ought to. The model appears to mix together an attitude toward a target, that being the organization, with an attitude toward a behavior, which is leaving or staying. They believe the studies should return to the original understanding of organizational commitment as an attitude toward the organization and measure it accordingly. Although the TCM is a good way to predict turnover, these psychologists do not believe it should be the general model. Because Eagly and Chaiken's model is so general, it seems that the TCM can be described as a specific subdivision of their model when looking at a general sense of organizational commitment. It becomes clear that affective commitment equals an attitude toward a target, while continuance and normative commitment are representing different concepts referring to anticipated behavioral outcomes, specifically staying or leaving. This observation backs up their conclusion that organizational commitment is perceived by TCM as combining different target attitudes and behavioral attitudes, which they believe to be both confusing and logically incorrect. The attitude-behavioral model can demonstrate explanations for something that would seem contradictory in the TCM. That is that affective commitment has stronger associations with relevant behavior and a wider range of behaviors, compared to normative and continuance commitment. Attitude toward a target (the organization) is obviously applicable to a wider range of behaviors than an attitude toward a specific behavior (staying). After their research, Sollinger, Olffen, and Roe believe Eagly and Chaiken's attitude-behavior model from 1993 would be a good alternative model to look at as a general organizational commitment predictor because of its approach at organizational commitment as a singular construct, which in turn would help predicting various behaviors beyond turnover.

## A Five Component Commitment Model

More recently, scholars have proposed a five component model of commitment, though it has been developed in the context of product and service consumption. This model proposes habitual and forced commitment as two additional dimensions which are very germane in consumption settings. It seems, however, that habitual commitment or inertial may also become relevant in many job settings. People get habituated to a job—the routine, the processes, the cognitive schemas associated with a job can make people develop a latent commitment to the job—just as it may occur in a consumption setting. The paper—by Keiningham and colleagues also compared applications of the TCM in job settings and in consumption settings to develop additional insights.

## Job Satisfaction

Job satisfaction is commonly defined as the extent to which employees like their work. Researchers have examined Job satisfaction for the past several decades. Studies have been devoted to figuring out the dimensions of job satisfaction, antecedents of job satisfaction, and the relationship between satisfaction and commitment. Satisfaction has also been examined under various demographics of gender, age, race, education, and work experience. Most research on job satisfaction has been aimed towards the person-environment fit paradigm. Job satisfaction has been found to be an important area of research because one of the top reasons individuals give for leaving a job is dissatisfaction.

Much of the literature on the relationship between commitment and satisfaction with one's job indicates that if employees are satisfied they develop stronger commitment to their work. Kalleberg studied work attitudes of workers in the USA and Japan and found a correlation of 0.73 between job satisfaction and organizational commitment of workers in Japan and a higher significant correlation of 0.81 among Americans. A study conducted by Dirani and Kuchinke produced results indicating a strong correlation between job commitment and job satisfaction and that satisfaction was a reliable predictor of commitment. Job satisfaction among employees—at least in retail settings—can also strengthen the association between customer satisfaction and customer loyalty.

### Perceiving a Calling

A study at the University of Florida found a positive correlation between the individual's perception of their career being a "calling" and the level of commitment to the job. This study looked at the relation between work commitment and participant's perception of meaning in their job. Participants were tested in the areas of; perceiving a calling, job satisfaction, and job commitment. Results showed a moderate correlation between participants perceiving a calling and job commitment and a weak correlation between perceiving a calling and job satisfaction.

## Other Factors

### Role Stress

Dysfunctions in role performance have been associated with a large number of consequences, almost always negative, which affect the well being of workers and functioning of organizations. An individual's experience of receiving incompatible or conflicting requests (role conflict) and/or the lack of enough information to carry out his/her job (role ambiguity) are causes of role stress. Role ambiguity and conflict decrease worker's performance and are positively related to the probability of the workers leaving the organization. Role conflict and ambiguity have been proposed as determining factors of workers' job satisfaction and organizational commitment.

### Empowerment

Empowerment in the workplace has had several different definitions over the years. It has been considered 'energizing followers through leadership, enhancing self efficacy by reducing powerlessness and increasing intrinsic task motivation.' A psychological view of empowerment describes it as 'a process of intrinsic motivation, perceived control, competence, and energizing towards achieving goals.' There are two prominent concepts of empowerment. The first is Structural Empowerment which comes from the Organizational/Management Theory and is described as the ability to get things done and to mobilize resources. The second is Psychological Empowerment which comes from Social Psychological models and is described as psychological perceptions/attitudes of employees about their work and their organizational roles. A study done by Ahmad et al. found support for the relationship between empowerment and job satisfaction and job commitment. The study looked at nurses working in England and nurses working in Malaysia. Taking cultural context into consideration, the study still showed a positive correlation between empowerment and job satisfaction/commitment.

### Job Insecurity and Employability

In a study conducted by De Cuyper research found that workers who were on fixed-term contracts or considered "temporary workers" reported higher levels of job insecurity than permanent workers. Job insecurity was found to negatively correlate with job satisfaction and affective organizational commitment in permanent workers. The study also found that job satisfaction and organizational commitment were highly correlated with being a permanent worker.

## Distribution of Leadership

A study conducted by Hulpia et al. focused on the impact of the distribution of leadership and leadership support among teachers and how that affected job satisfaction and commitment. The study found that there was a strong relationship between organizational commitment and the cohesion of the leadership team and the amount of leadership support. Previously held beliefs about job satisfaction and commitment among teachers was that they were negatively correlated with absenteeism and turnover and positively correlated with job effort and job performance. This study examined how one leader (usually a principal) effected the job satisfaction and commitment of teachers. The study found that when leadership was distributed by the 'leader' out to the teachers as well workers reported higher job satisfaction and organizational commitment than when most of the leadership fell to one person. Even when it was only the perception of distributed leadership roles workers still reported high levels of job satisfaction/ commitment.

## Shift to Organizational Change Commitment

By the end of the 1990s, leaders did not find the value in understanding whether or not their people were more or less committed to the organization. It was particularly frustrating that leaders could see that people committed to the organization were not as committed to strategic change initiatives, the majority of which failed to live up to expectations. John Meyer responded to this gap by proposing a model of organizational change commitment. The new model includes the same 3-components, but also includes a behavioral commitment scale: resistance, passive resistance, compliance, cooperation, and championing. Though Meyer does not cite him, a peer reviewed source for behavioral commitment comes from Leon Coetsee in South Africa. Coetsee brought the resistance-to-commitment model of Harvard consultant Arnold Judson to academic research and has continued developing the model as late as 2011.

## Guidelines to Enhance

Five rules help to enhance organizational commitment:

- Commit to people-first values: Put it in writing, hire the right-kind managers, and walk the talk.
- Clarify and communicate your mission: Clarify the mission and ideology; make it charismatic; use value-based hiring practices; stress values-based orientation and training; build tradition.
- Guarantee organizational justice: Have a comprehensive grievance procedure; provide for extensive two-way communications.
- Community of practice: Build value-based homogeneity; share and share alike; emphasize barnraising, cross-utilization, and teamwork; getting people to work together.
- Support employee development: Commit to actualizing; provide first-year job challenge; enrich and empower; promote from within; provide developmental activities; provide employee security without guarantees.

# Organizational Ethics

Organizational ethics is the ethics of an organization, and it is how an organization responds to an internal or external stimulus. Organizational ethics is interdependent with the organizational culture. Although it is akin to both organizational behavior and industrial and organizational psychology as well as business ethics on the micro and macro levels, organizational ethics is neither organizational behavior nor industrial and organizational psychology, nor is it solely business ethics (which includes corporate governance and corporate ethics). Organizational ethics express the values of an organization to its employees and/or other entities irrespective of governmental and/or regulatory laws.

Ethics are the principles and values used by an individual to govern his or her actions and decisions. An organization forms when individuals with varied interests and different backgrounds unite on a common platform and work together towards predefined goals and objectives. A code of ethics within an organization is a set of principles that is used to guide the organization in its decisions, programs, and policies. An ethical organizational culture consists of leaders and employees adhering to a code of ethics.

An organization's ethical philosophy can affect the organization in many ways including its reputation, productivity, and the bottom line of the organization. Ethics within an organization can offer many benefits. A positive ethical corporate culture improves the morale among the workers in an organization, which could increase productivity, employee retention and loyalty. Higher productivity improves the efficiency of the organizations and increased employee retention reduces the cost of replacing employees. Other essential benefits of an ethical culture include better internal communication and wider community development through corporate social responsibility. The Foreign Corrupt Practices Act restricts the United States business firms from engaging in bribery and other illegal practices internationally. There are laws that have the same type of prohibition for European companies which create a disadvantage competitively for both European and U.S. firms. Such laws are not a restricting element to organizations that have highly elevated ethical behavior as part of their values. Organizations that lack ethical practices as a mandatory basis of their business structure and corporate culture, have commonly been found to fail due to the absence of business ethics. Corporate downfalls would include, but are not limited to, the recent Enron and WorldCom scandals, two primary examples of unethical business practices concerning questionable accounting transactions.

Organizations focusing on encouraging ethical practices are commonly viewed with respect by their employees, the community, and corresponding industries. Ethical business practices of organizations have resulted in a solid financial bottom-line. This has been seen through greater sales and increased revenue by companies retaining talented personnel and attracting new skilled employees. More importantly, an ethical organization will have the ability to retain employees that are experienced and knowledgeable (generally referred to as human capital). This human capital results in less employee turnover, less training time for new employees, and greater output regarding services (or production of goods).

## Basic Ethical Elements

There are at least four elements that aim to create an ethical culture and behavior of employees within an organization. These elements are:

- A written code of ethics and standards (ethical code),
- Ethics training for executives, managers, and employees,
- The availability of ethical situational advice (i.E. Advice lines or offices),
- Confidential reporting systems.

Organizations are constantly striving for a better ethical atmosphere within the business climate and culture. Businesses must create an ethical business climate in order to develop an ethical organization. Otherwise said, companies must focus on the ethics of employees in order to create an ethical business. Employees must know the difference between what is acceptable and unacceptable in the workplace. These standards are found in the written code of ethics or may be referred to as the employee handbook. These standards are a written form of employee conduct and performance expectations.

Employee handbooks also commonly include rules concerning expectations and consequences that follow misconduct. Handbooks normally will clearly state the rules, guidelines, and standards of an organization as well as possible rules, regulations, and laws that they are bound by. Many company handbooks will include laws regarding sexual harassment, alcohol abuse, and drug/substance abuse.

## Intrinsic and Extrinsic Organizational Rewards

The intrinsic and extrinsic rewards of an ethical organization are bound to an organization's culture and ethics. Based on the reliability and support structure of each of the four areas needed for ethical behavior, the organizational ethics will be evident throughout the organization. The organization including the employees, managers, suppliers, customers, and other entities, will receive intrinsic and extrinsic rewards. Actions of employees can range from whistle blowing (intrinsic) to the extraordinary actions of hourly employee purchasing all the recently produced peanut butter (as produced by his employer), that has no resale value due to mislabeled jars. This employee was aware that his employer (extrinsic) would reimburse him in full for purchasing the mislabeled peanut butter.

## Ethical Theory and Leadership Empowerment

There are many theories and organizational studies that are related to "organizational ethics," but "organizations" and "ethics" are wide and varied in application and scope. These theories and studies can range from individual(s), team(s), stakeholder, management, leadership, human resources, group(s) interaction(s), as well as the psychological framework behind each area to include the distribution of job tasks within various types of organizations. As among these areas, the influence of leadership in any organization cannot go unexamined, because of a clear understanding of the organization's vision, goals (to include immediate and long-term strategic plans), and values. Leadership sets the tone for organizational management (strategic actions taken by an organization to create a positive image to both internal and external public). In turn, leadership directly influences the organizational symbolism (which reflects the culture, the language of the members, any meaningful objects, representations, and/or how someone may act or think within an organization). The values and ideals within an organization generally center upon "values for business" as the theoretical approach most leaders use to present to their "co-members" (which in truth maybe subordinates).

In fact, an examination of business reveals that most leaders approach the X(?) from the perspective of values for the business. Alongside presenting the vision, values, and goals of the organization, the leader should infuse empowerment and motivation to its members. Leaders using empowerment to motivate their subordinates, is based upon the view of: "Achieving organizational ownership of company values is a continuous process of communication, discussion, and debate throughout all areas of the organization" as.

## Stakeholder Theory

Whether it is a team, small group, or a large international entity, the ability for any organization to reason, act rationally, and respond ethically is paramount. Leaders must have the ability to recognize the needs and desires of members (or called "stakeholders" in some theories or models), and how they correspond to the organization. It is the stakeholder theory that implies that all stakeholders (or individuals) must be treated equally, regardless of the fact that some individuals will contribute more than others to the organization.

Leaders who motivate others must present the goals of an organization to the stakeholders with respect to particular benefits of the stakeholders. Leaders must set aside individual (or personal) ambitions (along with any prejudice) in order to present these goals properly. Furthermore, it is leadership that influences stakeholders towards ethical behavior for the organization. They must step behind a veil of ignorance and treat every stakeholder as a means with equal weight. Importantly, the leader (or stakeholder management) must possess the necessary skills and rank to ensure that each stakeholders voice is respected and heard within the organization to ensure that other voices are not expressing views (or needs as in respects to Maslow's Hierarchy of Needs). Therefore, stakeholder management must ensure an ethical system for their own management styles, personalities, systems, performances, plans, policies, strategies, productivity, openness, and even risk(s) within their cultures or industries.

## Ethical System Implementation

The function of developing and implementing business ethics into an organization is difficult. Due to each organization's culture and atmosphere being different, there is no clear or specific way to implement a code of ethics to an existing business. Business ethics implementation can be categorized into two groups; formal and informal measures. Formal measures include training and courses pertaining to ethics. Informal measures are led by example from either the manager or the social norm of the company.

There are several steps to follow when trying to implement an ethical system. Some of these steps include obtaining a commitment from the board of directors and senior managers, developing resources for ethics initiatives, and determining ethical risks and developing contingency plans. Other steps include developing an ethics program that addresses risks while still maintaining compliance with the ethical standards, providing insight for implementation and audits of the ethical programs, and communicating with stakeholders to create shared commitment and values for ethical conduct.

The implementation should be performed to the entirety of the business including all areas of operations. If it is not implemented pragmatically and with caution for the needs, desires, and personalities (consider the Big Five personality traits) of the stakeholders, the culture, and the employees, then problems may arise. Although a great deal of time may be required, stakeholder management should consider the Rational Decision-Making Model for implementation of various aspects, details, and standards of an ethical system to the stakeholders. If an implementation has been performed successfully, then all stakeholders have accepted the newly designed ethics system for the organization. With the implementation of an ethical system comes the implementation of new tasks and responsibilities. The responsibilities include leadership in ethics, delegating, and communicating as well as motivating the company's ethical position to its employees.

## Leadership in Organizations

"The ability to create a vision and influence, motivate, inspire and transform others to achieve certain goals towards that vision is known as leadership."

Leadership is the specific set of skills and attributes which can be acquired through learning.

A Leader is a person who guides others and motivates them to achieve specific goals to accomplish his vision.

Table: Difference between Managers and Leaders.

| Basis for Comparison | Manager | Leader |
|---|---|---|
| Position and Status | Managers are appointed personnel at official positions. | Any person can be a leader no matter what his position and status is. |
| Way of thinking | Controlled mindset | Out of the box thinking |
| Focus | Goal-oriented | People-oriented |
| Aim | Achieving targets | Accomplishing their vision |
| Objective | Getting the work done | Bringing some change |
| Tools | Power and control | Trust and honesty |
| Originality | Replica of one another, all doing the same thing | Original and individual personality |
| Attitude | Accept the existing situation and works accordingly | Challenge the existing situation and work to change the same |
| Perspective | Short term | Long term |

## Qualities of a Good Leader

- Proactive,
- Ability to Inspire,
- Clear Vision,
- Good Communication Skills,
- Confident,
- Self Driven,
- Decision Maker,
- Responsible,
- Learner,
- Patient Listener,
- Commitment,
- Never Give Up Attitude,
- Trustworthy.

## Leadership Process

- Evaluate and assess the organisation's position,
- Take initiative,

- Create a vision,
- Set objectives to accomplish the vision,
- Formulate strategies to achieve objectives,
- Develop a change process or tactics,
- Explain the need for change to the employees,
- Motivate and inspire the employees to bring the desired change,
- Implement the strategies,
- Analyze the results.

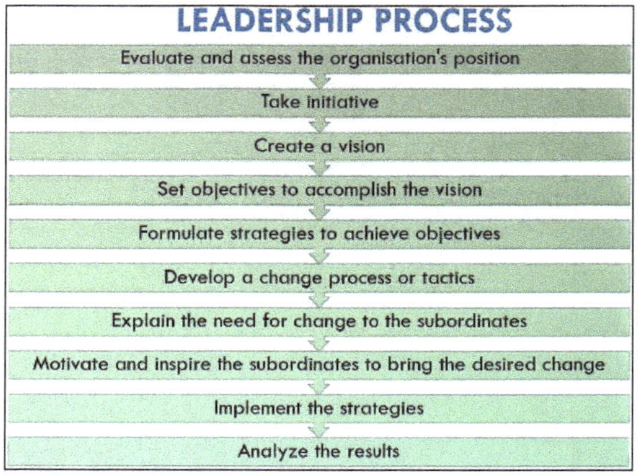


## Leadership Styles

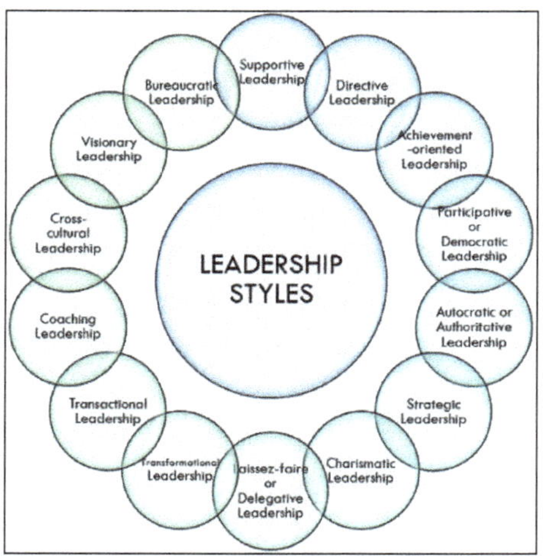


- Supportive Leadership: Leaders are more attentive towards the welfare and individual needs of the subordinates.
- Directive Leadership: Leaders establish the standards of performance for the subordinates and expect them to adhere to the rules and regulations. They provide complete guidance to the subordinates.

- Achievement-oriented Leadership: Leaders usually set challenging goals for the subordinates, expecting their constant improvement in performance. They have confidence that the subordinates will perform excellently.
- Participative or Democratic Leadership: Leaders invite opinions and suggestions from the subordinates while making decisions.
- Autocratic or Authoritative Leadership: Leaders have the complete hold over the subordinates and do not entertain opinions, suggestions, questions and complains. They take all the decisions solely without the participation of subordinates.
- Strategic Leadership: Strategic leaders frame a set of strategies towards their vision and motivate subordinates to accomplish that vision.
- Charismatic Leadership: Charismatic Leader has an extraordinary and powerful personality and acts as a role model for his followers who follow him blindly.
- Laissez-faire or Delegative Leadership: Leaders are lenient and assign authority and responsibility to the subordinates. The subordinates are free to work as they like to and take their own decisions with the minimal interference of the management. Laissez-faire is one of the least effective styles of leadership.
- Transformational Leadership: Transformational Leaders initiates a revolutionary change in the behavior, perception and attitude of the subordinates. They motivate and inspire the subordinates to develop their own skills to perform better and ultimately accomplish the vision of the organisation.
- Transactional Leadership: Transactional Leaders believe in motivating subordinates through rewards and incentives and discouraging them through punishments.
- Coaching Leadership: A Coaching Leader is well experienced in his role and is focussed on the long-term growth of his subordinates.
- Cross-cultural Leadership: In today's global scenario, Cross-cultural Leaders keep themselves updated and aware of the different cultures around the world, and uses this knowledge to lead culturally diverse teams.
- Visionary Leadership: A Visionary Leader communicates his vision for the organisation to his followers and intellectually influences them to become self-driven towards the shared vision.
- Bureaucratic Leadership: Bureaucratic leaders use their position to exercise power and strict control over the subordinates. The subordinates have to be in complete discipline and are promoted on the basis of their capability to comply with the rules and regulations of the organisation.

Behind the success of every organisation there lies an effective leadership. Leadership involves the exercise of influence by one person over others.

Leadership can be defined as an interpersonal influence directed toward the achievement of goals. Three important parts of this definition are the terms interpersonal, influence and goal.

Interpersonal means between persons and thus, a leader has more than one person or group to lead.

- Influence is the power to affect others.
- Goal is the end one attempts to attain.

## Characteristics of Leadership

- Empathy: Creating a legitimate rapport with your staff makes it less likely that personal issues and resentment can creep in and derail the group. When your team knows that you are empathetic to their concerns, they will be more likely to work with you and share in your vision, rather than foster negative feelings.
- Consistency: Being a consistent leader will gain you respect and credibility, which is essential to getting buy-in from the group. By setting an example of fairness and credibility, the team will want to act the same way.
- Honesty: Another characteristic of leadership that lends itself to credibility. Those who are honest, especially about concerns, make it far more likely that obstacles will be addressed rather than avoided. Honesty also allows for better assessment and growth.
- Direction: Having the vision to break out of the norm and aim for great things – then the wherewithal to set the steps necessary to get there – is an essential characteristic of good leadership. By seeing what can be and managing the goals on how to get there, a good leader can create impressive change.
- Communication: Effective communication helps keep the team working on the right projects with the right attitude. If you communicate effectively about expectations, issues and advice, your staff will be more likely to react and meet your goals.
- Flexibility: Not every problem demands the same solution. By being flexible to new ideas and open-minded enough to consider them, you increase the likelihood that you will find the best possible answer. You will set a good example for your team and reward good ideas.
- Conviction: A strong vision and the willingness to see it through is one of the most important characterizes of leadership. The leader who believes in the mission and works toward it will be an inspiration and a resource to their followers.

## Factors of Leadership

Leaders are people who are able to think and act creatively in abnormal situations and who set out to influence the ations, beliefs and feelings of others. There are four major factors in leadership.

## Leader

Leader must have an honest understanding about himself, what he know, and what he can do. Also, note that it is the followers, not the leader or someone else who determines if the leader is successful. If they do not trust or lack confidence in their leader, then they will be uninspired. To be successful you have to convince your followers, not yourself or your superiors, that you are worthy of being followed.

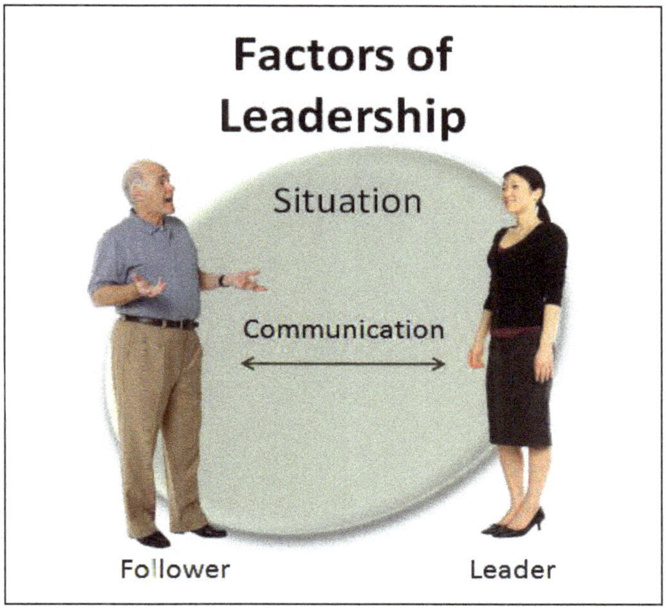


### Followers

Different people require different styles of leadership. For example, a new employee requires more supervision than an experienced employee does. A person who lacks motivation requires a different approach than one with a high degree of motivation. You must know your people! The fundamental starting point is having a good understanding of human nature, such as needs, emotions, and motivation. You must come to know your employees' be, know, and do attributes.

### Communication

Leadership is possible only through two-way communication. Much of it is nonverbal. For instance, when you "set the example," that communicates to your people that you would not ask them to perform anything that you would not be willing to do. What and how you communicate either builds or harms the relationship between you and your followers.

### Situation

All situations are different. What you do in one situation will not always work in another. Leader must use his judgment to decide the best course of action and the leadership style needed for each situation. For example, you may need to confront an employee for inappropriate behavior, but if the confrontation is too late or too early, too harsh or too weak, then the results may prove ineffective.

### Qualities of a Successful Leader

Leadership is the ability to influence the behavior of a group of individuals in a particular pattern. A leader should possess certain qualities which is helpful to influence the group for achieving the best results from individuals. Leadership traits can be divided in to two. They are personal traits and management traits:

- Personal traits:
    - Intelligence,
    - Self confidence,
    - Foresight and vision,
    - Initiative,
    - Sound physique,
    - Dynamic personality,
    - Objectivity,
    - Empathy,
    - Responsibility,
    - Emotional stability,
    - Tact.
- Managerial Traits:
    - Technical knowledge,
    - Organising ability,
    - Ability to deal with people.

## Importance of Leadership

Leadership plays an important role in making organisation successful. All organisations require leaders to lead the organisation. Leaders are able to build a team for achievement of organisational objectives. Without a good leader, organisation cannot function efficiently and effectively. The importance of good leadership are:

- Motivating employees,
- Better utilisation of human resources,
- Creating confidence,
- Promoting the spirit of co-ordination,
- Builds morale,
- Directing group activity,
- Develops good human relations,
- Helps to fulfil social responsibilities.

## Leadership Styles

From Mahatma Gandhi and Winston Churchill, to Martin Luther King and Steve Jobs, there can be as many ways to lead people as there are leaders. Fortunately, businesspeople and psychologists have developed useful frameworks that describe the main ways that people lead.

### Lewin's Leadership Styles

Psychologist Kurt Lewin developed his framework in the 1930s, and it provided the foundation of many of the approaches that followed afterwards. He argued that there are three major styles of leadership:

- Autocratic leaders make decisions without consulting their team members, even if their input would be useful. This can be appropriate when you need to make decisions quickly, when there's no need for team input, and when team agreement isn't necessary for a successful outcome. However, this style can be demoralizing, and it can lead to high levels of absenteeism and staff turnover. There are three types of autocratic leaders:
    - Strict autocrat: Who follows autocratic style in a very strict sense. He influences subordinates through negative motivation like criticing subordinates', imposing penalty etc.
    - Benevolent autocrat: Leader influences his subordinates through positive motivation. He uses reward and incentives in directing his subordinates towards these organisational goals.
    - Manipulative autocrat: The autocrat leader tries to make the subordinate to feel that they are actually participating in decision making even though he had already taken a decision.
- Democratic leaders make the final decisions, but they include team members in the decision-making process. They encourage creativity, and people are often highly engaged in projects and decisions. As a result, team members tend to have high job satisfaction and high productivity. This is not always an effective style to use, though, when you need to make a quick decision.
- Laissez-faire or free rein-leaders give their team members a lot of freedom in how they do their work, and how they set their deadlines. They provide support with resources and advice if needed, but otherwise they don't get involved. This autonomy can lead to high job satisfaction, but it can be damaging if team members don't manage their time well, or if they don't have the knowledge, skills, or self motivation to do their work effectively. (Laissezfaire leadership can also occur when managers don't have control over their work and their people).
- Paternalistic leaderships - under this style leader assumes that his function is paternl or fatherly. Their relationship is same as father and family. The leader guides and protects his subordinates as members of his family. As the head of the family, the leader provides good working conditions and fringe benefits to his subordinates.

## Leadership and Management

These are two notions that are often used interchangeably. Leadership and management must go hand in hand. They are not the same thing. But they are necessarily linked, and complementary. Any effort to separate the two is likely to cause more problems than it solves.

- The manager is a copy; the leader is an original.
- The manager maintains; the leader develops.
- The manager focuses on systems and structure; the leader focuses on people.
- The manager relies on control; the leader inspires trust.
- The manager has a short-range view; the leader has a long-range perspective.
- The manager asks how and when; the leader asks what and why.
- The manager has his or her eye always on the bottom line; the leader's eye is on the horizon.
- The manager imitates; the leader originates.
- The manager accepts the status quo; the leader challenges it.
- The manager is the classic good soldier; the leader is his or her own person.
- The manager administers; the leader innovates.
- The manager does things right; the leader does the right thing.

Perhaps there was a time when the calling of the manager and that of the leader could be separated. A foreman in an industrial area factory probably didn't have to give much thought to what he was producing or to the people who were producing it. His or her job was to follow orders, organize the work, assign the right people to the necessary tasks, coordinate the results, and ensure the job got done as ordered. The focus was on efficiency.

But in the new economy, where value comes increasingly from the knowledge of people, and where workers are no longer undifferentiated cogs in an industrial machine, management and leadership are not easily separated. People look to their managers, not just to assign them a task, but to define for them a purpose. And managers must organize workers, not just to maximize efficiency, but to nurture skills, develop talent and inspire results.

The late management guru Peter Drucker was one of the first to recognize this truth, as he was to recognize so many other management truths. He identified the emergence of the "knowledge worker," and the profound differences that would cause in the way business was organized.

## Leadership Theories

An organisation has the greatest chance f being successful when all of the employees work toward achieving its goals. Since leadership involves the exercise of influence by one person over others, the quality of leadership exhibited by supervisors is a critical determinant of organisational success. Thus, supervisors study leadership in order to influence the actions of employees towards the achievement of the goals of the organisation.

Effective leadership is a function of the characteristics of the leader, the style of leadership, the characteristics of the followers and the situation exists in the organisation. The leadership theories can be categorised as follows:

- Trait theories.
- Behavioral theories.
- Contingency theories.
- Transformational theories.

## Trait Thoeries of Leadership

The trait model of leadership is based on the characteristics of many leaders - both successful and unsuccessful - and is used to predict leadership effectiveness. The resulting lists of traits are then compared to those of potential leaders to assess their likelihood of success or failure.

Scholars taking the trait approach attempted to identify physiological (appearance, height, and weight), demographic (age, education and socioeconomic background), personality, self-confidence, and aggressiveness), intellective (intelligence, decisiveness, judgment, and knowledge), task-related (achievement drive, initiative, and persistence), and social characteristics (sociability and cooperativeness) with leader emergence and leader effectiveness.

Successful leaders definitely have interests, abilities, and personality traits that are different from those of the less effective leaders. Through many researches conducted in the last three decades of the 20th century, a set of core traits of successful leaders have been identified. These traits are not responsible solely to identify whether a person will be a successful leader or not, but they are essentially seen as preconditions that endow people with leadership potential.

Among the core traits identified are:

- Achievement drive: High level of effort, high levels of ambition, energy and initiative.
- Leadership motivation: an intense desire to lead others to reach shared goals.
- Honesty and integrity: trustworthy, reliable, and open.
- Self-confidence: Belief in one's self, ideas, and ability.
- Cognitive ability: Capable of exercising good judgment, strong analytical abilities, and conceptually skilled.
- Knowledge of business: Knowledge of industry and other technical matters.
- Emotional Maturity: well adjusted, does not suffer from severe psychological disorders.
- Others: charisma, creativity and flexibility.

## Strengths/Advantages of Trait Theory

- It is naturally pleasing theory.
- It is valid as lot of research has validated the foundation and basis of the theory.
- It serves as a yardstick against which the leadership traits of an individual can be assessed.
- It gives a detailed knowledge and understanding of the leader element in the leadership process.

## Limitations of the Trait Theory

- There is bound to be some subjective judgment in determining who is regarded as a 'good' or 'successful' leader.
- The list of possible traits tends to be very long. More than 100 different traits of successful leaders in various leadership positions have been identified. These descriptions are simply generalities.
- There is also a disagreement over which traits are the most important for an effective leader.
- The model attempts to relate physical traits such as, height and weight, to effective leadership. Most of these factors relate to situational factors. For example, a minimum weight and height might be necessary to perform the tasks efficiently in a military leadership position. In business organizations, these are not the requirements to be an effective leader.
- The theory is very complex.

## Implications of Trait Theory

The trait theory gives constructive information about leadership. It can be applied by people at all levels in all types of organizations. Managers can utilize the information from the theory to evaluate their position in the organization and to assess how their position can be made stronger in the organization. They can get an in-depth understanding of their identity and the way they will affect others in the organization. This theory makes the manager aware of their strengths and weaknesses and thus they get an understanding of how they can develop their leadership qualities.

The traits approach gives rise to questions: whether leaders are born or made; and whether leadership is an art or science. However, these are not mutually exclusive alternatives. Leadership may be something of an art; it still requires the application of special skills and techniques. Even if there are certain inborn qualities that make one a good leader, these natural talents need encouragement and development. A person is not born with self-confidence. Self-confidence is developed, honesty and integrity are a matter of personal choice, motivation to lead comes from within the individual, and the knowledge of business can be acquired. While cognitive ability has its origin partly in genes, it still needs to be developed. None of these ingredients are acquired overnight.

## Behavioral Theories

Behavioral theories of leadership are classified as such because they focus on the study of specific behaviors of a leader. For behavioral theorists, a leader behavior is the best predictor of his leadership influences and as a result, is the best determinant of his or her leadership success.

This behavior-focused approach provides real marketing potential, as behaviors can be conditioned in a manner that one can have a specific response to specific stimuli. As a result, we have gone from the supposition that leaders are born, (Great Man Theory) through to the possibility that we can measure your leadership potential (Trait Theory) via psychometrics measurements and then to the point that anyone can be made a leader (Behavioral Theories) by teaching them the most appropriate behavioral response for any given situation. There are two important Behavioral studies:

## Ohio State University

As leadership studies that were aimed at identifying the appropriate traits didn't yield any conclusive results, a group of people from Ohio State University developed a list of 150 statements from their generated responses that included 1,800 hundred statements. The list was designed to measure nine different behavioral leadership dimensions.

One of the primary purposes of the study was to identify common leadership behaviors. After compiling and analyzing the results, the study led to the conclusion that there were two groups of behaviors that were strongly correlated. These were defined as Consideration (People Oriented behavioral Leaders) and Initiating Structure (Task Oriented Leaders).

### Task Oriented Leaders

The task concerned leaders are focusing their behaviors on the organizational structure, the operating procedures and they like to keep control. Task-oriented leaders are still concern with their staff motivation; however it's not their main concern. They will favour behaviors that are in line with:

- Initiating,
- Organizing,
- Clarifying,
- Information Gathering.

### People Oriented Leaders

The people oriented leaders are focusing their behaviors on ensuring that the inner needs of the people are satisfied. Thus they will seek to motivate their staff through emphasizing the human relation. People oriented leaders still focus on the task and the results; they just achieve them through different means. Leaders with a people focus will have behaviors that are in line with:

- Encouraging,

- Observing,
- Listening,
- Coaching and Mentoring.

## University of Michigan

Lead by the famous organizational psychologist, Dr. Rensis Likert, the leadership studies at the University of Michigan identified three characteristics of effective leadership; two of which were previously observed in studies that had been conducted at Ohio State University. The study showed that task and relationship-oriented behaviors weren't of major significance within the world of organizational psychology. However it was the third observation that introduced a new concept, one of participative leadership.

## The Blake-Mouton Managerial Grid

The Blake-Mouton Managerial Grid was published in 1964, and it highlights the most appropriate style to use, based on concern for people and concern for production/tasks.

With a people-oriented style, focus is on organizing, supporting, and developing team members. This participatory style encourages good teamwork and creative collaboration.

With task-oriented leadership, focus is on getting the job done. We define the work and the roles required, put structures in place, and plan, organize, and monitor work.

According to this model, the best style to use is one that has both a high concern for people and a high concern for the task – it argues that you should aim for both, rather than trying to offset one against the other.

## Understanding the Model

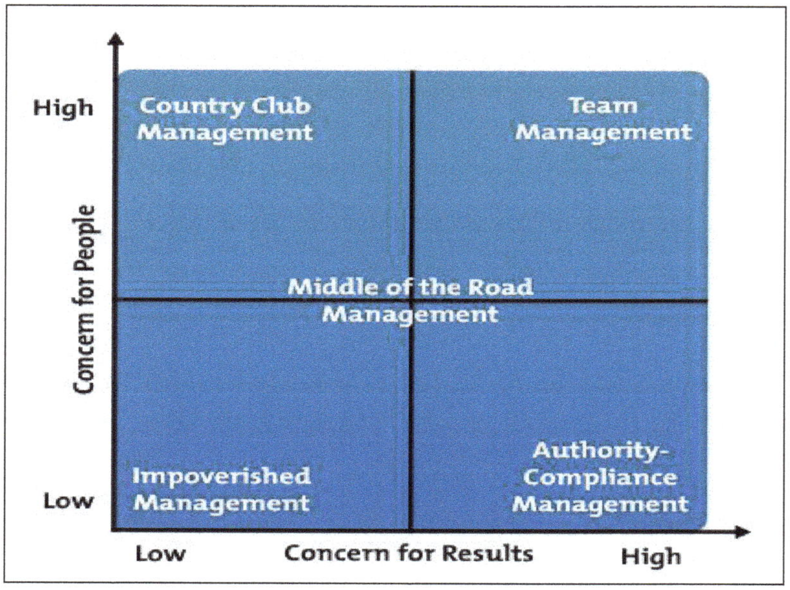


The Blake Mouton Managerial Grid.

The Managerial Grid is based on two behavioral dimensions:

- Concern for People: This is the degree to which a leader considers the needs of team members, their interests, and areas of personal development when deciding how best to accomplish a task.
- Concern for Results: This is the degree to which a leader emphasizes concrete objectives, organizational efficiency and high productivity when deciding how best to accomplish a task.

Using the axis to plot leadership 'concerns for results' versus 'concerns for people', Blake and Mouton defined the following five leadership styles:

### Impoverished Management – Low Results/Low People

This leader is mostly ineffective. He/she has neither a high regard for creating systems for getting the job done, nor for creating a work environment that is satisfying and motivating. The result is disorganization, dissatisfaction and disharmony.

### Country Club Management – High People/Low Results

This style of leader is most concerned about the needs and feelings of members of his/her team. These people operate under the assumption that as long as team members are happy and secure then they will work hard. What tends to result is a work environment that is very relaxed and fun but where production suffers due to lack of direction and control.

### Authority-compliance Management – High Results/Low People

Also known as Authoritarian or "Produce or Perish" Leaders, people in this category believe that employees are simply a means to an end. Employee needs are always secondary to the need for efficient and productive workplaces. This type of leader is very autocratic, has strict work rules, policies, and procedures, and views punishment as the most effective means to motivate employees.

### Middle-of-the-road Management – Medium Results/Medium People

This style seems to be a balance of the two competing concerns, and it may at first appear to be an ideal compromise. Therein lies the problem, though: When you compromise, you necessarily give away a bit of each concern, so that neither production nor people needs are fully met. Leaders who use this style settle for average performance and often believe that this is the most anyone can expect.

### Team Leadership – High Production/High People

According to the Blake Mouton model, this is the best managerial style. These leaders stress production needs and the needs of the people equally highly.

## Contingency Theories

These theories are based on the idea that the leader's ability to lead is a contingent upon various situational factors, including the leader's preferred style, the capabilities and behaviors of the followers and also various other situational factors.

Contingency theories are a class of behavioral theory that tells there is no best way of leading and that a leadership style that is effective in some situations may not be successful in others. The important contingency theories are:

## Fiedler's Contingency Model

This theory was developed by Fred E. Fiedler. This is the first comprehensive contingency theory of leadership. He believes that leader effectiveness depends upon both the leaders personality and the situation. Certain leaders are effective in one situation but not in others.

## Least preferred Co-worker (LPC) Scale

Fiedler identified the a Least Preferred Co-Worker scoring for leaders by asking them first to think of a person with which they worked that they would like least to work with again, and then to score the person on a range of scales between positive factors (friendly, helpful, cheerful, etc.) and negative factors (unfriendly, unhelpful, gloomy, etc.). A high LPC leader generally scores the other person as positive and a low LPC leader scores them as negative.

High LPC leaders tend to have close and positive relationships and act in a supportive way, even prioritizing the relationship before the task. Low LPC leaders put the task first and will turn to relationships only when they are satisfied with how the work is going.

Three factors are then identified about the leader, member and the task, as follows:

- Leader-Member Relations: The extent to which the leader has the support and loyalties of followers and relations with them are friendly and cooperative.
- Task structure: The extent to which tasks are standardised, documented and controlled.
- Leader's Position-power: The extent to which the leader has authority to assess follower performance and give reward or punishment.

The best LPC approach depends on a combination of these three. Generally, a high LPC approach is best when leader-member relations are poor, except when the task is unstructured and the leader is weak, in which a low LPC style is better.

The leadership style of the leader, thus, fixed and measured by what he calls the least preferred co-worker (LPC) scale, an instrument for measuring an individual's leadership orientation. The LPC scale asks a leader to think of all the people with whom they have ever worked and then describe the person with whom they have worked least well, using a series of bipolar scales of 1 to 8, such as the following:

| Unfriendly | 1 2 3 4 5 6 7 8 | Friendly |
|---|---|---|

| Uncooperative | 1 2 3 4 5 6 7 8 | Cooperative |
|---|---|---|
| Hostile | 1 2 3 4 5 6 7 8 | Supportive |
| .... | 1 2 3 4 5 6 7 8 | .... |
| Guarded | 1 2 3 4 5 6 7 8 | Open |

A high LPC score suggests that the leader has a "human relations orientation", while a low LPC score indicates a "task orientation". Fiedler assumes that everybody's least preferred co-worker in fact is on average about equally unpleasant. But people who are indeed relationship motivated, tend to describe their least preferred co-workers in a more positive manner, e.g., more pleasant and more efficient. Therefore, they receive higher LPC scores. People who are task motivated, on the other hand, tend to rate their least preferred co-workers in a more negative manner. Therefore, they receive lower LPC scores. So, the Least Preferred Co-worker (LPC) scale is actually not about the least preferred worker at all, instead, it is about the person who takes the test; it is about that person's motivation type.

## Situational Favorableness

According to Fiedler, the ability to control the group situation (the second component of the contingency model) is crucial for a leader. This is because only leaders with situational control can be confident that their orders and suggestions will be carried out by their followers. Leaders who are unable to assume control over the group situation cannot be sure that the members they are leading will execute their commands. Because situational control is critical to leadership efficacy.

The contingency theory allows for predicting the characteristics of the appropriate situations for effectiveness. Three situational components determine the favorableness of situational control:

- Leader-Member Relations: Referring to the degree of mutual trust, respect and confidence between the leader and the subordinates. When leader-member relations in the group are poor, the leader has to shift focus away from the group task in order to regulate behavior and conflict within the group.
- Task Structure: Referring to the extent to which group tasks are clear and structured. When task structure is low (unstructured), group tasks are ambiguous, with no clear solution or correct approach to complete the goal. In contrast, when task structure is high (structured), the group goal is clear, unambiguous and straightforward: members have a clear idea about the how to approach and reach the goal.
- Leader Position Power: Referring to the power inherent in the leader's position itself.

When there is a good leader-member relation, a highly structured task, and high leader position power, the situation is considered a "favorable situation." Fiedler found that low-LPC leaders are more effective in extremely favorable or unfavorable situations, whereas high-LPC leaders perform best in situations with intermediate favourability.

Leaders in high positions of power have the ability to distribute resources among their members, meaning they can reward and punish their followers. Leaders in low position power cannot control resources to the same extent as leaders in high power, and so lack the same degree of situational control.

For example, the CEO of a business has high position power, because she is able to increase and reduce the salary that her employees receive. On the other hand, an office worker in this same business has low position power, because although they may be the leader on a new business deal, they cannot control the situation by rewarding or disciplining their colleagues with salary changes.

## Leader-situation Match and Mismatch

Since personality is relatively stable though it can be changed, the contingency model suggests that improving effectiveness requires changing the situation to fit the leader. This is called "job engineering" or "job restructuring". The organization or the leader may increase or decrease task structure and position power, also training and group development may improve leader-member relations.

Examples:

- Task-oriented leadership would be advisable in natural disaster, like a flood or fire. In an uncertain situation the leader-member relations are usually poor, the task is unstructured, and the position power is weak. The one who emerges as a leader to direct the group's activity usually does not know subordinates personally. The task-oriented leader who gets things accomplished proves to be the most successful. If the leader is considerate (relationship-oriented), they may waste so much time in the disaster, that things get out of control and lives are lost.
- Blue-collar workers generally want to know exactly what they are supposed to do. Therefore, their work environment is usually highly structured. The leader's position power is strong if management backs their decision. Finally, even though the leader may not be relationship-oriented, leader-member relations may be extremely strong if they can gain promotions and salary increases for subordinates. Under these situations the task-oriented style of leadership is preferred over the (considerate) relationship-oriented style.

## Tri-dimensional Leader Effectiveness Model

Depending on employee's competencies in their task areas and commitment to their tasks, leadership style should vary from one person to another. They classified most of the activities of leaders into the following two distinct behavioral dimensions.

## Task Behavior

It is the extent to which leaders are likely to organise and define the roles of the members of their group and to explain what activities each is to do and when, where and how tasks are to be accomplished ; characterised by endeavouring to establish well defined patterns of organisation, channels of communication and ways of getting jobs accomplished.

The leader engages in one way communication with the workers by telling what each worker is to do. The communication is characterised as one way because there is no chance for workers to give feedback to the leader.

## Relationship Behavior

Relationship behavior on the other hand is the extent to which leaders are likely to maintain personal relationships between themselves and members of their group by opening up channels of communication, providing socio emotional support, active listening, psychological strokes, and facilitating behaviors. In this case the leaders and workers engage in two ways communication. There are sufficient opportunities for feedback.

In order to understand a persons leadership style there must be a combination of task and relationship behavior. They are directing/telling, coaching/selling, supporting/participating and delegating.

- Directing/telling: It is known as high task low relationship leadership behaviors directing. When the follower cannot do the job and is not motivated, then the leader takes a highly directive role, telling them what to do and without a great deal of concern for the relationship.
- Coaching/selling: High task-high relationship leadership behavior is referred to as coaching. Leaders still define roles and tasks, but seek ideas and suggestions from the follower. Decisions remain the leader's choice, but communication is much more two way.
- Supporting/Participating: Low task-High relationship leadership behavior is referred to as supporting. Leaders pass day to day decisions, such as task allocation and processes, to the follower. The leader facilitates and takes part in decisions, but control is with the follower. For people who have competence, but lack confidence or motivation does not need much direction because of their skills, but support is necessary to bolster their confidence and motivation.
- Delegating: Finally, low task-low relationship leadership behavior is referred to as delegating. When the follower can do the job and is motivated to do it, then the leader can basically leave them to it, trusting them to get on with the job. The leader allows group members considerable autonomy in completing the task. In the tri dimensional model it shows that the effectiveness of leaders depends on how appropriate their leadership style is to the situation in which they operate. The added effectiveness dimension also attempts to integrate the concepts of leader style with situation demands of a specific environment. So where the style is appropriate to a given situation it will be deemed effective, and where it is not appropriate it will be concluded ineffective.

## Leader Member Exchange Theory

Leader-Member Exchange Theory, also called LMX or Vertical Dyad Linkage Theory, describes how leaders in groups maintain their position through a series of tacit exchange agreements with their members.

## In-group and Out-group

In particular, leaders often have a special relationship with an inner circle of trusted lieutenants, assistants and advisors, to whom they give high levels of responsibility, decision influence, and access to resources. This in-group pay for their position. They work harder, are more committed to task objectives, and share more administrative duties. They are also expected to be fully committed and loyal to their leader. The out-group, on the other hand, are given low levels of choice or influence.

This also puts constraints upon the leader. They have to nurture the relationship with their inner circle whilst balancing giving them power with ensuring they do not have enough to strike out on their own.

## The LMX Process

These relationships, if they are going to happen, start very soon after a person joins the group and follow three stages.

## Role Taking

The member joins the team and the leader assesses their abilities and talents. Based on this, the leader may offer them opportunities to demonstrate their capabilities. Another key factor in this stage is the discovery by both parties of how the other likes to be respected.

## Role Making

In the second phase, the leader and member take part in an unstructured and informal negotiation whereby a role is created for the member and the often-tacit promise of benefit and power in return for dedication and loyalty takes place.

Trust-building is very important in this stage, and any felt betrayal, especially by the leader, can result in the member being relegated to the out-group.

This negotiation includes relationship factors as well as pure work-related ones, and a member who is similar to the leader in various ways is more likely to succeed. This perhaps explains why mixed gender relationships regularly are less successful than same-gender ones (it also affects the seeking of respect in the first stage). The same effect also applies to cultural and racial differences.

## Routinization

In this phase, a pattern of ongoing social exchange between the leader and the member becomes established.

## Success Factors

Successful members are thus similar in many ways to the leader (which perhaps explains why many senior teams are all white, male, middle-class and middle-aged). They work hard at building and sustaining trust and respect.

To help this, they are empathetic, patient, reasonable, sensitive, and are good at seeing the viewpoint of other people (especially the leader). Aggression, sarcasm and an egocentric view are keys to the out-group wash-room.

The overall quality of the LMX relationship varies with several factors. Curiously, it is better when the challenge of the job is extremely high or extremely low. The size of the group, financial resource availability and the overall workload are also important.

## Onwards and Upwards

The principle works upwards as well. The leader also gains power by being a member of their manager's inner circle, which then can then share on downwards. People at the bottom of an organization with unusual power may get it from an unbroken chain of circles up to the hierarchy.

## Path-goal Theory

The path-goal theory, also known as the path-goal theory of leader effectiveness or the path-goal model, is a leadership theory developed by Robert House, an Ohio State University graduate, in 1971 and revised in 1996. The theory states that a leader's behavior is contingent to the satisfaction, motivation and performance of her or his subordinates. The revised version also argues that the leader engages in behaviors that complement subordinate's abilities and compensate for deficiencies.

The path-goal model can be classified as a Transaction leadership theory. According to the first of all theory, the manager's job is viewed as guiding workers to choose the best paths to reach their goals, as well as the organizational goals. The theory argues that leaders will have to engage in different types of leadership behavior depending on the nature and the demands of a particular situation. It is the leader's job to assist followers in attaining goals and to provide the direction and support needed to ensure that their goals are compatible with the organization's goals.

A leader's behavior is acceptable to subordinates when viewed as a source of satisfaction, and motivational when need satisfaction is contingent on performance, and the leader facilitates, coaches, and rewards effective performance. The original path-goal theory identifies achievement-oriented, directive, participative, and supportive leader behaviors:

- The directive path-goal clarifying leader behavior refers to situations where the leader lets followers know what is expected of them and tells them how to perform their tasks. The theory argues that this behavior has the most positive effect when the subordinates' role and task demands are ambiguous and intrinsically satisfying.
- The achievement-oriented leader behavior refers to situations where the leader sets challenging goals for followers, expects them to perform at their highest level, and shows confidence in their ability to meet this expectation. Occupations in which the achievement motive was most predominant were technical jobs, sales persons, scientists, engineers, and entrepreneurs.
- The participative leader behavior involves leaders consulting with followers and asking for their suggestions before making a decision. This behavior is predominant when subordinates are highly personally involved in their work.
- The supportive leader behavior is directed towards the satisfaction of subordinates needs and preferences. The leader shows concern for the followers' psychological well being. This

behavior is especially needed in situations in which tasks or relationships are psychologically or physically distressing.

Path-goal theory assumes that leaders are flexible and that they can change their style, as situations require. The theory proposes two contingency variables, such as environment and follower characteristics, that moderate the leader behavior-outcome relationship.

Environment is outside the control of the follower-task structure, authority system, and work group. Environmental factors determine the type of leader behavior required if the follower outcomes are to be maximized. Follower characteristics are the locus of control, experience, and perceived ability. Personal characteristics of subordinates determine how the environment and leader are interpreted. Effective leaders clarify the path to help their followers achieve goals and make the journey easier by reducing roadblocks and pitfalls. Research demonstrates that employee performance and satisfaction are positively influenced when the leader compensates for the shortcomings in either the employee or the work setting. This theory is useful because it reminds leaders that their central purpose as a leader is to help subordinates define and reach their goals in an efficient manner.

## Leader-participation Model

The Vroom-Yetton-Jago model or Leader-Participation Model is a contingency approach to group decision making that is designed specifically to help leaders select the best approach to making decisions. The model identifies different ways a decision can be made by considering the degree of follower participation. It proposes a method for leaders to select the right approach to making a decision in a given set of circumstances.

The Vroom-Yetton-Jago model defines five different decision approaches that a leader can use. In order of participation from least to most, these are:

- AI – Autocratic Type 1: Decisions are made completely by the leader. Leaders make the decision on their own with whatever information is available.
- AII – Autocratic Type 2: The decision is still made by the leader alone, but the leader collects information from the followers. Followers play no other role in the decision- making process.
- CI – Consultative Type 1: The leader seeks input from select followers individually based on their relevant knowledge. Followers do not meet each other, and the leader's decision may or may not reflect followers' influence.
- CII – Consultative Type 2: Similar to CI, except the leader shares the problem with relevant followers as a group and seeks their ideas and suggestions. The followers are involved in the decision, but the leader still makes the decision.
- GII – Group-based Type 2: The entire group works through the problem with the leader. A decision is made by the followers in collaboration with the leader. In a GII decision, leaders are not at liberty to make a decision on their own.

The following questions must be answered to determine the appropriate leadership style in the leader participation model:

- Is there a quality requirement? Is the nature of the solution critical? Are there technical or rational grounds for selecting among possible solutions?
- Do I have sufficient information to make a high-quality decision?
- Is the problem structured? Are the alternative courses of action and methods for their evaluation known?
- Is acceptance of the decision by subordinates critical to its implementation?
- If I were to make the decision by myself, is it reasonably certain that it would be accepted by my subordinates?
- Do my subordinates share the organizational goals to be met by solving this problem?
- Is conflict among subordinates likely in obtaining the preferred solution?

By answering the questions honestly, the decision tree provides the leader with the preferred decision style for the given situation.

## Recent Appraoches to Leadership Theories

### Transformational Leadership

The leadership frameworks discussed so far are all useful in different situations, however, in business, "transformational leadership" is often the most effective style to use.

Transformational leaders have integrity and high emotional intelligence. They motivate people with a shared vision of the future, and they communicate well. They're also typically self-aware, authentic, empathetic, and humble.

Transformational leaders inspire their team members because they expect the best from everyone, and they hold themselves accountable for their actions. They set clear goals, and they have good conflict-resolution skills. This leads to high productivity and engagement.

However, leadership is not a "one size fits all" thing; often, you must adapt your approach to fit the situation. This is why it's useful to develop a thorough understanding of other leadership frameworks and styles; after all, the more approaches you're familiar with, the more flexible you can be.

### Charismatic Leadership

Charismatic leadership resembles transformational leadership: both types of leaders inspire and motivate their team members.

The difference lies in their intent. Transformational leaders want to transform their teams and organizations, while leaders who rely on charisma often focus on themselves and their own ambitions, and they may not want to change anything.

Charismatic leaders might believe that they can do no wrong, even when others warn them about the path that they're on.

## Transactional Leadership

This style starts with the idea that team members agree to obey their leader when they accept a job. The "transaction" usually involves the organization paying team members in return for their effort and compliance on a short-term task. The leader has a right to "punish" team members if their work doesn't meet an appropriate standard.

Transactional leadership is present in many business leadership situations, and it does offer some benefits. For example, it clarifies everyone's roles and responsibilities. And, because transactional leadership judges team members on performance, people who are ambitious or who are motivated by external rewards – including compensation – often thrive.

The downside of this style is that, on its own, it can be chilling and amoral, and it can lead to high staff turnover. It also has serious limitations for knowledge-based or creative work.

As a result, team members can often do little to improve their job satisfaction.

## Transformational Leadership

According to Hodgetts and Luttans, transformational leaders are visionary agents with a mission who are capable of motivating their followers to accept new goals and new ways of doing things. Over the last 30 years, transformational leadership has become one of the most prominent theories of organizational behavior. Transformational leadership has been defined by the ability of the leader to create a shared vision and a strong identification with team members that is based on more than just rewarding completion of project activities. Through this shared vision, the transformational leader is then able to mobilize commitment and transcendent performance of both the individual and the project as a whole. Such leaders are said to show charisma, as a means of motivating others to integrate into the collective vision, and a strong consideration of and support for individual team member needs.

In contrast to leadership based on individual gain and the exchange of rewards for effort, transformational leaders direct and inspire employee effort by raising their awareness of the importance of organizational values and outcomes. In doing so, such leaders activate the higher-order needs of their employees and encourage them to transcend their own self-interest for the sake of the organization and its clientele.

Research not only has validated the existence of transformational leadership but also consistently has linked the practice of these transformational leadership behaviors with employee performance and satisfaction. Transformational leaders use idealized influence, inspiration and motivation, intellectual stimulation and individualized consideration to achieve superior results.

## Leadership Substitutes

Leadership substitutes is one of the more recent theories on leadership. Although not many studies havebeen done so far to test them, these theories suggest certain different and interesting ways of looking at leadership.

The concept of substitutes for leadership was developed because leadership models and theories do not account for situation s in which leadershipis not needed. They simply try to specify what kind of a leader behavior is appropriate. The substitutes concept, hoever identifies situations in which leader behaviors are neutralised or replaced by characteristics of the subordinate, the task, and the organisation.

Under certain circumstances, leaders and leadership become unnecessary because they are no longer necessary for employees high performance and satisfaction.

Factors that can substitute for leadership include the following:

- Certain individual characteristics, including ability, knowledge, experience, training, independence, and indifference toward organisational rewards.
- Certain task characters, including routineness, high structure, frequent feedback, and intrinsic satisfaction.
- Certain organisation characteristics, including clear plans and goals, rules and procedures, cohesive work groups, rigid reward structure, and physical distance between leader and subordinates.

The distinction between maintenance focus and task focus is pertinent also when it comes to leadership of a team. Maintenance-focused leaders tend to pay attention to the cohesion of the group, ensuring that it remains harmonious while working towards team objectives. They are good at resolving conflict, and can delegate and supervise effectively. Such leaders, however, may be ineffective in some situations, such as when there is strong opposition within the group. Task-focused leaders, on the other hand, are focused on achieving objectives whatever the cost and they can drive change through resistance. They are not too concerned about cohesion or harmonious cooperation, focusing, instead, on achieving results. Their directive skills work best with subordinates rather than equals, and, generally, leading self-motivated people is not their strong point.

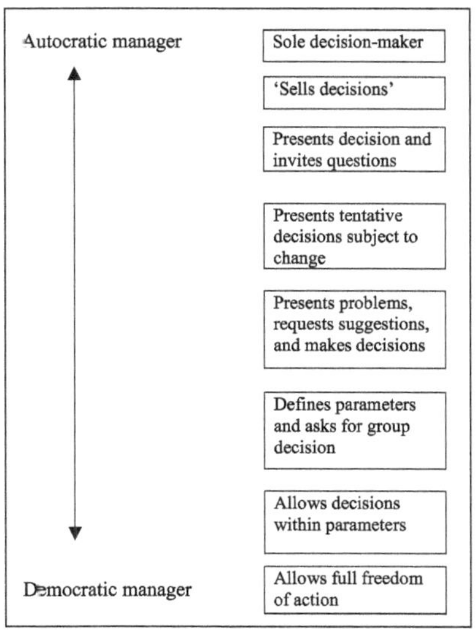


Leadership continuum.

Regardless of whether their focus is to maintain cohesion or to initiate tasks, effective team leaders share certain characteristics. According to Qubein, these common characteristics are:

- They value people: they acknowledge the importance and contribution of others.

- They listen actively: they make an effort to understand the needs and desires of others.
- They are tactful: they criticize sparingly, constructively and diplomatically.
- They give credit: they praise others and their contributions publicly.
- They are consistent: they control their personal moods, and are fair in their exchanges with others.
- They admit mistakes: they take the blame for errors they committed.
- They have a sense of humour: they maintain a pleasant disposition and pleasant manner.
- They set a good example: they follow their own regulations.

Like other managers, team leaders can exhibit styles of direction with varying degrees of dominance or control. These styles vary from contexts where the leader enforces his/her decision on team members, to the opposite extreme where the leader listens to all parties and allows for unlimited individual initiative. In many cases the leader's powers and responsibilities are inscribed in the organization's management structure, but, as in most facets of human behavior, they also depend on individual leader's interpretation of this structure. According to the leadership continuum model first proposed by R Tannebaum and W. H. Schmidt, leadership strategies range from autocratic to laissez-faire, and comprise several steps in- between. The leadership continuum is shown in the following diagram.

## References


- Organizational-behavior: investopedia.com, Retrieved 18 May, 2019
- Organizational-behaviour-definition-characteristics-and-nature, organization-organizational-behaviour- 63741: yourarticlelibrary.com, Retrieved 22 June, 2019
- What-is-organizational-behavior, mba: online.usi.edu, Retrieved 16 April, 2019
- Deery, S., Rayton, B., Walsh, J. & Kinnie, N. (2016). The Costs of Exhibiting Organizational Citizenship Behavior. Human Resource Management. doi: 10.1002/hrm.21815
- Organizational-behavior-management: online.aurora.edu, Retrieved 26 March, 2019
- Leadership: businessjargons.com, Retrieved 15 January, 2019
- Robbins, Stephen; Judge, Timothy (2016). Organizational Behavior (17 ed.). Pearson Education. ISBN 978-0-13-410398-3

# 4

# Human Resource Management

Human resource management includes recruitment and selection of employees, providing training, improving the performance of employees and maintaining relations with them. This chapter closely examines these aspects associated with human resource management to provide an extensive understanding of the subject.

Human resources is used to describe both the people who work for a company or organization and the department responsible for managing resources related to employees. The term human resources was first coined in the 1960s when the value of labor relations began to garner attention and when notions such as motivation, organizational behavior, and selection assessments began to take shape.

Human resource management is a contemporary, umbrella term used to describe the management and development of employees in an organization. Also called personnel or talent management (although these terms are a bit antiquated), human resource management involves overseeing all things related to managing an organization's human capital.

Human resource management is therefore focused on a number of major areas, including:

- Recruiting and staffing.
- Compensation and benefits.
- Training and learning.
- Labor and employee relations.
- Organization development.

Due to the many areas of human resource management, it is typical for professionals in this field to possess specific expertise in one or more areas. Just a few of the related career titles for HR professionals include:

- Training development specialist.
- HR manager.

- Benefits specialist.
- Human resource generalist.
- Employment services manager.
- Compensation and job analysis specialist.
- Training and development manager.
- Recruiter.
- Benefits counselor.
- Personnel analyst.

Human resource management involves developing and administering programs that are designed to increase the effectiveness of an organization or business. It includes the entire spectrum of creating, managing, and cultivating the employer-employee relationship.

For most organizations, agencies, and businesses, the human resources department is responsible for:

- Managing job recruitment, selection, and promotion.
- Developing and overseeing employee benefits and wellness programs.
- Developing, promoting, and enforcing personnel policies.
- Promoting employee career development and job training.
- Providing orientation programs for new hires.
- Providing guidance regarding disciplinary actions.
- Serving as a primary contact for work-site injuries or accidents.

Human resource management is about:

- Addressing current employee concerns: Unlike company managers who oversee the day-to-day work of employees, HR departments deal with employee concerns such as benefits, pay, employee investments, pension plans, and training. Their work may also include settling conflicts between employees or between employees and their managers.
- Acquiring new employees: The human resource management team recruits potential employees, oversees the hiring process (background checks, drug testing, etc.), and provides new employee orientation.
- Managing the employee separation process: The HR management team must complete a specific set of tasks if an employee quits, is fired, or is laid off. Paperwork must be completed to ensure that the process was completed legally. Severance pay may be offered or negotiated, benefits must be settled, and access to company resources must be

severed via the collection of keys, badges, computers, or sensitive materials from the employee.

- Improving morale: Effective HR teams encourage company employees to do their best, which contributes to the overall success of the company. Their work often involves rewarding employees for good performance and creating a positive work environment.

Human resource management (HRM or HR) is the strategic approach to the effective management of people in a company or organization such that they help their business gain a competitive advantage. It is designed to maximize employee performance in service of an employer's strategic objectives. Human resource management is primarily concerned with the management of people within organizations, focusing on policies and systems. HR departments are responsible for overseeing employee-benefits design, employee recruitment, training and development, performance appraisal, and reward management, such as managing pay and benefit systems. HR also concerns itself with organizational change and industrial relations, or the balancing of organizational practices with requirements arising from collective bargaining and governmental laws.

The overall purpose of human resources (HR) is to ensure that the organization is able to achieve success through people. HR professionals manage the human capital of an organization and focus on implementing policies and processes. They can specialize in finding, recruiting, training, and developing employees, as well as maintaining employee relations or benefits. Training and development professionals ensure that employees are trained and have continuous development. This is done through training programs, performance evaluations, and reward programs. Employee relations deals with the concerns of employees when policies are broken, such as cases involving harassment or discrimination. Managing employee benefits includes developing compensation structures, parental leave programs, discounts, and other benefits for employees. On the other side of the field are HR generalists or business partners. These HR professionals could work in all areas or be labor relations representatives working with unionized employees.

HR is a product of the human relations movement of the early 20th Century, when researchers began documenting ways of creating business value through the strategic management of the workforce. It was initially dominated by transactional work, such as payroll and benefits administration, but due to globalization, company consolidation, technological advances, and further research, HR as of 2015 focuses on strategic initiatives like mergers and acquisitions, talent management, succession planning, industrial and labor relations, and diversity and inclusion. In the current global work environment, most companies focus on lowering employee turnover and on retaining the talent and knowledge held by their workforce. New hiring not only entails a high cost but also increases the risk of a new employee not being able to adequately replace the position of the previous employee. HR departments strive to offer benefits that will appeal to workers, thus reducing the risk of losing employee commitment and psychological ownership.

## Practice

### Business Function

Dave Ulrich lists the functions of HR as: aligning HR and business strategy, re-engineering organization processes, listening and responding to employees, and managing transformation and change.

At the macro-level, HR is in charge of overseeing organizational leadership and culture. HR also ensures compliance with employment and labor laws, which differ by geography, and often oversees health, safety, and security. Based on the geographic location, there are various laws in place. There are several federal laws that are crucial for HR managers to be familiar with in order to protect both their company and its employees. Important federal laws and regulations include The Fair Labor Standards Act, which includes establishing a minimum wage and protecting the right for certain workers to earn overtime. The Federal Civil Rights Law protects against discrimination and prohibits making any hiring or firing decision based on race, age, sex, and gender. The Family and Medical Leave Act gives eligible employees up to twelve weeks of unpaid leave for family and medical reasons. Ensuring the company is compliant with all laws and regulations is an important aspect of HR and will protect the company from any sort of 'legal liability'. In circumstances where employees desire and are legally authorized to hold a collective bargaining agreement, HR will typically also serve as the company's primary liaison with the employee's representatives (usually a labor union). Consequently, HR, usually through representatives, engages in lobbying efforts with governmental agencies (e.g., in the United States, the United States Department of Labor and the National Labor Relations Board) to further its priorities.

Human Resource Management has four basic functions: staffing, training and development, motivation, and maintenance. Staffing is the recruitment and selection of potential employees, done through interviewing, applications, networking, etc. There are two main factors to staffing: attracting talented recruits and hiring resources. HR Managers must create detailed recruitment strategies and have a plan of action to put forward when recruiting. Next, managers can put strategies into place through hiring resources, by extending out to find the best possible recruits for the team. Recruiting is very competitive since every company wants the best candidates. Using tactics such as mass media can grab the attention of prospective recruits. Training and development is the next step and involves a continuous process of training and developing competent and adapted employees. Here, motivation is seen as key to keeping employees highly productive. This includes employee benefits, performance appraisals, and rewards. Employee benefits, appraisals, and rewards are all encouragements to bring forward the best employees. The last function, maintenance, involves keeping the employees' commitment and loyalty to the organization. Some businesses globalize and form more diverse teams. HR departments have the role of making sure that these teams can function and that people can communicate across cultures and across borders. The discipline may also engage in mobility management, especially for expatriates; and it is frequently involved in the merger and acquisition process. HR is generally viewed as a support function to the business, helping to minimize costs and reduce risk.

In startup companies, trained professionals may perform HR duties. In larger companies, an entire functional group is typically dedicated to the discipline, with staff specializing in various HR tasks and functional leadership engaging in strategic decision-making across the business. To train practitioners for the profession, institutions of higher education, professional associations, and companies have established programs of study dedicated explicitly to the duties of the function. HR is also a field of research study that is popular within the fields of management and industrial/organizational psychology.

One of the frequent challenges of HRM is dealing with the notion of unitarism (seeing a company as a cohesive whole, in which both employers and employees should work together for a common good) and securing a long-term partnership of employees and employers with common interests.

## Careers

There are half a million HR practitioners in the United States and millions more worldwide. The Chief HR Officer or HR Director is the highest ranking HR executive in most companies. He or she typically reports directly to the Chief Executive Officer and works with the Board of Directors on CEO succession.

Within companies, HR positions generally fall into one of two categories: generalist and specialist. Generalists support employees directly with their questions, grievances, and work on a range of projects within the organization. They "may handle all aspects of human resources work, and thus require an extensive range of knowledge. The responsibilities of human resources generalists can vary widely, depending on their employer's needs." Specialists, conversely, work in a specific HR function. Some practitioners will spend an entire career as either a generalist or a specialist while others will obtain experiences from each and choose a path later. The position of HR manager has been chosen as one of the best jobs in the US, with a #4 ranking by CNN Money in 2006 and a #20 ranking by the same organization in 2009, due to its pay, personal satisfaction, job security, future growth, and benefit to society.

Human resource consulting is a related career path where individuals may work as advisers to companies and complete tasks outsourced from companies. In 2007, there were 950 HR consultancies globally, constituting a US$18.4 billion market. The top five revenue generating firms were Mercer, Ernst & Young, Deloitte, Watson Wyatt (now part of Towers Watson), Aon (now merged with Hewitt), and PwC consulting. For 2010, HR consulting was ranked the #43 best job in America by CNN Money.

Some individuals with PhDs in HR and related fields, such as industrial and organizational psychology and management, are professors who teach HR principles at colleges and universities. They are most often found in Colleges of Business in departments of HR or Management. Many professors conduct research on topics that fall within the HR domain, such as financial compensation, recruitment, and training.

## Virtual Human Resources

Technology has a significant impact on HR practices. Utilizing technology makes information more accessible within organizations, eliminates time doing administrative tasks, allows businesses to function globally, and cuts costs. Information technology has improved HR practices in the following areas:

### E-recruiting

Recruiting has mostly been influenced by information technology. In the past, recruiters relied on printing in publications and word of mouth to fill open positions. HR professionals were not able to post a job in more than one location and did not have access to millions of people, causing the lead time of new hires to be drawn out and tiresome. With the use of e-recruiting tools, HR professionals can post jobs and track applicants for thousands of jobs in various locations all in one place. Interview feedback, background checks and drug tests, and onboarding can all be viewed online. This helps HR professionals keep track of all of their open jobs and applicants in a way that is faster and easier than before. E-recruiting also helps eliminate limitations of geographic location. Jobs can be posted and seen by anyone with internet access. In addition to recruiting portals, HR professionals often have social media presence through websites such as LinkedIn, allowing them to attract employees through the internet. On social media, they can help build the company's brand by posting company news and photos of company events.

### Human Resources Information Systems

HR professionals generally handle large amounts of paperwork on a daily basis, ranging from department transfer requests to confidential employee tax forms. Forms must be on file for a considerable period of time. The use of Human Resources Information Systems (HRIS) has made it possible for companies to store and retrieve files in an electronic format for people within the organization to access when needed, thereby eliminating the need for physical files and freeing up space within the office. HRIS also allows for information to be accessed in a timelier manner; files can be accessible within seconds. Having all of the information in one place also allows for professionals to analyze data quickly and across multiple locations because the information is in a centralized location.

### Training

Technology allows HR professionals to train new staff members in a more efficient manner. This gives employees the ability to access onboarding and training programs from virtually anywhere. This eliminates the need for trainers to meet new hires face-to-face when completing necessary paperwork for new employees. Training in virtual classrooms makes it possible for HR professionals to train a large number of employees quickly and to assess their progress through computerized testing programs. Some employers choose to incorporate an instructor with virtual training so that new hires are receiving training considered vital to the role. Employees have greater control over their own learning and development; they can engage in training at a time and place of their choosing, which can help them manage their work-life balance. Managers are able to track the training through the internet, which can help to reduce redundancy in training and training costs.

## Recruitment

Recruitment refers to the overall process of attracting, shortlisting, selecting and appointing suitable candidates for jobs (either permanent or temporary) within an organization. Recruitment can also refer to processes involved in choosing individuals for unpaid roles. Managers, human resource generalists and recruitment specialists may be tasked with carrying out recruitment, but in some cases public-sector employment agencies, commercial recruitment agencies, or specialist search consultancies are used to undertake parts of the process. Internet-based technologies which support all aspects of recruitment have become widespread.

## Process

- Job analysis for new jobs or substantially changed jobs, a job analysis might be undertaken to document the knowledge, skills, abilities and other characteristics (KSAOs) required or sought for the job. From these, the relevant information is captured in a person specification.
- Sourcing is the process of attracting or identifying candidates.
- Screening and selection.

## Sourcing

Sourcing is the use of one or more strategies to attract or identify candidates to fill job vacancies. It may involve internal and/or external recruitment advertising, using appropriate media, such as job portals, local or national newspapers, social media, business media, specialist recruitment media, professional publications, window advertisements, job centers, or in a variety of ways via the internet.

Alternatively, employers may use recruitment consultancies or agencies to find otherwise scarce candidates—who, in many cases, may be content in the current positions and are not actively looking to move. This initial research for candidates—also called name generation—produces contact information for potential candidates, whom the recruiter can then discreetly contact and screen.

## Referral Recruitment Programs

Referral recruitment programs allow both outsiders and employees to refer candidates for filling job openings. Online, they can be implemented by leveraging social networks.

## Employee Referral

An employee referral is a candidate recommended by an existing employee. This is sometimes referred to as Referral recruitment. Encouraging existing employees to select and recruit suitable candidates results in:

- Improved candidate quality ('fit'), and retention (which in the call center industry is around 45% annually). The one-to-one direct relationship between the candidate and the referring employee and the exchange of knowledge that takes place allows the candidate to develop a strong understanding of the company, its business and the application and recruitment process. The candidate is thereby enabled to assess their own suitability and likelihood of success, including "fitting in".

- Reduces the considerable cost of third parties service providers who would have previously conducted the screening and selection process. An op-ed in Crain's in April 2013 recommended that companies look to employee referral to speed the recruitment process for purple squirrels, which are rare candidates considered to be "perfect" fits for open positions.
- The employee typically receives a referral bonus, and is widely acknowledged as being cost effective. The Global Employee Referral Index 2013 Survey found that 92% of the participants reported employee referrals as one of the top recruiting sources for recruiting.
- As candidate quality improves and interview to job offer conversion rates increase, the amount of time spent interviewing decreases, which means the company's Human Resources headcount can be streamlined and be used more efficiently. Marketing and advertising expenditures decrease as existing employees source potential candidates from the existing personal networks of friends, family and associates. By contrast, recruiting through 3rd-party recruiting agencies incurs a 20–25% agency finder's fee – which can top $25K for an employee with $100K annual salary. Referral recruiting can be free (or cost a fraction).

There is, however, a risk of less corporate creativity: An "overly homogeneous" workforce is at risk for "fails to produce novel ideas or innovations."

## Social Network Referral

Initially, responses to mass-emailing of job announcements to those within employees' social network slowed the screening process.

Two ways in which this improved are:

- Making available screen tools for employees to use, although this interferes with the "work routines of already time-starved employees".
- "when employees put their reputation on the line for the person they are recommending".

## Screening and Selection

Various psychological tests can assess a variety of KSAOs, including literacy. Assessments are also available to measure physical ability. Recruiters and agencies may use applicant tracking systems to filter candidates, along with software tools for psychometric testing and performance-based assessment. In many countries, employers are legally mandated to ensure their screening and selection processes meet equal opportunity and ethical standards.

Employers are likely to recognize the value of candidates who encompass soft skills, such as interpersonal or team leadership, and the level of drive needed to stay engaged. In fact, many companies, including multinational organizations and those that recruit from a range of nationalities, are also often concerned about whether candidate fits the prevailing company culture and organization as a whole. Companies and recruitment agencies are now turning to video screening as a way to notice these skills without the need to invite the candidates in physical. Screening as a practice for hiring has undergone continual change over the years and often organizations are using video to maintain the aforementioned standards they set for themselves and the industry.

## Disabled Candidates

The word disability carries few positive connotations for most employers. Research has shown that employer biases tend to improve through first-hand experience and exposure with proper supports for the employee and the employer making the hiring decisions. As for most companies, money and job stability are two of the contributing factors to the productivity of a disabled employee, which in return equates to the growth and success of a business. Hiring disabled workers produce more advantages than disadvantages. There is no difference in the daily production of a disabled worker. Given their situation, they are more likely to adapt to their environmental surroundings and acquaint themselves with equipment, enabling them to solve problems and overcome adversity as with other employees. The U.S. IRS grants companies Disabled Access Credit when they meet eligibility criteria.

## Diversity

Many major corporations recognize the need for diversity in hiring to compete successfully in a global economy. The challenge is to avoid recruiting staff who are "in the likeness of existing employees" but also to retain a more diverse workforce and work with inclusion strategies to include them in the organisations.

## Recruitment Process Outsourcing

Recruitment process outsourcing (RPO) is a form of Business process outsourcing (BPO) where a company engages a third party provider to manage all or part of its recruitment process.

## Approaches

Internal recruitment or internal mobility (internal recruiters) refers to the process of a candidate being selected from the existing workforce to take up a new job in the same organization, perhaps as a promotion, or to provide career development opportunity, or to meet a specific or urgent organizational need. Advantages include the organization's familiarity with the employee and their competencies insofar as they are revealed in their current job, and their willingness to trust said employee. It can be quicker and have a lower cost to hire someone internally.

An employee referral program is a system where existing employees recommend prospective candidates for the job offered, and usually, if the suggested candidate is hired, the employee receives a cash bonus.

Niche firms tend to focus on building ongoing relationships with their candidates, as the same candidates may be placed many times throughout their careers. Online resources have developed to help find niche recruiters. Niche firms also develop knowledge on specific employment trends within their industry of focus (e.g., the energy industry) and are able to identify demographic shifts such as aging and its impact on the industry.

Social recruiting is the use of social media for recruiting.

Mobile recruiting is a recruitment strategy that uses mobile technology to attract, engage and convert candidates.

Some recruiters work by accepting payments from job seekers, and in return help them to find a job. This is illegal in some countries, such as in the United Kingdom, in which recruiters must not charge candidates for their services (although websites such as LinkedIn may charge for ancillary job-search-related services). Such recruiters often refer to themselves as "personal marketers" and "job application services" rather than as recruiters.

Using multiple-criteria decision analysis tools such as analytic hierarchy process (AHP) and combining it with conventional recruitment methods provides an added advantage by helping the recruiters to make decisions when there are several diverse criteria to be considered or when the applicants lack past experience; for instance, recruitment of fresh university graduates.

## Multi Tier Recruitment Model

In some companies where the recruitment volume is high, it is common to see a multi tier recruitment model where the different sub-functions are grouped together to achieve efficiency.

An example of a 3 tier recruitment model:

- Tier 1. Contact/Help desk: This tier acts as the first point of contact where recruitment requests are being raised. If the requests are simple to fulfil or are queries in nature, resolution may take place at this tier.
- Tier 2. Administration: This tier manages mainly the administration processes.
- Tier 3. Process: This tier manages the process and how the requests get fulfilled.

## Strategies

A recruitment strategy is a plan an organization enacts to form a recruiting process and establish a candidate pool. An organization uses recruitment strategies to identify a hiring vacancy, establish a timeline, and identify goals throughout the recruitment process. Recruitment strategies are typically the responsibility of the human resources department.

Organizations define their own recruiting strategies to identify who they will recruit, as well as when, where, and how that recruitment should take place. Common recruiting strategies answer the following questions:

- What type of individuals should be targeted?
- What recruitment message should be communicated?
- How can the targeted individuals best be reached?
- When should the recruitment campaign begin?
- What should be the nature of a site visit?

## Practices

Organizations develop recruitment objectives, and the recruitment strategy follows these objectives. Typically, organizations develop pre- and post-hire objectives and incorporate these objectives into a holistic recruitment strategy. Once an organization deploys a recruitment strategy it conducts recruitment activities. This typically starts by advertising a vacant position.

### Professional Associations

There are numerous professional associations for human resources professionals. Such associations typically offer benefits such as member directories, publications, discussion groups, awards, local chapters, vendor relations, government lobbying, and job boards.

Professional associations also offer a recruitment resource for human resources professionals.

## Human Resource Accounting

Human resource accounting is the process of identifying and reporting investments made in the human resources of an organization that are presently unaccounted for in the conventional accounting practices. It is an extension of standard accounting principles. Measuring the value of the human resources can assist organizations in accurately documenting their assets.

### Objectives

The human resource process was established to fulfill a number of objectives within the organization. These include:

- To furnish cost value information for making proper and effective management decisions about acquiring, allocating, developing, and maintaining human resources in order to achieve cost effective organizational objectives.
- To monitor effectively the use of human resources by the management.
- To have an analysis of the Human Asset, i.e. whether such assets are conserved, depleted, or appreciated.
- To aid in the development of management principles and proper decision making for the future, by classifying financial consequences of various practices.

### Methods

Approaches to human resource accounting H.R.A were first developed in 1691. The next approach was developed from 1691-1960, and the third phase was post-1960.

There are two approaches to HRA. Under the cost approach, also called the "human resource cost accounting method" or model, there is an acquisition cost model and a replacement cost model. Under the value approach, there is a present value of future earnings method, a discounted future wage model, and a competitive bidding model.

Considering the pros and cons of various models, Chennai based CA Lakshminarayanan Ramanujam has worked out a simple to use and easy to adopt, unique model titled GiveGET, for the Human Resource Valuation and Accounting, while accounting for PEACE.

## Cost Approach

This approach is also called an acquisition cost model. This method measures the organization's investment in employees using the five parameters: recruiting, acquisition, formal training and familiarization, informal training and informal familiarization, and experience and development. This model suggests that instead of charging the costs to profit and loss statement (p&l) accounting, it should be capitalized in the balance sheet. The process of giving a status of asset to the expenditure item is called capitalization.

In human resource management, it is necessary to amortize the capitalized amount over a period of time. So, here one will take the age of the employee at the time of recruitment and at the time of retirement. Out of these, a few employees may leave the organization before attaining the superannuation. This method is the only method of Human Resource Accounting that is based on sound accounting principles and policies.

## Limitations

- The valuation method is based on the false assumption that the dollar is stable.
- Since the assets cannot be sold there are no independent checks of valuation.
- This method measures only the costs to the organization, but ignores completely any measure of the value of the employee to the organization.
- It is too tedious to gather the related information regarding the human values.
- It may be possible that the employee is already fully trained and there is no need to incur any development, training, or recruitment costs. It will create difficulty for a company to find out CTC according to acquisition model.
- Does not account for software which can reduce the overall cost of human resources from by having integrated software completing the tasks of staff.

## Replacement Cost Approach

This approach measures the cost of replacing an employee. According to Likert (1985) replacement cost includes recruitment, selection, compensation, and training cost (including the income foregone during the training period). The data derived from this method could be useful in deciding whether to dismiss or replace the staff.

## Limitations

Substitution of replacement cost method for historical cost method does little more than update the valuation, at the expense of importing considerably more subjectivity into the measure. This method may also lead to an upwardly biased estimate because an inefficient firm may incur a greater cost to replace an employee.

## Present Value of Future Earnings

Lev and Schwartz proposed an economic valuation of employees based on the present value of future earnings, adjusted for the probability of employees' death/separation/retirement. This method helps in determining what an employee's future contribution is worth today.

## Limitations

- The measure is an objective one because it uses widely based statistics such as census income return and mortality tables.
- The measure assigns more weight to averages than to the value of any specific group or individual.

## Value to the Organization

Hekimian and Jones proposed that when an organization had several divisions seeking the same employee, the employee should be allocated to the highest bidder and the bid price incorporated into that division's investment base. For example, a value of a professional athlete's service is often determined by how much money a particular team, acting in an open competitive market, is willing to pay him or her.

## Limitations

The soundness of the valuation depends wholly on the information, judgment, and impartiality of the bidder.

## Expense Model

According to Mirvis and Mac, this model focuses on attaching dollar estimates to the behavioral outcomes produced by working in an organization. Criteria such as absenteeism, turnover, and job performance are measured using traditional organizational tools, and then costs are estimated for each criterion. For example, in costing labor turnover, dollar figures are attached to separation costs, replacement costs, and training costs.

## Model on Human Resource Accounting

This model prescribes the human resource accounting approach for two categories of employees:

- Employees, who are at strategic, key decision-making positions such as MD, CEO.
- Employees, who execute the decision taken by Top Executives (Vice President, Directors).
- Model arrives value of human resources as sum of below-mentioned three parts:
    - Real capital cost part.

- ◦ Present value of future salary/wages payments.
- ◦ Performance evaluation part.

## Limitations

- Calculation process is lengthy and cumbersome.
- Lev and Schwartz valuation principles have been used at one point of time, so this model contains a weakness from the Lev and Schwartz model.

Other limitations:

- Ravindra Tiwari has prescribed another approach to value human resources at the time of annual appraisal exercise, which suggests valuation of human resources on different appraisal parameters.

Human resource accounting is the accounting methods, systems, and techniques, which coupled with special knowledge and ability, assist personnel management in the valuation of personnel in their knowledge, ability and motivation in the same organization as well as from organization to organization. It means that some employees become a liability instead of becoming a human resource. HRA facilitates decision making about the personnel, i.e. either to keep or to dispense with their services or to provide mega-training. There are many limitations that make the management reluctant to introduce HRA. Some of the attributes are:

- There are no clear cut and specific procedures or guidelines for finding costs and value of human resources of an organization. The systems that are being adopted all have certain drawbacks.
- The period of existence of human resources is uncertain and hence valuing them under uncertainty in the future seems to be unrealistic.
- The much needed empirical evidence is yet to be found to support the hypothesis that HRA as a tool of management facilitates better and effective management of human resources.
- Since human resources are incapable of being owned, retained, and utilized, unlike physical assets, this poses a problem to treat them as assets in the strict sense.
- There is a constant fear of opposition from trade unions as placing a value on employees would make them claim rewards and compensations based on such valuations.
- In spite of all its significance and necessity, tax laws don't recognize human beings as assets.
- There is no universally accepted method of the valuation of human resources.

# Training and Development

Training and development involves improving the effectiveness of organizations and the individuals and teams within them. Training may be viewed as related to immediate changes in organizational effectiveness via organized instruction, while development is related to the progress of longer-term organizational and employee goals. While training and development technically have differing definitions, the two are oftentimes used interchangeably and/or together. Training and development has historically been a topic within applied psychology but has within the last two decades become closely associated with human resources management, talent management, human resources development, instructional design, human factors, and knowledge management.

The first training-related article was published in 1918 in the Journal of Applied Psychology. This explored an undergraduate curriculum designed for applied psychologists. World War II influenced the focus of applied psychology research to be on effectiveness of training programs, particularly in military contexts. By the 1960s and 70s, the field began developing theories and conducting theory-based research because up until that point, the field had been rooted in trial-and-error intervention research. This era also brought along the development of new training methods such as the use of computers, television, case studies, and role playing. The scope of training and development also expanded to include cross-cultural training, focus on the development of the individual employee, and the use of new organization development literature to frame training programs. The 1980s marked a shift to focus on how employees were receiving and implementing training programs, and encouraged the collection of data for evaluation purposes, particularly management training programs. The development piece of training and development became increasingly popular in the 1980s and 90s, with employees more frequently being influenced by the concept of "lifelong learning". It was in this decade that research revealing the impact and importance of fostering a training and development-positive culture (including management and co-worker) was first conducted. The turn of the century brought more research in topics such as team-training, for example cross-training. Cross-training emphasizes training in coworkers' responsibilities.

## Practice

Training and development encompasses three main activities: training, education, and development.

The "stakeholders" in training and development are categorized into several classes. The sponsors of training and development are senior managers. The clients of training and development are business planners. Line managers are responsible for coaching, resources, and performance. The participants are those who actually undergo the processes. The facilitators are Human Resource Management staff. And the providers are specialists in the field. Each of these groups has its own agenda and motivations, which sometimes conflict with the agendas and motivations of the others.

Especially in the last couple decades, training has become more trainee-focused, which allows those being trained more flexibility and active learning opportunities. For example, these active learning techniques include exploratory/discovery learning, error management training, guided exploration, and mastery training. Typical projects in the field include executive and supervisory/

management development, new-employee orientation, professional-skills training, technical/job training, customer-service training, sales-and-marketing training, and health-and-safety training. Training is particularly critical in high-reliability organizations, which rely on high safety standards in order to prevent catastrophic damage to employees, equipment, or the environment (e.g. nuclear power plants, operating rooms).

### Benefits

Training has been used in organizations for the past several decades. Although training and development requires investments of many types, there are cited benefits to integrating training and development into organizations:

- Increased productivity and job performance,
- Skills development,
- Team development,
- Decreasing safety-related accidents.

However, if the training and development is not strategic and pointed at specific goals, it can lead to more harm than good. Needs assessments, especially when the training is being conducted on a large-scale, are frequently conducted in order to gauge what needs to be trained, how it should be trained, and how extensively. Needs assessments in the training and development context often reveal employee and management-specific skills to develop (e.g. for new employees), organizational-wide problems to address (e.g. performance issues), adaptations needed to suit changing environments (e.g. new technology), or employee development needs (e.g. career planning). The degree of effectiveness of training and development programs can be predicted by the needs assessment and how closely the needs were met, the execution of the training (i.e. how effective the trainer was), and trainee characteristics (e.g. motivation, cognitive abilities). Effectiveness of training is typically done on an individual or team-level, with few studies investigating the impacts on organizations.

## Job Performance

Job performance assesses whether a person performs a job well. Job performance, studied academically as part of industrial and organizational psychology, also forms a part of human resources management. Performance is an important criterion for organizational outcomes and success. John P. Campbell describes job performance as an individual-level variable, or something a single person does. This differentiates it from more encompassing constructs such as organizational performance or national performance, which are higher-level variables.

### Features

There are several key features to Campbell's conceptualization of job performance which help clarify what job performance means.

## Outcomes

First, Campbell defines performance as behavior, which is something done by an employee. This concept differentiates performance from outcomes. Outcomes result partially from an individual's performance, but they are also the result of other influences. In other words, there are more factors determine outcomes than just an employee's behaviors and actions.

Campbell allows for exceptions when defining performance as behavior. For instance, he clarifies that performance does not have to be directly observable actions of an individual. It can consist of mental productions such as answers or decisions. However, performance needs to be under the individual's control, regardless of whether the performance of interest is mental or behavioral.

The difference between individual controlled action and outcomes is best conveyed through an example. In a sales job, a favorable outcome is a certain level of revenue generated through the sale of something (merchandise, or some service such as insurance). Revenue can be generated or not, depending on the behavior of employees. When the employee performs this sales job well, he is able to move more merchandise. However, certain factors other than employees' behavior influence revenue generated. For example, sales might slump due to economic conditions, changes in customer preferences, production bottlenecks, etc. In these conditions, employee performance can be adequate, yet sales can remain low. The first is performance and the second is the effectiveness of that performance. One can de-couple these two because performance is not the same as effectiveness.

Another closely related construct is productivity. One can think of productivity as a comparison of the amount of effectiveness that results from a certain level of cost associated with that effectiveness. In other words, effectiveness is the ratio of outputs to inputs—those inputs being effort, monetary costs, resources, etc.

Utility, another related construct, is defined as the value of a particular level of performance, effectiveness, or productivity. Utilities of performance, effectiveness, and productivity are value judgments.

## Organizational Goal Relevance

Another key feature of job performance is that it has to be goal relevant. Performance must be directed toward organizational goals that are relevant to the job or role. Therefore, performance does not include activities where effort is expended toward achieving peripheral goals. For example, the effort put toward the goal of getting to work in the shortest amount of time is not performance (except where it is concerned with avoiding lateness).

## Multidimensionality

Despite the emphasis on defining and predicting job performance, it is not a single unified construct. There are vastly many jobs each with different performance standards. Therefore, job performance is conceptualized as a multidimensional construct consisting of more than one kind of behavior. Campbell proposed an eight factor model of performance based on factor analytic research that attempts to capture dimensions of job performance existent (to a greater or lesser extent) across all jobs.

- The first factor is task specific behaviors which include those behaviors that an individual undertakes as part of a job. They are the core substantive tasks that delineate one job from another.
- On the other hand, non-task specific behaviors, the second factor, are those behaviors which an individual is required to undertake which do not pertain only to a particular job. Returning to the sales person, an example of a task specific behavior would be showing a product to a potential customer. A non-task specific behavior of a sales person might be training new staff members.
- Written and oral communication tasks refer to activities where the incumbent is evaluated, not on the content of a message necessarily, but on the adeptness with which they deliver the communication. Employees need to make formal and informal oral and written presentations to various audiences in many different jobs in the work force.
- An individual's performance can also be assessed in terms of effort, either day to day, or when there are extraordinary circumstances. This factor reflects the degree to which people commit themselves to job tasks.
- The performance domain might also include an aspect of personal discipline. Individuals would be expected to be in good standing with the law, not abuse alcohol, etc.
- In jobs where people work closely or are highly interdependent, performance may include the degree to which a person helps out the groups and his or her colleagues. This might include acting as a good role model, coaching, giving advice or helping maintain group goals.
- Many jobs also have a supervisory or leadership component. The individual will be relied upon to undertake many of the things delineated under the previous factor and in addition will be responsible for meting out rewards and punishments. These aspects of performance happen in a face to face manner.
- Managerial and administrative performance entails those aspects of a job which serve the group or organization but do not involve direct supervision. A managerial task would be setting an organizational goal or responding to external stimuli to assist a group in achieving its goals. In addition a manager might be responsible for monitoring group and individual progress towards goals and monitoring organizational resources.

Another taxonomy of job performance was proposed and developed for the US Navy by Murphy. This model is significantly broader and breaks performance into only four dimensions.

- Task-oriented behaviors are similar to task-specific behaviors in Campbell's model. This dimension includes any major tasks relevant to someone's job.
- Interpersonally oriented behaviors are represented by any interaction the focal employee has with other employees. These can be task related or non-task related. This dimension diverges from Campbell's taxonomy because it included behaviors (small talk, socializing, etc.) that are not targeting an organization's goal.

- Down-time behaviors are behaviors that employees engage in during their free time either at work or off-site. Down-time behaviors that occur off-site are only considered job performance when they subsequently affect job performance (for example, outside behaviors that cause absenteeism).
- Destructive/hazardous behaviors.

In addition to these models dividing performance into dimensions, others have identified different types of behaviors making up performance.

## Types

Another way to divide up performance is in terms of task and contextual (citizenship and counterproductive) behaviors. Whereas task performance describes obligatory behaviors, contextual behaviors are behaviors that do not fulfill specific aspects of the job's required role. Citizenship behaviors are defined as behaviors which contribute to the goals of the organization through their effect on the social and psychological conditions. Counterproductive behaviors, on the other hand, are intentional actions by employees which circumvent the aims of the organization.

## Determinants

Campbell also suggested determinants of performance components. Individual differences on performance are a function of three main determinants: declarative knowledge, procedural knowledge and skill, and motivation.

Declarative knowledge represents the knowledge of a given task's requirements. For instance, declarative knowledge includes knowledge of principles, facts, ideas, etc.

If declarative knowledge is knowing what to do, procedural knowledge and skill is knowing how to do it. For example, procedural knowledge and skill includes cognitive skill, perceptual skill, interpersonal skill, etc.

The third predictor of performance is motivation, which refers to "a combined effect from three choice behaviors—choice to expend effort, choice of level of effort to expend, and choice to persist in the expenditure of that level of effort". It reflects the direction, intensity, and persistence of volitional behaviors. Campbell emphasized that the only way to discuss motivation as a direct determinant of behavior is as one or more of these choices.

Campbell also mentioned several performance parameters that may have important implications for the job performance setting and should be investigated by industrial and organizational psychologists.

The first one is the distinction between speed and accuracy. This distinction is similar to the one between quantity and quality. Important questions that should be considered include: which is most valued by the organization, maximized speed, maximized accuracy, or some balance between the two? What kind of trade offs should an employee makes? The latter question is important because speed and accuracy for the same task may be independent of one another.

The second distinction is between typical and maximum performance. Sackett, Zedeck, and Fogli did a study on supermarket cashiers and found that there was a substantial difference between scores reflecting their typical performance and scores reflecting their maximum performance. This study suggested the distinction between typical and maximum performance. Regular work situations reflect varying levels of motivation which result in typical performance. Special circumstances generate maximum employee motivation which results in maximum performance.

Additionally, the impact of organizational justice perceptions on performance is believed to stem from Equity Theory. This would suggest that when people perceive injustice they seek to restore justice. One way that employees restore justice is by altering their level of performance. Procedural justice affects performance as a result of its impact on employee attitudes. Distributive justice affects performance when efficiency and productivity are involved. Improving justice perceptions improves productivity and performance.

## Results of Personnel Psychology

A meta-analysis of selection methods in personnel psychology found that general mental ability was the best overall predictor of job performance and training performance. While intelligence (general mental ability) is the strongest known predictor of job performance, that is less true for fields that are information-rich and require much instructional learning. Conscientiousness is another good predictor, but correlates with intelligence and is sometimes excluded from meta-analyses.

There are differences in the extent to which job performance is predicted by intelligence depending on the occupation. A 1998 meta-analysis of the predictors of job performance for salesperson found that extraversion and conscientiousness predicted both ratings and sales, but general cognitive ability and age correlated with ratings but not sales. Social skills, a good mentor and interpersonal virtues predict career success, a concept related to job performance, and happiness, better than high education, IQ or cerebral virtues, except for certain occupations like theoretical physics.

## Impact of Work Experience

The significance of work experience as a predictor of job performance is debatable as experience correlates with performance for people with 0-3 years' experience, but the correlation is attenuating to just 0.15 at 12+ years of experience. This suggests that experience doesn't increase performance after any more than a few years' experience.

## Detrimental Impact of Bullying

Bullying results in a loss of productivity. In one study a moderate negative correlation was found between self-rated performance and bullying, with the "currently bullied" on average reporting a decrease of productivity of approximately 7% compared with those who were neither bullied nor had witnessed bullying taking place.

## Core Self-evaluations

Job performance is a consistent and important outcome of core self-evaluations (CSE). The concept of core self-evaluations was first examined by Judge, Locke, and Durham as a dispositional predictor of job satisfaction, and involves four personality dimensions; locus of control, neuroticism, self-efficacy, and self-esteem. The way in which people appraise themselves using core self-evaluations has the ability to predict positive work outcomes, specifically, job satisfaction and job performance. The most popular theory relating the CSE trait to job performance argues that people with high CSE will be more motivated to perform well because they are confident they have the ability to do so. Motivation is generally the most accepted mediator of the core self-evaluations and job performance relationship. These relationships have inspired increasing amounts of research on core self-evaluations and suggest valuable implications about the importance this trait may have for organizations.

## Role Conflict

Role conflict can have many different effects on the work-life of an individual as well as their family-life. In a study in Taiwan, it was found that those suffering from role conflict also suffered greatly in their work performance, mainly in the form of lack of motivation. Those with role conflict did not do more than the bare minimum requirements at work. There was also a decline in the ability to assign tasks. Having multiple roles will often lead to job dissatisfaction.

Experiencing role conflict within the work place may also lead to workplace bullying. When companies undergo organizational change workers often experience either a loss or a gain in areas of a workers job, thus changing the expectations of the worker. Change is often very stressful for workers. Workers who might have lost a degree of power may feel like they lost their authority and begin to lash out at other employees by being verbally abusive, purposefully withholding work related items, or sometimes even physically to withhold their status.

While there are many de-motivational effects of role conflict on work, there is also a positive. Those undergoing role conflict often had an increase in work creativity. Due to multiple roles, there is an increase in flexibility, different sources of information, and these people have many different perspectives to bring to the table.

## Emotional Intelligence

Research of emotional intelligence (EI) and job performance shows mixed results: a positive relation has been found in some of the studies, in others there was no relation or an inconsistent one. This led researchers Cote and Miners to offer a compensatory model between EI and IQ, that posits that the association between EI and job performance becomes more positive as cognitive intelligence decreases, an idea first proposed in the context of academic performance (Petrides, Frederickson, & Furnham, 2004). The results of the former study supported the compensatory model: employees with low IQ get higher task performance and organizational citizenship behavior directed at the organization, the higher their EI.

A meta-analytic review by Joseph and Newman also revealed that both Ability EI and Trait EI tend to predict job performance much better in jobs that require a high degree of emotional labor (where 'emotional labor' was defined as jobs that require the effective display of positive emotion). In contrast, EI shows little relationship to job performance in jobs that do not require emotional labor. In other words, emotional intelligence tends to predict job performance for emotional jobs only.

A more recent study suggests that EI is not necessarily a universally positive trait. They found a negative correlation between EI and managerial work demands; while under low levels of managerial work demands, they found a negative relationship between EI and teamwork effectiveness. An explanation for this may suggest gender differences in EI, as women tend to score higher levels than men. This furthers the idea that job context plays a role in the relationships between EI, teamwork effectiveness, and job performance.

Another study assessed a possible link between EI and entrepreneurial behaviors and success. In accordance with much of the other findings regarding EI and job performance, they found that levels of EI only predicted a small amount of entrepreneurial behavior.

## The Advantages of the Human Resource Management Strategy

"Strategic human resource management (HRM) is the process of linking the human resource function with the strategic objectives of the organization in order to improve performance." Adopting an HR strategy that is concerned with the organization's larger mission and goals has multiple advantages and benefits for the company.

### Helps Evaluate HR Policies

The premise of strategic HRM is that the company's policies and procedures related to employees should fit into the organization's broader strategic plan. Developing these links between HR and strategy has the distinct advantage of helping the organization to evaluate its current HR policies and to replace outdated or inefficient policies with ones that promote a better workplace environment and employee relations.

As the company evaluates its HR policies, it can use the strategic plan's aims and objectives to evaluate each HR process. Those that fall out of the strategic vision can be reformulated or discarded in favor of better ones.

### Improves Team-building

Strategic HRM also helps to foster a sense of team spirit and camaraderie within the organization. A company's strategic vision will ideally rely on input from a broad range of stakeholders including managers, employees, customers and investors. Creating an HR strategy that aligns with this sense of open communication can have the major benefit of helping stakeholders feel like their opinions are valued and meaningful to the company's owners and executives.

### Helps Monitor Progress

While the strategic vision of the company can influence the creation and evaluation of HR policies, the reverse can also be true. Human resources can help the organization monitor its progress toward achieving its stated goals and objectives in the strategic plan. Much of the strategic plan is likely to rely on the cooperation and support of employees and individual departments or functions within the organization.

HR has a key role to play in making sure that all of these components of the strategic plan are implemented in a timely and effective way. The advantage of this marriage between strategy and HR management is that the company's executives and its HR function are consistently monitoring one another's progress and tweaking processes for the benefit of the company and its employees.

## Keeps the Organization Legal

A final advantage of the human resource management strategy is in keeping the organization compliant with laws relating to employees, salary, insurance and the like. The laws and policies governing business are complex and can vary between jurisdictions, but HR has a key role to play in making sure that the organization's strategic plan is not only presently legal but is also amendable enough that it can adapt to changing times and changing legal circumstances.

## References


- What-is-human-resources: humanresourcesedu.org, Retrieved 12 July, 2019
- Adam Sulich (2016-02-06). "Mathematical models and non-mathematical methods in recruitment and selection processes". Reviewed Papers Form 17th International Conference. Mekon 2015. 1. ISBN 978-80-248-3684-3
- Advantages-human-resource-management-strategy-66417: smallbusiness.chron.com, Retrieved 22 June, 2019
- Patrick J. Montana & Bruce H. Charnov (2000). "Training and Development". Management. Barron Educationally Series. p. 225. ISBN 9780764112768
- Karriker, JH; Williams, ML (2009). "Organizational Justice and Organizational Citizenship Behavior: A Mediated Multifoci Model". Journal of Management. 35: 112. doi:10.1177/0149206307309265

# 5
# Performance Management

Performance management focuses on the performance of an organization to meet their goals effectively and efficiently. Business performance management, enterprise performance management, behavior systems analysis, etc. comes within it. This chapter delves into the concepts related to performance management.

Performance Management can be defined as a process which continuously identifies, measures and develops the performance of the workforce in the organization. And to do so, each individual's performance and objectives are connected with the overall mission and goals of the enterprise. Hence, the two key elements of performance management are:

- Continuous process,
- Link to mission and goals.

In performance management, the managers try to figure out, the existing performance level of the employees and works on improving that level. It is a systematic assessment of the performance of an employee and using the assessment to better the performance over time.

Performance Management Cycle.

Performance management is commonly misconstrued with performance appraisal, which is a process of evaluating the performance of the workforce and includes feedback/review on an employee job performance. However, getting feedback is not sufficient. There are three more steps involved in the accomplishment of the process, which are:

- Performance Interview,
- Archiving Performance Data,
- Use of Appraisal Data.

These three activities along with the feedback are the essence of the process, which when undertaken in an organized way, the process turns out as Performance Management System (PMS).

### Concept of Performance Management

As a communication system, it is developed to assist employees in succeeding. It not just requires direction, from the end of managers and supervisors, but also needs active participation on the part of employees.

It makes sure that employees are known about their key job functions, aware of the performance level expected, get constant feedback on their performance, have opportunities for training and development, get ratings on their performance and reward thereon, in just and fair manner.

## Performance Improvement

Performance improvement is measuring the output of a particular business process or procedure, then modifying the process or procedure to increase the output, increase efficiency, or increase the effectiveness of the process or procedure.

In organizational development, performance improvement is organizational change in which the managers and governing body of an organization put into place and manage a program which measures the current level of performance of the organization and then generates ideas for modifying organizational behavior and infrastructure which are put into place to achieve higher output.

Performance improvement can be applied to either individual performance such as an athlete or organizational performance such as a racing team or a commercial business. Performance improvement at the operational or individual employee level usually involves processes such as statistical quality control. At the organizational level, performance improvement usually involves softer forms of measurement such as customer satisfaction surveys which are used to obtain qualitative information about performance from the viewpoint of customers.

The primary goals of organizational improvement are to increase organizational effectiveness and efficiency to improve the ability of the organization to deliver goods and or services. A third area sometimes targeted for improvement is organizational efficacy, which involves the process of setting organizational goals and objectives. Performance improvement can occur at different levels: an individual performer, a team, an organizational unit, or the organization itself.

The United States Coast Guard has published the Performance Improvement Guide (PIG), which describes various processes and tools for performance management at the individual and organizational levels.

There are two main ways to improve performance: improving the measured attribute by using the performance platform more effectively, or by improving the measured attribute by modifying the performance platform, which in turn allows a given level of use to be more effective in producing the desired output.

For instance, in several sports such as tennis and golf, there have been technological improvements in the apparatuses used in these sports. The improved apparatus in turn allows players to achieve better performance with no improvement in skill by purchasing new equipment. The apparatus, the golf club and golf ball or the tennis racket, provide the player with a higher theoretical performance limit.

Performance is a measure of the results achieved. Performance efficiency is the ratio between effort expended and results achieved. The difference between current performance and the theoretical performance limit is the performance improvement zone.

Another way to think of performance improvement is to see it as improvement in four potential areas. First are the resource input requirements (e.g., reduced working capital, material, replacement or reorder time, and set-up requirements). Second, is the THROUGHPUT requirements, often viewed as process efficiency; this is measured in terms of time, waste, and resource utilization. Third, OUTPUT requirements, often viewed from a cost/price, quality, functionality perspective. Fourth, OUTCOME requirements, did it end up making a difference.

Performance is an abstract concept and must be represented by concrete, measurable phenomena or events to be measured. Baseball athlete performance is abstract covering many different types of activities. Batting average is a concrete measure of a particular performance attribute for a particular game role, batting, for the game of baseball.

Performance assumes an actor of some kind but the actor could be an individual person or a group of people acting in concert. The performance platform is the infrastructure or devices used in the performance act.

## Science: Behavior Modification

In his study of innate human needs, renowned psychologist Abraham Maslow in his concept of a hierarchy of needs identified esteem and social fulfillment, garnered by recognition by family and peers, as a basic human need, and therefore able to be tied to structured programs that increase performance. Abraham Maslow, on "Third Force" psychology, combines aspects of behavioral, cognitive, and emotional psychology, and accounts for the impact of culture and society on behavior.

## Corporate or Commercial

In business, human performance in sales, operations and employee engagement is able to be improved through psychologically rewarding experiences "which can trigger a host of intrinsic human emotions and behavior as identified by Maslow. Including rewards in a performance improvement solution is a proven strategy to engage employees and align them with the company's goals. Awards can be cash or non-cash. Both stimulate human behavior. The addition of non-cash awards to the total rewards package creates a unique manner of unlocking the performance potential of people because it separates a reward from being used as or perceived as ordinary salary income. Non-cash awards break through the clutter to motivate higher achievement of and drive greater returns on investment. Cash as a reward can also be spent on day-to-day items like food or gas and does not create the increased "psychological reward" of achieving special items, or points to acquire items. By connecting with all levels of the organization, a complete rewards package can amplify performance across the organization and bring personal goals into alignment with organizational goals." Reward programs supporting improvement in sales and operations can be effectively paid for from the increase in revenue or profits which flow from the program, and without spending to reward for your current levels.

There is substantial evidence that monetary rewards are not effective outside the context of very rote work. In some cases, monetary incentive plans may decrease employee morale, as in Microsoft's stack-ranking system, where the total reward amount is fixed and employees are graded on an artificially fitted distribution.

### Cycle

Business performance management and improvement can be thought of as a cycle:

- Performance planning where goals and objectives are established.
- Performance coaching where a manager intervenes to give feedback and adjust performance.
- Performance appraisal where individual performance is formally documented and feedback delivered.

## Organizational Performance

Organizational performance comprises the actual output or results of an organization as measured against its intended outputs (or goals and objectives).

According to Richard et al. organizational performance encompasses three specific areas of firm outcomes: (a) financial performance (profits, return on assets, return on investment, etc.); (b) product market performance (sales, market share, etc.); and (c) shareholder return (total shareholder return, economic value added, etc.). The term Organizational effectiveness is broader.

Specialists in many fields are concerned with organizational performance including strategic planners, operations, finance, legal, and organizational development.

In recent years, many organizations have attempted to manage organizational performance using the balanced scorecard methodology where performance is tracked and measured in multiple dimensions such as:

- Financial performance (e.g. shareholder return),
- Customer service,
- Social responsibility (e.g. corporate citizenship, community outreach),
- Employee stewardship,
- Organizational performance,
- Performance measurement systems,
- Performance improvement,
- Organizational engineering.

## Balanced Scorecard

The balanced scorecard is a strategy performance management tool – a semi-standard structured report, that can be used by managers to keep track of the execution of activities by the staff within their control and to monitor the consequences arising from these actions.

The phrase 'balanced scorecard' primarily refers to a performance management report used by a management team, and typically this team is focused on managing the implementation of a strategy or operational activities – in a recent survey 62% of respondents reported using Balanced Scorecard for strategy implementation management, 48% for operational management. Balanced Scorecard is also used by individuals to track personal performance, but this is less common – only 17% of respondents in the survey using Balanced Scorecard in this way, however it is clear from the same survey that a larger proportion (about 30%) use corporate Balanced Scorecard elements to inform personal goal setting and incentive calculations.

The critical characteristics that define a balanced scorecard are:

- Its focus on the strategic agenda of the organization concerned,
- The selection of a small number of data items to monitor,
- A mix of financial and non-financial data items.

### Use

Balanced scorecard is an example of a closed-loop controller or cybernetic control applied to the management of the implementation of a strategy. Closed-loop or cybernetic control is where actual performance is measured. The measured value is compared to a reference value and based on the difference between the two corrective interventions are made as required. Such control requires three things to be effective:

- A choice of data to measure,

- The setting of a reference value for the data,
- The ability to make a corrective intervention.

Within the strategy management context, all three of these characteristic closed-loop control elements need to be derived from the organisation's strategy and also need to reflect the ability of the observer to monitor performance and subsequently intervene – both of which may be constrained. Balanced Scorecard was initially proposed as a general purpose performance management system. Subsequently, it was promoted specifically as an approach to strategic performance management. Balanced scorecard has more recently become a key component of structured approaches corporate strategic management.

Two of the ideas that underpin modern balanced scorecard designs concern making it easier to select which data to observe, and ensuring that the choice of data is consistent with the ability of the observer to intervene.

## Characteristics

The characteristic feature of the balanced scorecard and its derivatives is the presentation of a mixture of financial and non-financial measures each compared to a 'target' value within a single concise report. The report is not meant to be a replacement for traditional financial or operational reports but a succinct summary that captures the information most relevant to those reading it. It is the method by which this 'most relevant' information is determined (i.e., the design processes used to select the content) that most differentiates the various versions of the tool in circulation. The balanced scorecard indirectly also provides a useful insight into an organisation's strategy – by requiring general strategic statements (e.g. mission, vision) to be precipitated into more specific/tangible forms.

The first versions of Kaplan and Norton's interpretation of the balanced scorecard asserted that relevance should derive from the corporate strategy, and proposed design methods that focused on choosing measures and targets associated with the main activities required to implement the strategy. As the initial audience for this were the readers of the Harvard Business Review, the proposal was translated into a form that made sense to a typical reader of that journal – managers of US commercial businesses. Accordingly, initial designs were encouraged to measure three categories of non-financial measure in addition to financial outputs – those of "customer," "internal business processes" and "learning and growth." These categories were not so relevant to public sector or non-profit organisations, or units within complex organizations (which might have high degrees of internal specialization), and much of the early literature on balanced scorecard focused on suggestions of alternative 'perspectives' that might have more relevance to these groups(e.g.), Ahn, Elefalke, Brignall, Irwin, Radnor et al.

Modern balanced scorecards have evolved since the initial ideas proposed in the late 1980s and early 1990s, and the modern performance management tools including Balanced Scorecard are significantly improved – being more flexible (to suit a wider range of organisational types) and more effective (as design methods have evolved to make them easier to design, and use).

## Variants

Since the balanced scorecard was popularized in the early 1990s, a large number of alternatives to the original 'four box' balanced scorecard promoted by Kaplan and Norton in their various articles and books have emerged. Most have very limited application, and are typically proposed either by academics as vehicles for expanding the dialogue beyond the financial bottom line – e.g. Brignall or consultants as an attempt at differentiation to promote sales of books and / or consultancy (e.g. Neely et al., Bourne, Niven).

Variants that feature adaptations of the structure of balanced scorecard to suit better a particular viewpoint or agenda are numerous. Examples of the focus of such adaptations include the triple bottom line, decision support, public sector management, and health care management. The performance management elements of the UN's Results Based Management system have strong design and structural similarities to those used in the 3rd Generation Balanced Scorecard design approach.

Balanced scorecard is also linked to quality management tools and activities. Although there are clear areas of cross-over and association, the two sets of tools are complementary rather than duplicative.

Balanced scorecard is also used to support the payments of incentives to individuals, even though it was not designed for this purpose and is not particularly suited to it.

## Design

Design of a balanced scorecard is about the identification of a small number of financial and non-financial measures and attaching targets to them, so that when they are reviewed it is possible to determine whether current performance 'meets expectations'. By alerting managers to areas where performance deviates from expectations, they can be encouraged to focus their attention on these areas, and hopefully as a result trigger improved performance within the part of the organization they lead.

The original thinking behind a balanced scorecard was for it to be focused on information relating to the implementation of a strategy, and over time there has been a blurring of the boundaries between conventional strategic planning and control activities and those required to design a balanced scorecard. This is illustrated well by the four steps required to design a balanced scorecard included in Kaplan & Norton's writing on the subject in the late 1990s:

- Translating the vision into operational goals.
- Communicating the vision and link it to individual performance.
- Business planning, index setting.
- Feedback and learning, and adjusting the strategy accordingly.

These steps go far beyond the simple task of identifying a small number of financial and non-financial measures, but illustrate the requirement for whatever design process is used to fit within broader thinking about how the resulting balanced scorecard will integrate with the wider business management process.

Although it helps focus managers' attention on strategic issues and the management of the implementation of strategy, it is important to remember that the balanced scorecard itself has no role in the formation of strategy. In fact, balanced scorecards can co-exist with strategic planning systems and other tools.

## First Generation

The first generation of balanced scorecard designs used a "four perspective" approach to identify what measures to use to track the implementation of strategy. `The original four "perspectives" proposed were:

- Financial: encourages the identification of a few relevant high-level financial measures. In particular, designers were encouraged to choose measures that helped inform the answer to the question "How do we look to shareholders?" Examples: cash flow, sales growth, operating income, return on equity.
- Customer: encourages the identification of measures that answer the question "What is important to our customers and stakeholders?" Examples: percent of sales from new products, on time delivery, share of important customers' purchases, ranking by important customers.
- Internal business processes: encourages the identification of measures that answer the question "What must we excel at?"Examples: cycle time, unit cost, yield, new product introductions.
- Learning and growth: encourages the identification of measures that answer the question "How can we continue to improve, create value and innovate?". Examples: time to develop new generation of products, life cycle to product maturity, time to market versus competition.

The idea was that managers used these perspective headings to prompt the selection of a small number of measures that informed on that aspect of the organisation's strategic performance. The perspective headings show that Kaplan and Norton were thinking about the needs of non-divisional commercial organisations in their initial design. These categories were not so relevant to public sector or non-profit organisations, or units within complex organizations (which might have high degrees of internal specialization), and much of the early literature on balanced scorecard focused on suggestions of alternative 'perspectives' that might have more relevance to these groups(e.g. Butler et al., Ahn, Elefalke, Brignall, Irwin, Flamholtz, Radnor et al.).

These suggestions were notably triggered by a recognition that different but equivalent headings would yield alternative sets of measures, and this represents the major design challenge faced with this type of balanced scorecard design: justifying the choice of measures made. "Of all the measures you could have chosen, why did you choose these?" These issues contribute to dis-satisfaction with early Balanced Scorecard designs, since if users are not confident that the measures within the Balanced Scorecard are well chosen, they will have less confidence in the information it provides.

Although less common, these early-style balanced scorecards are still designed and used today. In short, first generation balanced scorecards are hard to design in a way that builds confidence that they are well designed. Because of this, many are abandoned soon after completion.

## Second Generation

In the mid-1990s, an improved design method emerged. In the new method, measures are selected based on a set of "strategic objectives" plotted on a "strategic linkage model" or "strategy map". With this modified approach, the strategic objectives are distributed across the four measurement perspectives, so as to "connect the dots" to form a visual presentation of strategy and measures.

In this modified version of balanced scorecard design, managers select a few strategic objectives within each of the perspectives, and then define the cause-effect chain among these objectives by drawing links between them to create a "strategic linkage model". A balanced scorecard of strategic performance measures is then derived directly by selecting one or two measures for each strategic objective. This type of approach provides greater contextual justification for the measures chosen, and is generally easier for managers to work through. This style of balanced scorecard has been commonly used since 1996 or so: it is significantly different in approach to the methods originally proposed, and so can be thought of as representing the "2nd generation" of design approach adopted for the balanced scorecard since its introduction.

## Third Generation

In the late 1990s, the design approach had evolved yet again. One problem with the "second generation" design approach described above was that the plotting of causal links amongst twenty or so medium-term strategic goals was still a relatively abstract activity. In practice it ignored the fact that opportunities to intervene, to influence strategic goals are, and need to be, anchored in current and real management activity. Secondly, the need to "roll forward" and test the impact of these goals necessitated the creation of an additional design instrument: the Vision or Destination Statement. This device was a statement of what "strategic success", or the "strategic end-state", looked like. It was quickly realized that if a Destination Statement was created at the beginning of the design process, then it was easier to select strategic activity and outcome objectives to respond to it. Measures and targets could then be selected to track the achievement of these objectives. Design methods that incorporate a Destination Statement or equivalent (e.g. the results-based management method proposed by the UN in 2002) represent a tangibly different design approach to those that went before, and have been proposed as representing a "third generation" design method for balanced scorecards.

Design methods for balanced scorecards continue to evolve and adapt to reflect the deficiencies in the currently used methods, and the particular needs of communities of interest (e.g. NGO's and government departments have found the third generation methods embedded in results-based management more useful than first or second generation design methods).

This generation refined the second generation of balanced scorecards to give more relevance and functionality to strategic objectives. The major difference is the incorporation of Destination Statements. Other key components are strategic objectives, strategic linkage model and perspectives, measures and initiatives.

## Popularity

In 1997, Kurtzman found that 64 percent of the companies questioned were measuring performance from a number of perspectives in a similar way to the balanced scorecard. Balanced scorecards have been implemented by government agencies, military units, business units and corporations as a whole, non-profit organizations, and schools.

Balanced scorecard has been widely adopted, and consistently has been found to be the most popular performance management framework in a widely respected annual survey (e.g. see results from 2003 and 2013).

Theorists have argued from the earliest days of discussion of Balanced Scorecard usage that much of the benefit of the balanced scorecard comes from the design process itself. Indeed, it is argued that many failures in the early days of balanced scorecard could be attributed to this problem, in that early balanced scorecards were often designed remotely by consultants – it is suggested that by not being involved in the design, the relevant managers who were to use the device did not trust, and so failed to engage with and use the devices.

Academic criticism of the balanced scorecard can be broken into three distinct (but overlapping) areas of concern.

- The first kind of criticism focuses on the empirical nature of the framework, and when it was originally proposed the lack of any formal validation of the ideas. Kaplan and Norton notoriously failed to include any citations of earlier articles in their initial papers on the topic, an absence noted, for example, by Norreklit. Others identified technical flaws in the methods and design of the original balanced scorecard or concerning the lack of validation for the approach – for example Flamholtz observed that no validation was provided for the choice of the "four perspectives" of the 1st Generation design.
- The second kind of criticism is that the balanced scorecard does not provide a bottom line score or a unified view with clear recommendations: it is simply a list of metrics (e.g. Jensen 2001). These critics usually include in their criticism suggestions about how the 'unanswered' question postulated could be answered, but typically the unanswered question relate to things outside the scope of balanced scorecard itself (such as developing strategies) (e.g. Brignall).
- The third kind of criticism is that the model fails to fully reflect the needs of stakeholders – putting bias on financial stakeholders over others. Early forms of Balanced Scorecard proposed by Kaplan & Norton focused on the needs of commercial organisations in the USA – where this focus on investment return was appropriate. This focus was maintained through subsequent revisions. Even now over 20 years after they were first proposed, the four most common perspectives in Balanced Scorecard designs mirror the four proposed in the original Kaplan & Norton paper. There have been many studies that suggest other perspectives might better reflect the priorities of organisations – particularly but not exclusively relating to the needs of organisations in the public and Non Governmental sectors. For instance, the balanced scorecard does not address important aspects of nonprofit strategy such as social dimensions, human resource elements, political issues and the distinctive nature of competition and collaboration in nonprofit settings. More modern design approaches such as 3rd Generation Balanced Scorecard, the Public Sector Scorecard and the UN's Results Based Management methods explicitly consider the interests of wider stakeholder groups, and perhaps address this issue in its entirety.

In response to these concerns there have been many studies seeking to provide (retrospective) academic underpinnings for the Balanced Scorecard concept, and to provide case study and validation information for the various design generations. There are relatively few reliable assessments of the effectiveness of the approaches embodied in Balanced Scorecard, but some studies demonstrate a link between the use of balanced scorecards and better decision making or improved financial performance of companies.

Broadcast surveys of usage have difficulties in this respect, due to the wide variations in definition of 'what a balanced scorecard is' (making it hard to work out in a survey if you are comparing like with like). Single organization case studies suffer from the 'lack of a control' issue common to any study of organizational change – what the organization would have achieved if the change had not been made isn't known, so it is difficult to attribute changes observed over time to a single intervention (such as introducing a balanced scorecard). However, such studies as have been done have typically found balanced scorecard to be useful.

Consideration has been given to the effect of organisation size on Balanced Scorecard effectiveness:

- For large organisations this work has focused on how to translate aggregate corporate strategies into performance management tools relevant to individual teams / units within the organisation.
- In SMEs Balanced Scorecard has been found to be effective, but that focus is required on balancing design complexity and relevance with the availability of resource to do the design work. Others have argued that the Balanced Scorecard is unsuitable for SMEs for a variety of reasons, including the belief that SMEs lack a long-term strategic focus, that changes in an SME's strategy are too frequent, and that SMEs have limited knowledge about performance measurement in general and therefore do not recognise the benefits that might accrue from use of the tool, but it is also important to note that none of these studies attempts to theorise the reasons behind their negative findings.

## Software Tools

It is important to recognize that the balanced scorecard by definition is not a complex thing – typically no more than about 20 measures spread across a mix of financial and non-financial topics, and easily reported manually (on paper, or using simple office software).

The processes of collecting, reporting, and distributing balanced scorecard information can be labor-intensive and prone to procedural problems (for example, getting all relevant people to return the information required by the required date). The simplest mechanism to use is to delegate these activities to an individual, and many Balanced Scorecards are reported via ad-hoc methods based around email, phone calls and office software.

In more complex organizations, where there are multiple balanced scorecards to report and/or a need for co-ordination of results between balanced scorecards (for example, if one level of reports relies on information collected and reported at a lower level) the use of individual reporters is problematic. Where these conditions apply, organizations use balanced scorecard reporting software to automate the production and distribution of these reports.

# Business Performance Management

Business performance management is a set of performance management and analytic processes that enables the management of an organization's performance to achieve one or more pre-selected goals. Synonyms for "business performance management" include "corporate performance management (CPM)" and "enterprise performance management". Gartner has officially retired the concept of, "CPM" and reclassified into, "financial planning and analysis (FP&A)" and, "financial close" to reflect two significant trends - increased focus on planning, and the emergence of a new category of solutions supporting the management of the financial close.

Business performance management is contained within approaches to business process management.

Business performance management has three main activities:

- Selection of goals.
- Consolidation of measurement information relevant to an organization's progress against these goals.
- Interventions made by managers in light of this information with a view to improving future performance against these goals.

Although presented here sequentially, typically all three activities will run concurrently, with interventions by managers affecting the choice of goals, the measurement information monitored, and the activities being undertaken by the organization.

Because business performance management activities in large organizations often involve the collection and reporting of large volumes of data, many software vendors, particularly those offering business intelligence tools, market products intended to assist in this process. As a result of this marketing effort, business performance management is often incorrectly understood as an activity that necessarily relies on software systems to work, and many definitions of business performance management explicitly suggest software as being a definitive component of the approach.

This interest in business performance management from the software community is sales-driven - "The biggest growth area in operational BI analysis is in the area of business performance management."

Since 1992, business performance management has been strongly influenced by the rise of the balanced scorecard framework. It is common for managers to use the balanced scorecard framework to clarify the goals of an organization, to identify how to track them, and to structure the mechanisms by which interventions will be triggered. These steps are the same as those that are found in BPM, and as a result, balanced scorecard is often used as the basis for business performance management activity with organizations.

In the past, owners have sought to drive strategy down and across their organizations, transform these strategies into actionable metrics, and use analytics to expose the cause-and-effect relationships that, if understood, could give insight into decision-making.

Business performance management consists of a set of management and analytic processes, supported by technology, that enable businesses to define strategic goals and then measure and manage performance against those goals. Core business performance management processes include financial planning, operational planning, business modeling, consolidation and reporting, analysis, and monitoring of key performance indicators linked to strategy.

Business performance management involves consolidation of data from various sources, querying, and analysis of the data, and putting the results into practice.

## Frameworks

Various frameworks for implementing business performance management exist. The discipline gives companies a top-down framework by which to align planning and execution, strategy and tactics, and business-unit and enterprise objectives. Reactions may include the Six Sigma strategy, balanced scorecard, activity-based costing (ABC), Objectives and Key Results (OKR), Total Quality Management, economic value-add, integrated strategic measurement and Theory of Constraints.

## Metrics and Key Performance Indicators

Some of the areas from which bank management may gain knowledge by using business performance management include:

- Customer-related numbers:
  - New customers acquired.
  - Status of existing customers.
  - Attrition of customers (including breakup by reason for attrition).
- Turnover generated by segments of the customers - possibly using demographic filters.
- Outstanding balances held by segments of customers and terms of payment - possibly using demographic filters.
- Collection of bad debts within customer relationships.
- Demographic analysis of individuals (potential customers) applying to become. customers, and the levels of approval, rejections and pending numbers.
- Delinquency analysis of customers behind on payments.
- Profitability of customers by demographic segments and segmentation of customers by profitability.
- Campaign management.
- Real-time dashboard on key operational metrics.
  - Overall equipment effectiveness.

- Clickstream analysis on a website.
- Key product portfolio trackers.
- Marketing-channel analysis.
- Sales-data analysis by product segments.
- Callcenter metrics.

Though the above list describes what a bank might monitor, it could refer to a telephone company or to a similar service-sector company.

Items of generic importance include:

- Consistent and correct KPI-related data providing insights into operational aspects of a company.
- Timely availability of KPI-related data.
- KPIs designed to directly reflect the efficiency and effectiveness of a business.
- Information presented in a format which aids decision-making for management and decision-makers.
- Ability to discern patterns or trends from organized information.

Business performance management integrates the company's processes with CRM or ERP. Companies should become better able to gauge customer satisfaction, control customer trends and influence shareholder value.

## Application Software Types

People working in business intelligence have developed tools that ease the work of business performance management, especially when the business-intelligence task involves gathering and analyzing large amounts of unstructured data.

Tool categories commonly used for business performance management include:

- MOLAP — Multidimensional online analytical processing, sometimes simply called "analytics" (based on dimensional analysis and the so-called "hypercube" or "cube").
- Scorecarding, dashboarding and data visualization.
- Data warehouses.
- Document warehouses.
- Text mining.
- DM — data mining.
- BPO — business performance optimization.
- EPM — enterprise performance management.

- EIS — executive information systems.
- DSS — decision support systems.
- MIS — management information systems.
- SEMS — strategic enterprise management software.
- EOI — Operational intelligence Enterprise Operational Intelligence Software.

## Design and Implementation

Questions asked when implementing a business performance management program include:

- Goal-alignment queries: Determine the short- and medium-term purpose of the program. What strategic goal(s) of the organization will the program address? What organizational mission/vision does it relate to? A hypothesis needs to be crafted that details how this initiative will eventually improve results / performance (i.e. a strategy map).
- Baseline queries: Assess current information-gathering competency. Does the organization have the capability to monitor important sources of information? What data is being collected and how is it being stored? What are the statistical parameters of this data, e.g., how much random variation does it contain? Is this being measured?
- Cost and risk queries: Estimate the financial consequences of a new BI initiative. Assess the cost of the present operations and the increase in costs associated with the BPM initiative. What is the risk that the initiative will fail? This risk assessment should be converted into a financial metric and included in the planning.
- Customer and stakeholder queries: Determine who will benefit from the initiative and who will pay. Who has a stake in the current procedure? What kinds of customers / stakeholders will benefit directly from this initiative? Who will benefit indirectly? What quantitative / qualitative benefits follow? Is the specified initiative the best or only way to increase satisfaction for all kinds of customers? How will customer benefits be monitored? What about employees, shareholders, and distribution channel members?
- Metrics-related queries: Information requirements need operationalization into clearly defined metrics. Decide which metrics to use for each piece of information being gathered. Are these the best metrics and why? How many metrics need to be tracked? If this is a large number (it usually is), what kind of system can track them? Are the metrics standardized, so they can be benchmarked against performance in other organizations? What are the industry standard metrics available?
- Measurement methodology-related queries: Establish a methodology or a procedure to determine the best (or acceptable) way of measuring the required metrics. How frequently will data be collected? Are there any industry standards for this? Is this the best way to do the measurements? How do we know that?
- Results-related queries: Monitor the BPM program to ensure that it meets objectives. The program itself may require adjusting. The program should be tested for accuracy, reliability,

and validity. How can it be demonstrated that the BI initiative, and not something else, contributed to a change in results? How much of the change was probably random?

## Performance Measurement

Performance measurement is the process of collecting, analyzing and/or reporting information regarding the performance of an individual, group, organization, system or component.

Definitions of performance measurement tend to be predicated upon an assumption about why the performance is being measured.

- Moullin defines the term with a forward looking organisational focus—"the process of evaluating how well organisations are managed and the value they deliver for customers and other stakeholders".
- Neely et al. use a more operational retrospective focus—"the process of quantifying the efficiency and effectiveness of past actions".
- In 2007 the Office of the Chief Information Officer in the USA defined it using a more evaluative focus—"Performance measurement estimates the parameters under which programs, investments, and acquisitions are reaching the targeted results".

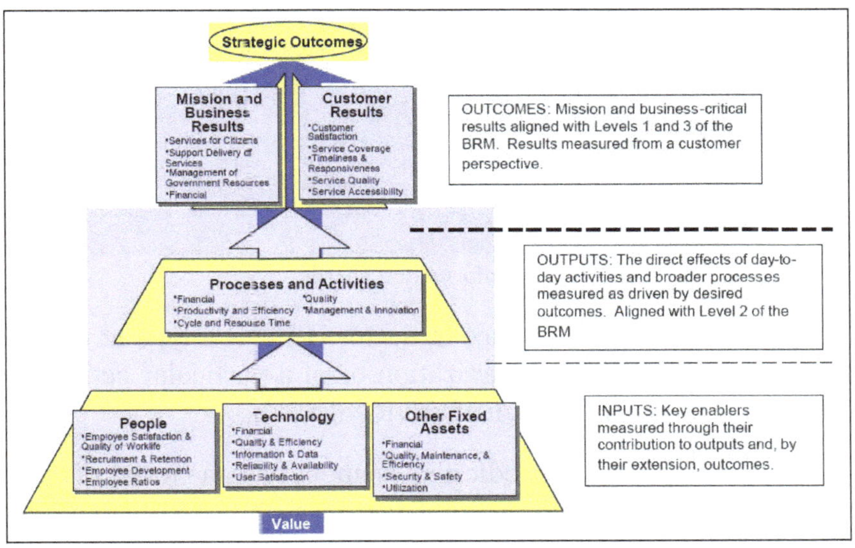


Performance Reference Model of the Federal Enterprise Architecture.

Beyond a simple agreement about it being linked to some kind of measurement of performance there is little consensus about how to define or use performance measures. In the light of this what has happened is the emergence of organising frameworks that incorporate performance measures and often also proscribe methods for choosing and using the appropriate measures for that application. The most common such frameworks include:

- Balanced scorecard—used by organisations to manage the implementation of corporate strategies.

- Key performance indicator—a method for choosing important/critical performance measures, usually in an organisational context.

Operational standards often include pre-defined lists of standard performance measures. For example EN 15341 identifies 71 performance indicators, whereof 21 are technical indicators, or those in a US Federal Government directive from 1999.

Defining performance measures or methods by which they can be chosen is also a popular activity for academics—for example a list of railway infrastructure indicators is offered by Stenström et al., a novel method for measure selection is proposed by Mendibil et al.

Academic articles that provide critical reviews of performance measurement in specific domains are also common—e.g. Ittner's observations on non-financial reporting by commercial organisations, or Boris et al.'s observations about use of performance measurement in non-profit organisations.

## Performance Indicator

KPI information boards.

A performance indicator or key performance indicator (KPI) is a type of performance measurement. KPIs evaluate the success of an organization or of a particular activity (such as projects, programs, products and other initiatives) in which it engages.

Often success is simply the repeated, periodic achievement of some levels of operational goal (e.g. zero defects, 10/10 customer satisfaction), and sometimes success is defined in terms of making progress toward strategic goals. Accordingly, choosing the right KPIs relies upon a good understanding of what is important to the organization. What is deemed important often depends on the department measuring the performance – e.g. the KPIs useful to finance will differ from the KPIs assigned to sales.

Since there is a need to understand well what is important, various techniques to assess the present state of the business, and its key activities, are associated with the selection of performance indicators. These assessments often lead to the identification of potential improvements, so performance indicators are routinely associated with 'performance improvement' initiatives. A very common way to choose KPIs is to apply a management framework such as the balanced scorecard.

## Categorization of Indicators

Key performance indicators define a set of values against which to measure. These raw sets of values, which can be fed to systems that aggregate the data, are called indicators. There are two categories of measurements for KPIs.

- Quantitative facts without distortion from personal feelings, prejudices, or interpretations presented with a specific value - objective- preferably numeric measured against a standard.
- Qualitative values based on or influenced by personal feelings, tastes, or opinions and presented as any numeric or textual value that represents an interpretation of these elements.

An 'indicator' can only measure what 'has' happened, in the past tense, so the only type of measurement is descriptive or lagging. Any KPI that attempts to measure something in a future state as predictive, diagnostic or prescriptive is no longer an 'indicator' it is a 'prognosticator' - at this point it is analytics (possibly based on a KPI).

## Points of Measurement

Performance focuses on measuring a particular element of an activity. An activity can have four elements: input, output, control, and mechanism. At a minimum, an activity is required to have at least an input and an output. Something goes into the activity as an input; the activity transforms the input by making a change to its state; and the activity produces an output. An activity can also have enabling mechanisms that are typically separated into human and system mechanisms. It can also be constrained in some way by a control. Lastly, its actions can have a temporal construct of time.

- Input indicates the inputs required of an activity to produce an output.
- Output captures the outcome or results of an activity or group of activities.
- Activity indicates the transformation produced by an activity (i.e., some form of work).
- Mechanism is something that enables an activity to work (a performer), either human or system.
- Control is an object that controls the activity's production through compliance.
- Time indicates a temporal element of the activity.

## Identifying Indicators of Organization

Performance indicators differ from business drivers and aims (or goals). A school might consider the failure rate of its students as a key performance indicator which might help the school understand its position in the educational community, whereas a business might consider the percentage of income from returning customers as a potential KPI.

The key stages in identifying KPIs are:

- Having a pre-defined business process (BP).

- Having requirements for the BPs.
- Having a quantitative/qualitative measurement of the results and comparison with set goals.
- Investigating variances and tweaking processes or resources to achieve short-term goals.

Key performance indicators (KPIs) are ways to periodically assess the performances of organizations, business units, and their division, departments and employees. Accordingly, KPIs are most commonly defined in a way that is understandable, meaningful, and measurable. They are rarely defined in such a way such that their fulfillment would be hampered by factors seen as non-controllable by the organizations or individuals responsible. Such KPIs are usually ignored by organizations.

KPIs should follow the SMART criteria. This means the measure has a Specific purpose for the business, it is Measurable to really get a value of the KPI, the defined norms have to be Achievable, the improvement of a KPI has to be Relevant to the success of the organization, and finally it must be Time phased, which means the value or outcomes are shown for a predefined and relevant period.

In order to be evaluated, KPIs are linked to target values, so that the value of the measure can be assessed as meeting expectations or not.

## Examples of Performance Indicators

Key performance indicators are the non-financial measures of a company's performance - they do not have a monetary value but they do contribute to the company's profitability.

### Accounts

Some examples are:

- Percentage of overdue invoices.
- Percentage of purchase orders raised in advance.
- Number of retrospectively raised purchase orders.
- Finance report error rate (measures the quality of report).
- Average cycle time of workflow.
- Number of duplicate payments.

### Marketing and Sales

- New customer acquisition.
- Demographic analysis of individuals (potential customers) applying to become customers, and the levels of approval, rejections, and pending numbers.
- Status of existing customers.

- Customer attrition.
- Turnover (i.e., revenue) generated by segments of the customer population.
- Outstanding balances held by segments of customers and terms of payment.
- Collection of bad debts within customer relationships.
- Profitability of customers by demographic segments and segmentation of customers by profitability.

Many of these customer KPIs are developed and managed with customer relationship management software.

Faster availability of data is a competitive issue for most organizations. For example, businesses which have higher operational/credit risk (involving for example credit cards or wealth management) may want weekly or even daily availability of KPI analysis, facilitated by appropriate IT systems and tools.

## Manufacturing

Overall equipment effectiveness is a set of broadly accepted non-financial metrics which reflect manufacturing success.

- OEE: Availability x performance x quality.
- Availability: Run time / total time, by definition this is the percentage of the actual amount of production time the machine is running to the production time the machine is available.
- Performance: Total count / target counter, by definition this is the percentage of total parts produced on the machine to the production rate of machine.
- Quality: Good count / total count, by definition, this is the percentage of good parts out of the total parts produced on the machine.
- Cycle time ratio (CTR): Standard cycle time / real cycle time.
- Capacity utilization.
- Rejection rate.

## Professional Services

Most professional services firms (for example: management consultancies, systems integration firms, or digital marketing agencies) use three key performance indicators to track the health of their businesses. They typically use professional services automation (PSA) software to keep track of and manage these metrics.

- Utilization rate: The percentage of time employees spend generating revenue.
- Project profitability: The difference between revenue generated by a project and the cost of delivering the work.
- Project success rate: The percentage of projects delivered on time and under budget.

### System Operations

- Availability / uptime,
- Mean time between failure,
- Mean time to repair,
- Unplanned availability,
- Average time to repair.

### Project Execution

- Earned value,
- Cost variance,
- Schedule variance,
- Estimate to complete,
- Manpower spent / month,
- Money spent / month,
- Planned spend / month,
- Planned manpower / month,
- Average time to delivery,
- Tasks / staff,
- Project overhead / ROI,
- Planned delivery date vs actual delivery date.

### Supply Chain Management

Businesses can utilize KPIs to establish and monitor progress toward a variety of goals, including lean manufacturing objectives, minority business enterprise and diversity spending, environmental "green" initiatives, cost avoidance programs and low-cost country sourcing targets.

Any business, regardless of size, can better manage supplier performance with the help of KPIs robust capabilities, which include:

- Automated entry and approval functions,
- On-demand, real-time scorecard measures,
- Rework on procured inventory,

- Single data repository to eliminate inefficiencies and maintain consistency,
- Advanced workflow approval process to ensure consistent procedures,
- Flexible data-input modes and real-time graphical performance displays,
- Customized cost savings documentation,
- Simplified setup procedures to eliminate dependence upon IT resources.

Main SCM KPIs will detail the following processes:

- Sales forecasts,
- Inventory,
- Procurement and suppliers,
- Warehousing,
- Transportation,
- Reverse logistics.

Suppliers can implement KPIs to gain an advantage over the competition. Suppliers have instant access to a user-friendly portal for submitting standardized cost savings templates. Suppliers and their customers exchange vital supply chain performance data while gaining visibility to the exact status of cost improvement projects and cost savings documentation.

## Government

The provincial government of Ontario, Canada has been using KPIs since 1998 to measure the performance of higher education institutions in the province. All post secondary schools collect and report performance data in five areas – graduate satisfaction, student satisfaction, employer satisfaction, employment rate, and graduation rate.

## Further Performance Indicators

- Duration of a stockout situation:

$$\text{ROC} = \frac{\text{Close} - \text{Close (Past)}}{\text{Close (Past)}} \times 100$$

- Customer order waiting time.

## Human Resource Management

- Employee turnover,
- Employee performance indicators,
- Cross functional team analysis.

### Problems

In practice, overseeing key performance indicators can prove expensive or difficult for organizations. Some indicators such as staff morale may be impossible to quantify. As such, dubious KPIs can be adopted that can be used as a rough guide rather than a precise benchmark.

Key performance indicators can also lead to perverse incentives and unintended consequences as a result of employees working to the specific measurements at the expense of the actual quality or value of their work.

Sometimes the collecting of statistics can become a substitute for a better understanding of the problems so the use of dubious KPIs can result in progress in aims and measured effectiveness becoming different. For example, US soldiers during the Vietnam War were shown to be effective in kill ratios and high body counts, but this was misleading when used to measure aims as it did not show the lack of progress towards the US goal of increasing South Vietnamese government control of its territory. Another example would be to measure the productivity of a software development team in terms of lines of source code written. This approach can easily result in large amounts of dubious code being added, thereby inflating the line count but adding little of value in terms of systemic improvement. A similar problem arises when a footballer kicks a ball uselessly in a match in order to build up his statistics.

## Enterprise Performance Management

Enterprise performance management (EPM) is a field of business performance management which considers the visibility of operations in a closed-loop model across all facets of the enterprise. Specific to financial activities in the office of the chief financial officer, EPM also supports financial planning and analysis (FP&A). "Corporate performance management (CPM)" is a synonym for "enterprise performance management". Gartner has officially retired the concept of, "CPM" and reclassified into, "financial planning and analysis (FP&A)" and, "financial close" to reflect two significant trends - increased focus on planning, and the emergence of a new category of solutions supporting the management of the financial close.

There are several domains in the EPM field which are driven by corporate initiatives, academic research, and commercial approaches. These include:

- Strategy formulation,
- Business planning and forecasting,
- Financial management,
- Supply chain effectiveness.

Based on the mission and vision of an organization, different strategic needs may drive how EPM domains are leveraged and promoted within an organization. For example, a professional services firm based in Canada may view the need to have effective and transparent supply chain operations very differently from a clothing manufacturer with operations throughout the world. What is common in the EPM approach is the closed-loop EPM process model advocated by Kaplan and Norton and their management approaches to strategy formulation, including balanced scorecard and strategy map techniques.

The four domains, or disciplines, referred to above exist to define and cover the six stages of the closed-loop EPM process model. The six stages of the closed-loop EPM process model are: strategy development, strategy translation, organization alignment, operations planning, learning and monitoring, and testing and adaptation.

## Strategy Formulation

Strategy formulation refers to activities of an organization which determine the direction of its agenda. This is generally constructed of the mission, vision, and strategic goals and objectives of an organization. Once the direction is established, an organization monitors its progress against those activities and takes corrective actions to reach a particular target state.

While execution is the key to any operational objective, the strategy formulation surrounding why execution should occur and the context by which execution should be performed is also important. In recent years, organizations embed formal approaches to risk management to address market opportunities that organizations pursue. In this way strategy is aligned, performance is predictable, and executives can make better business decisions.

Executives live in a financially driven environment, where operational processes are traditionally a means of organizing resources inside the company and its value chain and employees are the responsible actors to execute those processes. The strategy gap that some industry watchdogs have noted is real and growing. Innovative technologies provide one approach to collapsing this gap and allowing corporate strategic outcomes to be fully realized and risk management programs to be fully described.

The first two steps of the closed-loop EPM process model involve developing the strategy and then to translate the strategy into particular actions that the organization can undertake. Strategy development as a subset of strategy formulation represents the articulation of the key components of strategy: mission, vision, strategic goals, and strategic objectives. There are several approaches to strategy development which may be considered. However this may occur the executive leadership of the organization approve the strategy and typically review this strategy every 3–5 years based upon a 10-20 year horizon. Some business and national cultures may consider a longer-range strategy horizon.

Strategy translation then takes the often obscure direction and statements defined in the first step and considers how to make these directions actionable. In the case of strategic goals, these are lofty targets given generally 3–5 years to achieve. Strategic objectives then identify specific progress against goals in a given time period. For example, "product ABC will achieve a market share of x% over the next two fiscal years." would be a strategic objective. Key performance indicators assigned to these goals are determined which can monitor the organization progress towards achieving goals and objectives.

## Business Planning and Forecasting

Business planning and forecasting refers to the set of activities where business is planned against the strategy and what forecast activities or results of the organization may occur from operational execution during a particular time period. This discipline corresponds to the third and sixth steps of the closed-loop EPM process model. Financial forecasts are a forecast of how a business will perform financially over, say, the year ahead.

Preparing forecasts will help a business to assess its likely sales income, costs, external financing needs and profitability. Financial forecasts are essential if a business needs to raise money from a third party, such as a bank. But they also provide businesses with the means to monitor performance on, say, a monthly basis and thereby exercise effective financial control - arguably the second most important management function in running a business.

### Financial Management

Financial management refers to the set business processes done to close the financial records of an organization at the end of a period in an accurate and timely fashion according to a generally accepted basis of accounting, including the financial statement presentation of results to both internal and external stakeholders, as well as providing appropriate explanations and insights to the nature of the financial results and all supporting documentation.

### Supply Chain Effectiveness

Supply chain effectiveness refers to capabilities to not only manage an enterprise supply chain, but also to provide transparency to all parts of the value chain. This includes the ability to see the sales pipeline and create demand plans organized with suppliers to fulfill those demand plans. Another area of key focus is sales and operations planning (S&OP).

## Behavioral Systems Analysis

Behavioral Systems Analysis (BSA) applies behavior analysis and systems analysis to human performance in organizations.

BSA Builds competitive business and organizational performance through the application of applied behavioral research and systems analysis.

Managers, executives and practitioners apply Behavioral Systems Analysis by:

- A behavioral systems based assessment of factors leading to productive and non-productive performance.
- Identifying process and system changes necessary for improved performance.
- Redesigning systems and processes to generate high levels of discretionary effort.

It stands on a foundation of basic and applied research with proven effectiveness in building:

- Profitability,
- Productivity.

- Performance of:
  - Organizations,
  - Work teams,
  - Individual employees,
  - Supervisors.
- Leadership and executive coaching,
- Injury reduction,
- Quality improvement,
- Change Management,
- Incentive and reward systems.

BSA is demonstrably effective in building outcomes such as productivity, safety, quality, cycle times and customer service in many industries, including:

- Banking and financial,
- Chemical and petro-chemical,
- Human services,
- Manufacturing,
- Paper,
- Transportation,
- Utilities.

A closer look: Behavioral Systems Analysis focuses on performance improvement in organizations through the methods and principles of behavior analysis and systems analysis.

Behavior Analysis is a scientific discipline that studies the behavior of individuals. Behavior Analysis maintains that behavior is the product of individual's interaction with his or her environment (e.g., physical environment, social environment, genetic environment) and the history of that interaction. All social organizations are comprised of individuals' behaviors and their products.

Systems Analysis is a scientific discipline that studies the operations of complex systems such as organizations, and focuses on the interactions between parts of those systems. A system can be understood as interrelated components or parts that interact toward a common purpose. Accordingly, the behavior or functioning of one part or parts affect(s) the behavior or functioning of other parts. In systems analysis, a system is not considered to be reducible to its parts. Therefore, the parts can only be understood in terms of their interaction with other parts of the system.

Behavioral Systems Analysis draws upon basic and applied research on behavior and the research and practice in Organizational Behavior Management, Performance Management and Systems Analysis.

Behavioral Systems Analysis views organizational performance as a scientific subject matter. From this perspective, an individual's behavior in organizations is a naturally occurring phenomenon. Moreover, the discovery orderly relations between behavior and the system in which it occurs gives us opportunities for Behavioral Systems Applications to improve individual and system performance.

Behavioral Systems Analysis is an approach to organizational design and management. It is based on the premise that organizations are complex systems. As such, changes in one aspect of performance in an organization necessarily affects performance in another parts of an organization. A primary goal of BSA is to create a balanced applications in which areas of poor performance are improved, areas of high performance are maintained, and employee performance outcomes are directed towards organizational goals. This is done through the careful use of behavioral and systems theories, and the application of research based principles of behavior, such as reinforcement, punishment, stimulus control, discrimination and generalization.

## References


- Performance-management: businessjargons.com, Retrieved 02 January, 2019
- Neely, Andy; Adams C.; Kennerley M. (27 May 2002). The Performance Prism: The Scorecard for Measuring and Managing Business Success: The Scorecard for Measuring and Managing Stakeholder Relationships. London: Prentice Hall. ISBN 978-0-273-65334-9
- Kaplan, Robert S.; Norton, D. P. (1 July 2008). The Execution Premium: Linking Strategy to Operations. Boston, MA.: Harvard Business School Press. ISBN 978-1-4221-2116-0
- Boris, E. T., & Kopczynski Winkler, M. (2013). The Emergence of Performance Measurement as a Complement to Evaluation Among U.S. Foundations. New Directions For Evaluation, 2013(137), 69-80. doi:10.1002/ev.20047
- Carol Taylor Fitz-Gibbon (1990), "Performance indicators", BERA Dialogues (2), ISBN 978-1-85359-092-4

# Permissions

All chapters in this book are published with permission under the Creative Commons Attribution Share Alike License or equivalent. Every chapter published in this book has been scrutinized by our experts. Their significance has been extensively debated. The topics covered herein carry significant information for a comprehensive understanding. They may even be implemented as practical applications or may be referred to as a beginning point for further studies.

We would like to thank the editorial team for lending their expertise to make the book truly unique. They have played a crucial role in the development of this book. Without their invaluable contributions this book wouldn't have been possible. They have made vital efforts to compile up to date information on the varied aspects of this subject to make this book a valuable addition to the collection of many professionals and students.

This book was conceptualized with the vision of imparting up-to-date and integrated information in this field. To ensure the same, a matchless editorial board was set up. Every individual on the board went through rigorous rounds of assessment to prove their worth. After which they invested a large part of their time researching and compiling the most relevant data for our readers.

The editorial board has been involved in producing this book since its inception. They have spent rigorous hours researching and exploring the diverse topics which have resulted in the successful publishing of this book. They have passed on their knowledge of decades through this book. To expedite this challenging task, the publisher supported the team at every step. A small team of assistant editors was also appointed to further simplify the editing procedure and attain best results for the readers.

Apart from the editorial board, the designing team has also invested a significant amount of their time in understanding the subject and creating the most relevant covers. They scrutinized every image to scout for the most suitable representation of the subject and create an appropriate cover for the book.

The publishing team has been an ardent support to the editorial, designing and production team. Their endless efforts to recruit the best for this project, has resulted in the accomplishment of this book. They are a veteran in the field of academics and their pool of knowledge is as vast as their experience in printing. Their expertise and guidance has proved useful at every step. Their uncompromising quality standards have made this book an exceptional effort. Their encouragement from time to time has been an inspiration for everyone.

The publisher and the editorial board hope that this book will prove to be a valuable piece of knowledge for students, practitioners and scholars across the globe.

# Index

CPSIA information can be obtained
at www.ICGtesting.com
Printed in the USA
LVHW062018100122
708212LV00002B/314

9 781682 859858